The
Hermetic Art
of Memory

The Hermetic Art of Memory

Martin Faulks and Paul Ferguson

ἐγὼ δὲ τὴν εὐεργεσίαν τοῦ Ποιμάνδρου ἀνεγραψάμην εἰς ἐμαυτόν, καὶ πληρωθεὶς ὧν ἤθελον ἐξηυφράνθην. ἐγένετο γὰρ ὁ τοῦ σώματος ὕπνος τῆς ψυχῆς νῆψις, καὶ ἡ κάμμυσις τῶν ὀφθαλμῶν ἀληθινὴ ὅρασις, καὶ ἡ σιωπή μου ἐγκύμων τοῦ ἀγαθοῦ, καὶ ἡ τοῦ λόγου ἐκφορὰ γεννήματα ἀγαθῶν. θεόπνους γενόμενος τῆς ἀληθείας ἦλθον.

I inscribed in my memory the benefaction of the Divine Mind, and I was exceedingly glad, for I was full with that for which I craved. My bodily sleep had come to be my soul's wakefulness; and the closing of my eyes, true vision; and my silence, pregnant with good; and my barrenness of speech, a brood of holy thoughts. Becoming God-inspired, I attained the abode of Truth.

The Divine Pimander, Book I, section 30.

Cover image and design by Robert Wilcockson

First published 2020

ISBN 978 0 85318 573 4

Published by Lewis Masonic

an imprint of Ian Allan Publishing Ltd, Shepperton, Middx TW17 8AS.
Printed in England.

Visit the Lewis Masonic website at www.lewismasonic.co.uk

Contents

Acknowledgements

We would like to thank Tim Kirtley (Librarian of Wadham College,
University of Oxford) and the staff of the Bibliothèque Nationale
at Tolbiac for their kind assistance in supplying complete pages
from the *Thamus*.

Martin Faulks Salutes The Reader

A Guide to Understanding the Hermetic Art of Memory

How to Practice the Hermetic Art of Memory
The art of memory is a method whereby intense concentration is used to create an imaginary building in the mind. This 'memory palace' is then used as a filing system to record information to be recalled at a later point. This powerful method involves the repeated practice of walking the same route and stopping at the same locations in the imagination. Once this becomes effortless you can then begin to place symbolic, exciting, representative objects in each of these locations to trigger your memory. Once put in place, simply walk through the memory palace to find the powerful aide-memoire in each position, so that all you wish to recall comes back to mind with incredible ease and accuracy.[1]

But there is much more to this art. To contemporary readers of the original work, the word 'memory' had some very different connotations and associations than we have now. The term not only referred to the recall of past events, but could also refer to the creation of anything in the mind's eye. Perhaps the closest concept in the modern day would be that of creative visualisation. At the time, much of what we now associate with visualisation, self-hypnosis and autosuggestion was also linked to memory in a similar vein. This was because it was thought that what was committed to the mind would become a part of the personality. So, by memorising images of virtues or talents, then those good habits, qualities or attitudes would become part of normal functioning. Likewise, if information and knowledge were arranged systematically, this would allow for quick, logical and rational thinking. For this reason, memory manuals and emblem books were published for the educated to contemplate upon as forms of self-improvement.

But how could memory be magical?
Renaissance Hermeticists believed the whole of existence was constructed from pure consciousness. To them, the thoughts created in the mind were less dense than the material objects you could hold but

were made of the very same substance. It was believed that all emanated from the original thoughts of God, ideas of the divine consciousness itself. The process of human imagination was seen as a microcosm of the same process by which divinity created the whole of existence. Thus memory was a tool that could be used to 'create', however, the images created in your own consciousness would not initially have the same potency or ability to manifest as those of the divine mind.

So, from the Hermetic point of view, a memory created with great force in the mind of a practitioner would cause an inner transformation. If, by using the same method, you were to create or project this memory/transformation into the underlying consciousness of the universe, this would manifest in external events.

An imprint in your mind is called 'memory', and an imprint in the great consciousness is called 'magic'.

But there's more…

The Hermetic creation story tells us of a single, pre-existing force that shines forth a divine light. This emanation is the first form of consciousness, and within this consciousness, original thoughts appear. Within philosophical circles these thoughts are often called 'forms', but those of a religious disposition may call them 'gods'. These original thoughts then emanate the ideas that condense into matter. So, for example, behind all horses there is an idea of 'horse', or behind all loves there is one divine 'love'. Inspired by the Hermetic texts, in Renaissance magical practices these forces were invoked into statues using natural substances that tradition told would hold the charge of the idea, things that would be in sympathy with the divine rays. For instance, if you wanted to bring Venus into a statue you could make the statue out of a sacred gemstone which was pink in colour and was said to take in the energy from the rays of Venus (the divine idea of love); you would put herbs of love and oils of love on it and say harmonious prayers to her. In the Hermetic art of memory, this process is made internal. Just as the Eastern practice of yoga holds that meditation on a specific subject until a union is reached can bring about an inner transformation and spiritual powers, so too does the Hermetic memory art. By meditating on a series of memorised images related to a divine force you can become at one with it.

The Hermetic art of memory is a form of meditation whereby mental images, words and associations are used to tune into divine powers.

Using complicated and detailed images really helps keep the mind on the subject and bring forth oneness.[2] In a sense, it's a form of invocation just as with ancient traditions when a God was drawn into a person (albeit in a far more abstract and exacting manner). This divine force transforms the substance of the mind as it connects, and lifts them to a higher standard in line with the qualities of the divine presence. So in the case of our example of Venus, you would become more loving and able to bring about love and attain divine powers related to this quality.

When drawing blessings from divine powers into yourself, Hermetic mnemonics are a form of meditation. When influencing the world around you, a magic circle and a memory palace become one.

In modern terminology, the location/subject is the magical energy, the image/adjunct the intention, and the memory/shadow the magical effect.

So if a practitioner wished to bring forth magical strength, they could meditate on an image of an elephant and, once at one with this idea, could add an image or series of images of strength, and when this influence was felt could direct this shadow to an actual act of strength.[3]

Likewise, to bring about an inner transformation, you could follow the same procedure and 'sit' in the shadow. Hermetic teachers in Dicsone's day would be able to guide a student in this process with great care and dedication. They would sit together in contemplation on a specific star or constellation, drawing the divine radiance within. In imitation of the scenes of tuition in the original ancient Hermetic texts, this practice would constitute a direct transmission of the art. The teacher would powerfully demonstrate the exact force to be connected with and the exact manner and mindset needed to receive it, and so this would be energetically reflected in the student.

This threefold process is a law of consciousness that echoes the Hermetic creation myth. It is not only the same for magic and memory, but also reflects the process of logical deduction (hence the name of the work).[4]

First Steps in the Hermetic Art of Memory

Alexander Dicsone and his teacher Giordano Bruno lived at a time when the memory arts were common practice amongst the educated classes, and those who trained in the Hermetic art tended to be very advanced practitioners. Likewise, in those days magical tuition was often direct, with a teacher studiously bestowing all the details of the art directly, mouth to ear, teacher and student sitting in the shadows together and perfecting the art.

A modern practitioner working alone who has not had such an education may need to do some preparatory training in order to be able to practice the art effectively.

We need to start with a new view of the mind. Imagine that every thought and experience, every memory in your consciousness, creates its own vibration: we must be careful to make sure that what we put in our consciousness is beneficial. Make sure your inner being has only inspiring, uplifting vibrations and that you cut out any unnecessary input or stimulus that would use up your mental processing time and ability.

Practice using your memory. Embrace each opportunity to improve your mental skills during everyday life. If someone gives you a list of things to purchase or undertake, take a while to really memorise that list before starting on the first mission. If there are any numbers or addresses you keep needing to look up, it's time to firmly commit them to memory. If you have something to work out, don't use a calculator, but rather do it in your head. Really embrace any opportunity given to do mental work. When you drive somewhere don't use a sat nav, but look at the route first on a map and as you go along make an effort to memorise it. Remove all barriers to learning and take a keen interest in grammar, spelling and science. Whenever you hear a new word or a foreign phrase, embrace the chance to learn this with enthusiasm, repetition, and any mnemonic hook you find useful.

Then, move to creating memory palaces in locations that already exist and you know well. These are natural memory palaces, as it were, which require very little work in the creation of memory images. By using a pre-existing place you already know, you can simply just hook the things you want to remember on to existing locations, objects or pictures that are readily available.

So, if you wanted to learn about botany, you could first practice walking your garden in a set route, stopping at each plant, shrub, or tree in turn, slowly building up to learning and memorising each of the plants' names and then qualities. If you found any of the information hard to recall, you could apply mnemonic techniques, creating strong images and placing them upon the plant in your imagination. Another easy memory palace would be your local church or sacred space, using every icon, statue and decoration as a hook for a biblical or moral lesson, building each one up with repeated practise and with exacting precision. Many churches or monasteries were designed with this practice in mind, so you may find that the figures you see already have small details created to help you recall specific facts, lessons or references.

Extend this practice to all areas of your life. Mnemosyne, the Greek goddess of memory, is traditionally the mother of the muses. The art of memory brings about inspiration, so be sure to be creative. Really embrace this as a time to cultivate this aspect of your personality.

Would it be possible to use a picture of the staff at your workplace for you to memorise the names, hobbies and birthdays of every one of your colleagues? How about a series of yoga postures to learn Hindu mythology?

Gardens, constellations, houses, museums, paintings, planets, temples, art galleries, and picture albums all make perfect natural memory palaces.

Keep with this practice until you see an improvement in your memory and imagination. Get into the mindset that each positive image that becomes part of your mind becomes a new blessing inside, and that any images warning of danger or negativity act like gargoyles, warding off all you would wish to avoid. When you have formed ten of these natural memory palaces, you can move on to creating specific memory palaces of your own, containing things you would like to remember, or blessings and virtues you wish to draw into your life.[5] The initial goal in the Hermetic art of memory was to bring about inner balance and harmony. This first stage was known by the Hermetic practitioners as the "Square Art".

To do this start by creating a building which holds each of the archangels in order, building up detailed images of each one with symbolic clothing, objects and colours showing their powers. Make a temple of the nine muses and the alchemical metals belonging to each one. Allow inspiration to fill you when creating your memory palaces, looking for images of virtues, divine powers and elemental balance. Take advantage of the traditions you feel the most affinity to. For a western Hermetic practitioner this is likely to include the elements, the planets, the Zodiac, the Greek or Egyptian pantheons, the principles of logic, the scales of colour and light. Really practice building up the details on each memory figure so as to cover more areas of knowledge and to extend your time of unwavering focus on it. Allow yourself to become at one with the vibration, using this method to gain an ecstatic union with the energy. Fill your soul with this divinity and goodness. Make your heart a cornucopia of kindness and your mind a kaleidoscope of colourful inspiration.

If at any point you find an image hard to form in your mind's eye, persist, as this may be an energy or quality within your consciousness that needs to be healed, evolved or transformed. Use these difficult images to bring about inner balance and tranquillity.

Then and only then is it time to move on from the square to the curved art. This next step as the name suggests involves the creation of a new curved or circular memory palace. Within this sacred, inner space divine cosmic forces are drawn down and impressed firmly into your being. Renaissance Hermeticists favoured specific areas of the heavens for this. Stars holding angels, clusters and constellations directing fate or shining forth virtues would have special traditional memory images to allow you to tune in to the divine power of each 'face' or 'station' in the heavens, thus covering all of the powers.

A magus needed to master and create a system covering the whole path to apotheosis. The most common of these were the 32 decans and the 28 mansions of the moon.

Master Dicsone states:
'The commanders and princes of the tribes should be selected from among the images of the lunar mansions. A permanent decemvirate should take responsibility for the administration, and golden chains should be provided for them in the individual stations. But make sure you keep all these things under careful observation, so that those that wish to can remain in position and stand fast. Those who want their efforts in this task to be rewarded must act with great care and meticulousness.'

This very mysterious paragraph may require some explanation for the modern reader. Dicsone is suggesting that the first filing system or memory palace to use is the twenty-eight mansions of the moon, those being the areas of the zodiac that the moon passes through each day of the lunar month.

'Continual decemvirate' is a reference to a particular time in Roman history when ten governors ruled together, taking turns to head the state. In this context it's both a recommendation to the reader to make the moon's mansions constant in the mind, but also points out that though the moon always rules, at any one time it is one of the eight phases in command (New Moon, Waxing Crescent, First Quarter, Waxing Gibbous, Full Moon, Waning Gibbous, Third Quarter, Waxing Crescent). Thus you should make sure to be in tune with and working with the influence of the current phase.

'Furnish them with golden chains' is an alchemical code, instructing you to link the image formed in your mind with the divine powers themselves. The allusion is to a passage in Homer's *Iliad* (i. 19-30), where Zeus says, '*If a golden chain were let down from heaven, and all the gods and goddesses pulled at one end, they would not be able to pull him [Zeus] down to earth; whereas he could lift with ease all the deities and all created things besides with his single might.*'

Master Dicsone then goes on to recommend that the practitioner works diligently until the image can be held clearly in the mind's eye. In modern terminology, we would say for the practitioner to learn to visualize them clearly without fading or movement in the image.

From the Hermetic point of view, the moon is the ideal memory palace for someone starting this art, as it is considered to be a transmitter of higher forces.

As this quote from the Picatrix summarises: '*Wherefore draw your attention to that which we have said before concerning her being fortunate and unfortunate, increasing [waxing] and diminishing [waning] in light, because after separating from the Sun she secures his strength then she moves to be in a sextile, square, trine and opposition aspect. And she receives strength from the stars and planets when she is connected by the aspects we have mentioned before.*'

By working with the moon phases, the Hermetic Mnemonic Magus would be able to get used to the higher powers in a more gentle and safer way, at least to start with, while still developing aspects of the self.

The key to success is in the feel of the whole exercise. Firmly fix in your intention the idea that the moon is your ally and that your goal is to be in tune with the energy of each phase.

Before you can start to draw the divine blessing of the moon into yourself by creating 'shadows' of the higher powers in your consciousness, you need to tune in. Spend time standing in its light.

Watch the phases go round. Learn about how the phases work and function. Study all aspects of the moon and its phases. Learn to think in terms of lunar months, discover how farmers time things by the moon, explore the myths surrounding this satellite. The more fastidious you are with this undertaking, the greater success you will realise later on in this exercise.

Once you have all this in place, you should start to form a memory palace with the phases of the moon. To do this, you should sit each and every day in a meditative state, imagining each of the phases in turn in your mind's eye. To begin with, you can time the phases with your breathing. With each inhalation imagine one image changing to the next, hold your breath as you imagine it as clearly as possible, and then breathe out before moving to the next. As time progresses you can increase the duration of each phase, working up the number of breaths you sustain at each phase. When you can visualise each of the moon phases in order like this, it is time to start to work with the mansions.

Working with the Mansions of the Moon
If you are serious about the Hermetic Art of Memory, it is at this stage that it may be worth seeking out a teacher to guide you. Both Bruno and Dicsone taught students directly. A teacher who has already gone through this system can introduce the student directly to the energies. If you do not have access to a teacher, you need to make the moon's mansions the subject of your daily study. Read everything you can find on the subject and be sure to learn each and every aspect thoroughly. Make this your daily dedication to the path.

The mindset needed for this operation is as follows. Imagine that the moon is the transmitter of divine transformative forces which can be brought into your being through 'memory'. Your goal is to use the memory image and actual gazing at the specific area of the zodiac as a mode of meditation. Once you feel the force of that area, you are to direct yourself to becoming at one with it. With time you will start to feel the golden chain form. Persist, and you will begin to notice your inner qualities transform, and abilities related to the specific energies will start to appear.

The memory images in the appendix of this book should be made firm so that you can go through them all in turn as a form of meditation. With practice, you will be able to feel the influence and direct the forces into memorable images that have a magical effect.

Once this starts to take hold, you may feel called to look to the stars associated with each mansion and meet with the angels by building detailed memory images of them for meditation inspired by the qualities they hold. Consider each angel you attune with a divine aid to your good works in the world.

[1] In Dicsone's system specific terminology is used for each of these: 'subject' for location; 'adjunct' for the object or memory hook; and 'shadow' for the thing to remember.

[2] See *The Serpent Power: The Secrets of Tantric and Shaktic Yoga* (Dover Paperback – 2 Jan 2000). One Indian Tantric example of this very same approach using complicated images of the Chakras.

[3] "Through Meditation on the strength of the elephant you can gain the strength of an elephant." Chapter 3 paragraph 25 The yoga sutras of patanjali Swami Sivananda Translation

[4] Premise/Location, Proposition/image = Conclusion/Memory For more on this see the chapter 'Deconding Dicsone' by Paul Ferguson

[5] See my book *A Mosaic Palace* for further clarification on the process of creating a memory palace.

Decoding Dicsone

*'Statues, Asclepius, yes. See how little trust you have! I
mean statues ensouled and conscious, filled with spirit and
doing great deeds; statues that foreknow the future and
predict it by lots, by prophecy, by dreams and by many
other means; statues that make people ill and cure them,
bringing them pain and pleasure as each deserves.'*
Asclepius, 81.

Some biographical background.
Alexander Dicsone (or Dicson or Dickson, or Italianised as Alessandro
Dicsono; pseudonymously Heius Scepsius) was born in Perthshire in
1558 and educated at the University of St. Andrew's. He was to become
the leading disciple in the British Isles of the late 16ᵗʰ century Italian
Dominican friar, philosopher, mathematician, poet, cosmological
theorist, Hermetic occultist and memory-expert Giordano Bruno, who
spent the years 1583-1585 in England, during which period the two men
may well have met.

We do not know what first piqued Dicsone's interest in
mnemotechnics. His sideline as a double-agent shuttling between the
Catholic rebel Francis Hay (the Earl of Erroll) and the Scottish Kirk no
doubt required a retentive memory, and he may also have been, like
many men of his generation, an enthusiastic card-player (we know that
some at least of his Art of Memory pupils were card-sharps). Whatever
the case, his interest in the subject was sufficiently strong for him to
publish two treatises of his own, the *De Umbra* (London 1583) and the
Thamus (Leiden, 1597) which, in true Brunonian fashion, combine
mnemotechnics with Neoplatonic and esoteric themes. The present
volume contains transcriptions and new annotated translations of both
works.

Sadly, later commentators have not been kind to either work. J. Lewis
McIntyre, in his 1903 biography of Bruno (p. 36), describes the *De
Umbra* as 'extremely sketchy, occasionally diffuse and of little value
even were there anything of value in the Art of Memory which it
teaches', while William Boulting, in his 1916 biography *Giordano*

Bruno, his life, thought and martyrdom (p. 98), dismisses it as 'a mnemonic and Neoplatonic work of little value, being but a poor imitation of Bruno's *Shadows of Ideas*.' Frances Yates is equally unimpressed, and also disparages the later *Thamus* as a mere re-working of the *De Umbra*, when it is in fact a separate work, albeit displaying considerable overlap with the *De Umbra*.

It must be said that Dicsone is his own worst enemy. One problem with both texts is their compressed and elliptical style: they give the impression of being truncated versions of much longer and more detailed works. Perhaps they were intended purely as sketches or aides-memoires for his students, or perhaps he was simply erring on the side of caution: after all, less than three years after the publication of the *Thamus* in 1597, Bruno was burned at the stake for his unorthodoxy. What is more, Dicsone's Latin, though stylish, is often ambiguous and confusing, and his terminology very much his own.

But whatever his shortcomings as a writer Dicsone does seem to have inspired feelings of great affection in at least some of his contemporaries. Like Bruno he seems to have won the respect of Sir Philip Sidney, and he was indeed a member of his intellectual circle[1]. As for Bruno himself, he mentions Dicsone in the First Dialogue of *De la Causa, Principio et Uno*, saying he is 'dearer to him than his own eyes'[2]. And after Dicsone's death, his friend the Scottish court poet Thomas Murray (1564-1623) published the following moving elegy:

In Verissimam Alexandri Dicsoni et authoris amicitiam.

Una erat in binis semper mens, una voluntas,
  Unus et in bino corpore sensus erat.
Unus erat binis dolor, oblectatio binis
  Unaque, spes binis una, metusque fuit.
Unus amor binis; una aversatio binis;
  Una etiam binis ira; odiumque fuit.
Unus erat nobis labor, una et cura duobus;
  Una etiam nobis vita duobus erat.
Sic duo non duo sunt; unus non unus; at unus
  Est duo; nunc duo sunt unus; utrumque simul.
Sic ego Dicsonus; fuit ille Moravius, et, sic
  Unus uterque fuit; neuter uterque fuit.

On the truest friendship between the author and Alexander Dickson.

In the two of us there was always just one mind, one will,
  And in our two bodies there was just one sentiment.
In the two of us there was just one sorrow, and just one delight,
  In the two of us just one hope and fear,
In the two of us just one love and one dislike,
  In the two of us just one anger and one hatred.
For the two of us there was just one task and one concern.
  For the two of us life itself was just one.
The two of us are not two, and one is not one,
  But one is two, and now two are one, both at once.
So I am Dickson, and he was Murray,
  So one was both, and neither of us was just one of two.[3]

Dicsone is also the subject of an intriguing reference in Henry Adamson's *The Muses Threnodie; or Mirthful Mournings on the Death of Mr Gall* (1638), a poem made famous by its reference to Masonry and Rosicrucianism:

Right over against is that wood Earnside,
  And fort where Wallace ofttimes did reside:
While we beheld all these, the tide did flow,
  A lie the rudder goes; about we row,
Up to the town again we make our course,
  Sweetly convoy'd with Tays reflowing source.
There we beheld where Wallace ship was drown'd,
  Which he brought out of France, whose bottome found
Was not long since, by Master Dickeson's art,
  That rare ingeniour, skil'd in everie part
Of Mathemathicks.

So it would seem that Dicsone was a man of many parts, on this occasion involved in the location and salvage of Scottish hero Sir William Wallace's ship, though how and with what motive we know not[4].

   Apart from his talent for friendship, Dicsone's mnemotechnic writings also won a measure of praise from some of his contemporaries. Thomas Watson's non-esoteric treatise *Compendium Memoriæ Localis* of 1585, for example, refers to Dicsone's *De Umbra* as 'skilful' (*artificiosa*). However, the *De Umbra* also led him into an ideological dispute with English supporters of the Protestant convert, logician and educational reformer Petrus Ramus (1515-1572), himself an exponent of the Art of Memory and something of a poster-boy for the English Puritans. Frances Yates effectively summarises the root of the quarrel:

'The French dialectician [Ramus] whose simplification of teaching methods made such a stir was born in 1515 and died in 1572, massacred as a Huguenot in the Massacre of St. Bartholomew. This end recommended him to Protestants, to whom his pedagogical reforms were also welcome as a means of sweeping out the complexities of scholasticism. Amongst the complexities of which Ramus made a clean sweep were those of the old art of memory. Ramus abolished memory as a part of rhetoric, and with it he abolished the artificial memory. This was not because Ramus was not interested in memorising. On the contrary, one of the chief aims of the Ramist movement for the reform and simplification of education was to provide a new and better way of memorising all subjects. This was to be done by a new method whereby every subject was to be arranged in 'dialectical order'. This order was set out in schematic form in which the 'general' or inclusive aspects of the subject came first, descending thence through a series of dichotomised classifications to the 'specials' or individual aspects. Once a subject was set out in its dialectical order it was memorised in this order from the schematic presentation – the famous Ramist epitome' (p. 232)

and

'Though many surviving influences of the old art of memory may be detected in the Ramist 'method' of memorising through dialectical order, yet he deliberately gets rid of its most characteristic feature, the use of the imagination. No more will places in churches or other buildings be vividly impressed on the imagination. And, above all, gone in the Ramist system are the images, the emotionally striking and stimulating images the use of which had come down through the centuries from the art of the classical rhetor. The 'natural' stimulus for memory is now *not the emotionally exciting memory image; it is the abstract order of dialectical analysis* which is yet, for Ramus, 'natural', since dialectical order is natural to the mind' (p. 234, our emphasis).

All this was of course completely at odds with the image-based memory-systems of Bruno and Dicsone, which the iconoclastic Puritans saw as smacking of idolatry, heresy, Papism and even obscenity (as the practitioner was encouraged to use strikingly memorable images which occasionally breached the contemporary bounds of decency). Yates surmises (p. 273) that the ludicrous Socrates-figure of the dialogues in the two Dicsone texts is a portrait of Ramus: we certainly know that Dicsone's assault on Ramism was sufficiently blatant to draw a response from an anonymous Cambridge don, possibly William Perkins. His *Antidicsonus*[5] of 1584 attacked both Dicsone and other mnemotechnic writers of the same ilk, including Cosmas Rossellius, the author of the *Thesaurus Artificiosæ Memoriæ* (Venice 1579). Dicsone's later *Thamus* is in no way a riposte to Perkins, but shows no signs of apology either: it must be considered a reworking of the earlier material in the light of Dicsone's recent reading, especially of Lucretius and works of natural philosophy.

But however much of a stir Dicsone may have caused in his own time, he has been much neglected since. In general the academic world has shown an understandable reserve towards some of the more esoteric aspects of the Renaissance. Accordingly, although the works of the much more famous Giordano Bruno have been extensively studied by academics, it has almost always been from the perspective of the historian of science or of ideas[6]. As a result, Bruno's true historical significance has been underappreciated, and some of his most interesting works (e. g. the *De imaginum, signorum et idearum compositione* of 1591) have been relatively neglected.

It is unsurprising therefore that the works of his Scottish pupil should have shared a similar fate. Though a transcription and translation of his *De Umbra* will be found at the University of Birmingham's *Philological Museum* site[7], their transcription contains a number of errors, including several line-skips, and these seem to have wrong-footed the translator. We have therefore felt justified in bringing a fresh transcription and a new annotated translation before the public. We have added the later *Thamus* for good measure, as this is a significant re-working of the earlier text.

But while the foregoing statement about the academic world's attitude towards esoterica is hard to dispute, there are certain refreshing exceptions to the rule. One is the thesis *Applied Imagination: Giordano Bruno and the Creation of Magical Images*[8] by Michael Storch which, in the words of the author, 'is a departure from much of the current scholarship on Bruno which has focused on his contribution to scientific thought, and downplayed or ignored the Hermetic and magical elements which pervade his work', for 'creating images is fundamentally an act of magic' and 'to control the images is to control reality. Bruno presents a comprehensive program to both create and manipulate infinite images in order not only to understand and explain the cosmos, but to change it' (page 12). 'The M-word [magic] is embarrassing to many modern scholars of philosophy and religion. The modern West is unique in its denial of the ontological status of magic' (p. 46). 'Modernity itself is greatly involved in the presupposition of the separation between humanity and nature, whereas magic is built on integration' (p. 48). As Storch explains (p. 18), Bruno took the *mystical* memory techniques of Raymond Lull and turned them into a *magical* system: 'Throughout his writings, Bruno speaks very positively of magic. *De Magia, [De] Vinculis [in Genere]*, and *De Imaginum* are very clearly and overtly instruction manuals on the correct use of magic' (p. 36).

We also think that Stephen Clucas's paper on two Brunonian texts (Mnemosine in London: The Art of Memory and Giordano Bruno's Spaccio de la bestia trionfante and Degli eroici furori. In: XVII-XVIII. *Bulletin de la société d'études anglo-américaines des XVIIᵉ et XVIIIᵉ siècles*. N° 58, 2004. pp. 7-23[9]) addresses the esoteric aspects of Bruno's system with exemplary clarity and insight, and we are happy to quote from it here:

'Bruno's art of memory...was conceived...as a method of ordering the intellect (a logic), a means of effecting a moral transformation of the subject (an ethical art) and as a form of magic. In fact these three aims are seen by Bruno as complementary, and are united in Bruno's overarching project: the perfection of man and the transformation of the self into a state of god-like being. In the theoretical introduction to *De Umbris Idearum*...Bruno suggests that while his art of memory could be used effectively by the rude and untutored it held particular benefits for those who were versed in the metaphysics and doctrines of the Platonists. Practitioners of different intellectual abilities could utilise it according to their capacities...The end of the 'higher and [more] general form' of his art was the 'ordering all the operations of the soul' – by which he understood not only the intellectual operations governed by traditional logic, but also appetition (and thus ethics). It was, in fact, seen as 'the origin of many methods' which are compared to 'various organs' by which one could 'explore (or discover) artificial memory'. [In] the 'Thirty intentions of the shadows'...Bruno outlines what is basically a Neoplatonic theory of knowledge derived from Plotinus (as schematised by Ficino). Essentially, Bruno argues, the original principle of the universe – the One – propagates itself like light, descending through increasingly imperfect forms until it reaches the lowest degree of matter. The universe is subject to a 'constant movement from the Light towards the darkness [of matter]'. As the 'Light' descends it diversifies, 'progressively descending from supersubstantial unity by way of increasing multiplicity into infinite multiplicity.' The forms descend from the One to the many by means of an analogical series of similitudes. There is an 'order and connection in all things such that inferior bodies follow intermediate bodies, and intermediate bodies follow superior bodies.' This analogous series, the 'ladder of nature' or 'golden chain' of resemblances, extends 'from the superessential itself to the essences, from the essences to those things which exist, from those to their vestiges, images, simulacra and shadows' which can be found in matter – which bears 'the final vestige of it from the light which is called the First Act' – and in the human mind, where the shadows exist in a superior form, because 'something is better apprehended by means of the species which is in the intellect than by means of the species which is in the physical subject, since it is more immaterial.' By reascending along the chain of intermediaries, the soul can raise itself towards superior things: 'to the sound of Apollo's harp inferior things are gradually recalled to superior things, and inferior things acquire the nature of superior things through intermediary things.' The aim of the art is to allow its practitioner to use inferior things to raise the soul upwards towards divinity. 'Let us resolutely aim for that [goal],' says Bruno, 'like those who, through remarkable operations of the soul, have the ladder of nature before their eyes, let us always strive to proceed from motion and multiplicity, through inward operations, towards stasis and unity.' It is the cultivation of these 'inward operations' which is the primary purpose of Bruno's memory art. It is an instrument designed to help the mind trace the multitudinous species of the universe back towards the unity of the superessential form' (pp. 7-9).

We feel that Storch and Clucas provide a sound basis for our examination of Dicsone's two treatises, as we have no reason to suppose that Dicsone's view of the Art of Memory differed substantially from Bruno's. It is, however, a poor pupil who cannot surpass his master, and Dicsone's system does show some signs of originality in both terminology and procedure.

The Method.

For Dicsone memory *(memoria)* is 'a power, an action, a shadow, and a beating of the wings of the mind' in which the mind is free of the influence of the body and the senses.

Memory rests on two solid foundations: 'goodness' *(bonitas)* in the sense that the materials with which it works are ideal rather than rational, and 'judgement' *(iudicium)*, by which Dicsone means the ability to retain things in the memory even though they might not be entirely congenial to the memoriser.

Memory proceeds from God, but is expressed through three media: God; the divine afflatus ('rays from above'); and our thinking capacity, both innate and acquired, which is understood as being in a symbiotic relationship with Nature.

Memory consists of two parts: foreknowledge *(providentia)* and discrimination *(criterium)*. Foreknowledge is the groundwork that must be performed to achieve a successful result (Dicsone uses the analogy of the planting and maintenance of a fruit-tree). Discrimination is the 'regular stimulus' process by which the visual and cognitive apparatus insinuates into the memory 'whatever is perceived as a result of the impulse of the faculties or which was fashioned by the work of the senses'.

Objects *(res)* are memorised through the use of shadows *(umbræ)*, which are 'the representation *(efficta species* or just *species)* of an object which is assigned *(credita)* to a subject' *(subiectum)* and 'so selected *(assumpta)* as to ensure a firm perception *(firma perceptio)* of that object' *(De Umbra, Ch. XI; Thamus, 'Shadows')*.

A subject is 'a sort of pocket *(sinus)* or receptacle *(receptaculum)* into which the shadows are placed' (*De Umbra*, Ch. VI; *Thamus*, 'Subjects').

Subjects can be either absolute *(absolutum)* or adjuvant *(adiuvans)*. It is the absolute subjects that contain the shadows.

Absolute subjects can be either simple *(simplex)* or conjoined *(coniunctum)*.

Absolute subjects are fixed and immobile *(fixum et immotum)*, whereas adjuvant subjects can be moved.

Adjuvant subjects are used 'to increase the absolute subject and also to ensure a firm perception of the shadows' (*De Umbra*, Ch. VIII).

For Dicsone all adjuvant subjects are 'mathematical' in that they indicate the number and sequence of the subjects.

Subjects should be 1) of a reasonable and constant size; 2) neither too bright nor too dark; 3) separated by moderate and constant intervals without too much space between them.

Subjects should neither be too much alike nor too different from one another.

Subjects should follow their natural sequence if they have one or, if they do not, should be carefully and logically arranged.

Ideally each subject should have just one prevailing idea, but this can be (and may need to be) subdivided, thus allowing different aspects of an idea to be examined and memorised.

In Dicsone's microcosmic 'mind map', possibly inspired by St. Augustine, the memory seems to occupy the key 'solar' position at the centre of the mental universe, while the various parts of the sensory and cognitive apparatus are located at the boundary *(horizon)*, also known as the periphery *(peripheria)*. 'The memory is at the centre, for the sensory faculties are on the boundary, and nothing can be moved to the centre except by means of all the intermediate orbs'.

Shadows can be simple, modified or absolute.

Simple shadows are sensory, while modified shadows are conceptual.

Simple shadows are conveyed from the boundary, i.e. they are moved from the sensory or cognitive apparatus towards the memory, while modified shadows are represented within the senses.

If a simple shadow is not available then a representation of sufficient likeness, known as a simulacrum *(simulachrum)*, can be substituted.

Modified shadows can be further subdivided into those that involve

1) modification of objects, 2) mathematical modification, and 3) verbal modification.

1) Objects are modified if they cannot be visualised but can be grasped by the other senses or by the mind. This is known as a construction (*conformatio*).

Absolute shadows are those that do not involve any difference of number.

Absolute shadows can be either simple or conjoined.

Absolute shadows that cannot be apprehended by the senses can be modified by a metaphorical process of the borrowing (*mutuatio*) of an object that *can* be apprehended by the senses. This can involve the use of:

a) One object to evoke many.

b) An object to evoke its correlative (e.g. tenant/landlord, son-in-law/father-in-law).

c) An object to evoke its opposite.

d) Metaphor (e.g. a ship in a storm standing for a struggling republic).

e) Objects that differ in quality.

f) Distribution (*synecdoche*).

2) Mathematical objects (numbers) cannot project either simple or modified shadows.

In such cases the Zodiac should be used.

3) Where objects are lacking (as in the case of words), verbal modification (inflection) can be used. Dicsone's sections on this subject (e.g. Chapter XVII of the *De Umbra*) are not very lucid, and it is not even obvious whether he is referring to the memorising of English (or Scots) or Latin texts, but the procedure seems clear enough in outline.

All shadows, whatever their origin, are subject to a process of approval (*commendatio*) by the vision, i.e. they must satisfy certain visual criteria and be assimilable by the practitioner.

Thus far, Dicsone's system can be used solely for mnemotechnic purposes. However, the addition of the stage of animation (*animatio*) brings it within the bounds of magic. And if any reader is sceptical about the extension of a mnemonic system into the esoteric realm, let them ponder Aleister Crowley's remark in Book O, II.5, that 'the whole magical apparatus and ritual is a complex system of mnemonics'.

The word *animatio* was rarely used in Classical Latin and, only then, to signify the infusion of life by the divinity, but by Dicsone's time, under the influence of Renaissance esoteric writers, the word had acquired a different significance. Bruce MacLennan, relying on Frances Yates, admirably summarises this semantic trajectory in his paper *Neoplatonism in Science, Past and Future*[10]:

'Already in the Pythagorean revival of late antiquity memory was connected with spiritual practices, and biographers attributed a prodigious memory to such figures as Pythagoras and Apollonius of Tyana (Yates 1966, p. 56). Also beginning in antiquity was the use of cosmologically significant structures, such as the zodiac, decans, and planetary spheres, to organize ideas and their images (Yates 1966, p. 54). In this way the art of memory allowed the macrocosm to be reflected in the microcosm of the individual mind. In the Middle Ages there was increasing use of the art of memory to internalize religiously significant ideas, such as the articles of faith, the virtues and vices, and the paths to salvation and damnation (Yates 1966, pp.67–9)... Albertus Magnus said that the images of the virtues, for example, contained their own *intentiones*, which were efficacious for imparting the virtues (Yates 1966, p. 76). Further, Aquinas introduced a devotional focus into the art of memory by suggesting that the images should be contemplated with solicitude and affection (Yates 1966, pp. 83–7). (Contributing to this development was the medieval practice of *Ars Notaria*, a magical art of memory, attributed to Pythagoras, in which one sought illumination by contemplating esoteric figures while reciting magical prayers; Yates 1966, pp. 56–7.) In the Renaissance these developments reached their culmination in the spiritual magic of Ficino and Pico, who took practices from the Asclepius and other Hermetica for the "ensouling" (ἐμψύχωσις, *animatio*) of images, and synthesized them with the art of memory, the astral magic of the Picatrix, and the Neoplatonic theurgy of Iamblichus and Proclus. In this art properly structured memory images were regarded as "inner talismans", which through their theurgic power could draw down celestial influences and unite the divine part of the human mind with the divine powers of the cosmos' (Yates 1966, pp. 149–62).

In Dicsone's system animation is a process of the cognitive faculties. It is a process of 'negation [presumably of the Self] and, most certainly, a dual transformation, namely of you into the object itself, and of the object into itself' (*De Umbra*, Ch. XXI), adding that 'every skill is something to be admired, but this, which causes inanimate objects to appear as if they are living and breathing, is especially worthy of our admiration'.

In the *Thamus* Dicsone expands upon this statement:

'this is that quickened power of the mind, and a carefully-achieved loosening of the mind from the body. Thus an (as yet unformed) thought-process, that of the shadows, forsakes matter and time and grasps the ideas and rationales, since it has a natural propensity for such an understanding'.

In Chapter XVI of the *De Umbra* Dicsone advocates the use of images appropriate to the Zodiac together with, if necessary, the wandering planets and the Lunar Dragon. In his pseudonymous *Defensio pro Alexander Dicsono Arelio* of 1584 (the year after the publication of the *De Umbra*) he retracted this suggestion, presumably under Puritan pressure, but his *Thamus* of 1597 returns to the astrological theme, albeit more discreetly, saying that the objects should be distributed among the 'third-parts', i.e. the third-parts of an astrological sign, the decans, and that 'the commanders and princes of the third-parts may, if you wish, be selected from among the images of the lunar mansions'. Most modern Hermetic practitioners would probably use the Sephiroth of the Tree of Life or the Tarot as the images for their Memory Palace.

Two of the most obscure parts of Dicsone's system are the veiling (*velificatio*) and the Golden Chain.

Assuming our translation of *velificatio* is correct, and Dicsone is using it in its specialised iconographic sense to mean the arch-like cloak which divinities hold over their heads in classical sculpture to symbolise the vault of the firmament, then we may assume that this is a way of emphasising the numinous and 'shadowy' character of the divinity being addressed.

The reference to the Golden Chain is perhaps less obscure. Presumably it is the Plotinian ladder rising to the ideal forms whereby the more ambitious practitioner can ascend from his or her chosen image as far as their imaginative powers will allow.

The following quotations from Israel Regardie's *Tree of Life* are intended merely as pointers as to how we think Dicsone's system might have been used:

'As experience increases, the Magician retaining within his memory a comprehensive alphabet of correspondences, and as he becomes more familiar with the nature of that plane, he will become aware instantaneously as to whether the vision proceeds aright, and his growing intuition will warn him when some danger to coherency threatens. It cannot be too frequently uttered that the checking of the vision by reference to the magical alphabet [the 'set' of images] is one of the most important tasks devolving upon the Magician. To neglect this scientific verification and critical examination of the vision is to find oneself sooner or later wallowing in the clogging mire of astral intoxication, with the prospect of advance and progress imperceptibly vanishing into thin air.' [p. 158]

And from p. 164:

'The technique, briefly, is as follows. Seating himself comfortably in a chair – or if he be trained in the assumption of a Yoga posture and is easy therein, so much the better-and tranquillizing his mind and emotions as far as may be possible, the Magician should try to imagine standing before him an exact duplicate of his own body. Should the Magician have engaged in much practice of the *tattva* symbols or the spiritual exercises of St. Ignatius and those described in a former section of this study, no great difficulty will be encountered in formulating this image. The Theurgist should conceive vividly that a simulacrum of his own body stands before him in the mind; and that it is clothed as the Magician is clothed, in magical robe with wand or sword, as the case may be, and that it stands upright, or seated on a chair, or curled in an easy and comfortable *Asana*. Should the Magician be seated, the image likewise should be seen to be seated. By a supreme effort of will that image should be made to move in the mind and, observed very closely all the time, to rise standing upright on its feet. The most difficult part of the Magician's task now approaches. To the Body of Light he must transfer his own consciousness, and it is this transfer which may prove a little difficult, for sometimes it simply will not go'[wherein the shadow should be substituted for the 'duplicated body' of the Magician].

We think we have done enough to show that Dicsone's system does have magical applications as well as some points of originality. Further investigation of his sources and of events in his life should help to dispel some of the shadows currently surrounding his work. We like to think that, with these texts, we have provided a useful starting-point for such an endeavour.

1   http://www.philological.bham.ac.uk/dickson/intro.html

2   '...che il Nolano [Bruno] ama, quanto gli occhi suoi'. See Wagner, *Opere di Giordano Bruno*, Leipzig 1830, vol. 1, p. 227.

3   To be found in *Delitiæ Poetarum Scotorum huius ævi illustrium* (DPS, Amsterdam, 1637). The sentiments expressed are strangely reminiscent of what the Enochian angels are alleged to have said to Dr. John Dee and Edward Kelley: 'You are but one body in this work'. One wonders if Dicsone and Murray were perhaps conjoined in some form of magical enterprise. It is interesting to note that a manuscript of this poem was catalogued as 2477.71 by Dr. von Heinemann in his 1898 catalogue of the Herzog August Library in Wolfenbüttel.

4   See Paul Ferguson, 'Where is the Ship of William Wallace?': https://www.academia.edu/37917652/WHERE_IS_THE_SHIP_OF_WILLI AM_WALLACE.

5   *Antidicsonus Cujusdam Cantabrigiensis G.P. Accessit Libellus, in Quo ... Explicatur Impia Dicsoni Artificiosa Memoria.*

6 'Academics tend to look on "esoteric," "occult," or "magical" beliefs with contempt, but are usually ignorant about the religious and philosophical traditions to which these terms refer, or their relevance to intellectual history. Wouter J. Hanegraaff tells the neglected story of how intellectuals since the Renaissance have tried to come to terms with a cluster of "pagan" ideas from late antiquity that challenged the foundations of biblical religion and Greek rationality. 'Expelled from the academy on the basis of Protestant and Enlightenment polemics, these traditions have come to be perceived as the Other by which academics define their identity to the present day' (part of the blurb for Wouter J. Hanegraaff's *Esotericism and the Academy: Rejected Knowledge in Western Culture*, CUP, 2012).

7 http://www.philological.bham.ac.uk/dickson/

8 Available online at http://digitool.library.mcgill.ca/R/?func=dbin-jump-full&object_id=102846&local_base=GEN01-MCG02

9 Available online at https://www.persee.fr/doc/xvii_0291-3798_2004_num_58_1_1969

10 https://www.academia.edu/3014531/Neoplatonism_in_Science. His references are to the 1966 edition of *The Art of Memory* by Frances Yates (ISBN 978-0-226-95001-3).

The Shadow of Reason[1] and Judgement

or

The Virtue of Memory:

A Prosopopœia[2]

by

Alexander Dicsone of Errol[3]

TO THE MOST ILLUSTRIOUS LORD ROBERT DUDLEY,
EARL OF LEICESTER[4], etc.

I sat down under his shadow

with great delight[5].

LONDON,
Published by Thomas Vautrollier[7.] Printer.
1583.

[Motto on printer's device:] THE ANCHOR OF HOPE[6].

PREFACE BY ALEXANDER DICSONE OF ERROL

TO THE MOST ILLUSTRIOUS LORD ROBERT DUDLEY, EARL OF LEICESTER, etc.

So, my most illustrious Earl, can you really spare enough time from your own business[8] (or rather, from the affairs of State) to look at my *Shadow*, even though it might turn out to be the work of someone who's just acting the fool? For no doubt you'll accuse me of making fun of you or might even say that I'm insane, adding that it's tantamount to the former if I'm peddling trifles and to the latter if I'm not.

For my part I shall only say, 'I determine nothing'[9]. My judgement and evaluation of the matter in hand tell me that it is better to make such a statement than to run the risk of being suspected of either vanity or stupidity by disclosing information in some respects and concealing it in others. After all, if anyone puts forward ideas of his own and then proceeds to praise them or, alternatively, disparages them simply to appear more modest and polite then, in either case, he shows himself to be nothing more than a pompous ass, for the former is typical of the unsophisticated and the excessively frank and the latter of starvelings and knaves.

Even if my meditation, whatever it might consist of, does show due regard for your very burdensome responsibilities then it might still of course outstay its welcome, and you should therefore take great care should it appear to be drunk[10] when it comes knocking at your door. If, however, we are to make due allowance for the natural order of things and for the customs of our time then what, I ask, should the legitimate focus of a philosophical meditation be other than that divinity who was the common parent of letters[11]? I, for my part, shall certainly be grateful if you would allow such a meditation to dwell in the *shadow* of your glorious name, and shall definitely try to ensure that its ultimate fruit will be an argument that is likely to engender, at the very least, a not unpleasant *memory*.

Farewell.

January 1st [1584].

ALEXANDER DICSONE SALUTES THE READER

What, I hear you say, do I find so fascinating about the contents of the shadow that is cast by a light-source? Surely the former merely defines the boundary[12] of the latter?

It is beyond dispute that we encounter two things in Nature: memory as an idea in itself, and the way in which our reasoning faculty accesses that memory[13.] I am happy to leave the former topic to the brave, for everyone unconditionally agrees that the virtue of memory is unique. However, it's the latter topic that I'm concerned with in this book, for it is a legitimate subject of enquiry whether there is any power of reason involved in accessing the memory and, if so, what we shall be likely to first encounter when we start investigating it.

Those who have been blessed with greater stamina than I will certainly make their presence felt in the former area of enquiry, but I myself shall not be working in that field. As for those without such powers of endurance, they will prefer either to tell me what they already know or will decide that what they don't know should perhaps be left for me to find out. As I seem to have satisfied the latter I shall not be wasting my time flattering the tastes of the former, for since such people are superficial and possess only a minimal degree of cunning, they will naturally assume that it is easy to speculate about my own personality on the basis of their own. Consequently they'll prefer to ask a physician to help them develop a good memory or else will seek the source of my theory of memory in the Creator. Such people consider the Art of Memory to be a thing of naught or, at least, something boring and tiresome. Finally, they will see me personally as vain or, perhaps, even weak-minded.

But they do all this with impunity, for I simply refuse to lose my temper when I'm pecked at by such tiny birds as these. I ignore such wretches, and turn instead to my more cherished (and also more refined) friends, those who feel that they must:

Priusquam noscere queant, exigunt:[14]
'...investigate things thoroughly before they can pronounce judgement'.

I occasionally encounter a second type of person, namely those who complain that what I have to say is too obscure. If they are kindly disposed towards me then they'll infer causes from circumstances[15]*; if not, and if they choose to go on the offensive against me, then they should obviously heed the words of the poet:*

Ole quid ad te,
De cute quid faciat ille, vel ille sua.
'What does it matter to you, Olus, what this man or that woman does with their own skin?'[16]

Well, it's my skin, and it's my money too, so it's certainly no business of Olus.

Finally, if it's true that 'I have my Zoilus[17]*' as the saying goes, then I expect I'll also encounter people who will feel that my frankness in attacking and explaining Socratic deceit goes too far. So be it – so what, I say, as long as they in their turn acknowledge the poverty of their own judgement, for acknowledge it they must unless they want me to turn my attentions to them. For it matters a great deal, dear reader:*

Davusne loquatur, herusne,
Maturusne senex, an adhuc florente iuventa
Fervidus.
'whether it's Davus that's speaking, or the master of the house, or an old man, or a hot-blooded fellow in the bloom of youth',[18]

for if any literary form is difficult to make convincing then it's the prosopopœia, partly because, in this form of narrative, you need to ensure that what the characters are saying matches their personalities while at the same time being on the alert that, in your desire to achieve conformity between character and utterance, you do not neglect the former. It's also inevitable that, from time to time, you'll fail in one respect or the other, though it certainly seems preferable to try to preserve the consistency of the character whom you've just introduced to the reader. Anyway, if you think I've been careless in attending to the attributes and demands of this literary form then I'm sure I can count on your benevolence.

Farewell.

JOHN ADAM[19] OF LINCOLN SALUTES THE READER

A commonplace to be found in many discourses is that sound and honest merchandise doesn't need the services of a charlatan to sell it, any more than a good wine needs an ivy-wreathed bowl to persuade you to drink it.

Thanks to the diligence and meticulousness of our friend Dicsone, and following a number of attempts of various kinds, his ideas about the virtue of memory are now finally with us, and they do not seem to me to need my recommendation, promotion or dissimulation, for his argument is unusual, finely-wrought and useful, as everyone will be happy to admit without demur.

His book is also mature and finished in form, and decidedly philosophical: every syllable will be found to have its appropriate emphasis, every word its meaning, and every sentence its correct weight – what more could you want? This is certainly a very solid piece of work, and not just a sketchy and unconvincing simulacrum of a serious philosophical treatise.

Once upon a time the benefits of a good memory suddenly found themselves rendered superfluous by the invention of writing, and even when they finally started to attract more attention in our own times they were deemed unworthy of generous support, as if they were afflicted with a strange and severe melancholy and deformity.

Then along came Dicsone who, as it were, restored a patch of fallow land to its original vigour and purpose by measuring it out with daily ploughing, renewal and second ploughings and, indeed, with every known form of cultivation and sowing of seed.

Not only did Dicsone restore it, he also popularised it, to the great advantage of us mortals. Unfortunately that execrable monstrosity of our age, the curse of envy, is now spreading far and wide, so that you'll find nothing in this world of ours that's of rare ingenuity or polished craftsmanship that's not insolently attacked, snapped at and lacerated. So little however does our author allow himself to be upset by these paltry daggers that he is even accustomed to taking pity upon their leaden tips. So, dear reader, embrace with open arms this sweet and pleasant *shadow*, so worthy of your efforts, and bestow your favour upon it.

Farewell.

A PROSOPOPŒIA

ON

THE SHADOW OF REASON

BY

ALEXANDER DICSONE OF ERROL

DRAMATIS PERSONÆ: THAMUS[20], MERCURY[21], THEUTATES[22]

THAMUS. But Mercury, those things *are* true, because as far as absolutely anything in the universe is concerned there's nothing quite like the Odd, the One and the Single. The One embodies just one idea, and has just one sign to indicate that it is the One. That idea is certainly incorporeal, but through the process of embodiment it produces all the ideas of the world, of time and of the generative process. But can we really use our imaginations to understand the vessel[23] of anything that we usually grasp with the intellect alone? This is true of everything that perishes beneath the rising of the sun, and perhaps it is even true of the generative process itself, given that it may not be able to endure the rays shed by such a great light. Accordingly, the perversity of ignorance has washed over the Earth, so that it now carries a huge burden of matter. This is pure evil, and since it's a fire that transforms a pyramid into a type of cube[24] it does not allow any connection with the upper spheres, but nor is it stopped in its tracks at that point. Oh how absurd this is! There's just one generative process, one time, one world, one eternity – but how many different things have the philosophers asserted that One Thing to be? But at least they did genuinely reflect upon the subject unless, of course, they preferred just to spew the whole thing forth[25].

MERCURY. But they have had their hands immersed in the waters[26], for they bestow that cloak upon people. But when will the time come when those people wish to tear that cloak asunder and escape from it. And are they even able to do so?

THAM. Cloak?

MERC. Isn't that what you said? But how many cloaks are there which aren't fashioned in the image of the tomb!

THAM. What you're referring to is the web of ignorance, and the robber that's a sojourner in its dark expanse[27]. But that's quite enough of all that! Besides, since it's a holiday and we've been given permission to go for a walk, would you not like, while you're listening to the rest of this conversation, to proceed to the jaws of Hell and its wide expanse? Maybe you're obliged to do this anyway as part of the duty you have to tell us about the shadows – unless you want to do something else that is.

MERC. But the Senate's already in session and has already summoned me several times! Just in case you didn't know, there's a motion before the Senate relating to wild animals of a certain kind, and my presence there may be required to enable a decision to be made upon it.

THAM. What's all this about wild animals? Surely they're entirely extinct upon the Earth, along with their bodies?

MERC. People certainly believe that, but in fact the Underworld *only* accepts wild animals.

THAM. But it's an everyday occurrence to see humans going down into the Underworld. We certainly don't see any wild animals going down there!

MERC. You are ignorant, Thamus, simply ignorant. Those *are* wild animals – they're just pretending to have the human form of the creature in question[28].

THAM. Well, what you're telling me is simply incredible, but I suppose we're obliged to believe anything that Mercury says, although I would say that this phenomenon could perhaps be attributed to people's bestial habits. But do continue.

MERC. The Earth is a place of sin, and Mother Nature deceives us in her mimicry, for the form of a true man is intellect. In the shadow of the light the mind clothes itself in matter through the mind and with the assistance of the spirit. Positioned at the boundary of the image it inclines towards matter but is driven back to those things that fall within the scope of the intelligence – the things that actually exist. The mind is not afflicted by the senses but, untroubled by the defenders of matter[29], tries to rise towards that which actually exists, as if from a dark and, as it were, night-like day. Those who have bound up their soul within the body and have therefore cast it aside are savage beasts, who should perhaps be frightened of coming back in the next life as animals.[30]

THAM. I think I understand. But what do you mean by 'the defenders of matter'? Can you be a bit more explicit?

MERC. I mean that such a man is in the duodenary, and has been driven away from the denary[31]. But I'm in a hurry, and your excessive inquisitiveness is making me late.

THAM. But... Oh, he's gone. But who's this? Why, it's Theutates! I recognise his staff, his numbers, his counting-stones and tablets, and his alphabets as well. Yes indeed, it *is* him. Was what we've been talking about something you're familiar with, Theutates? Have you, as a god, also endured the Underworld?

THEUTATES. Theutates most certainly is a god, Thamus, and nor are your beloved Egyptians in any doubt that he is, but I'm just his shadow.

THAM. But what about Æacus[32]? You tricked him in a similar way, didn't you[33]?

THEUT. Yes I did.

THAM. I approve of that wholeheartedly by the way. You are most certainly a god!

THEUT. Are you laughing at me, my good man? If you'd been a member of high society in Naucratis[34] then you wouldn't have these absurd doubts about my divinity.

THAM. But I certainly would have been absurd if I'd ceased to have any doubts. But you're quite wrong: you're not a man after all, but a wild beast, as Mercury has just been explaining to me.

THEUT. You're slandering me, Thamus. Do literacy and our various mathematical discoveries really strike you as nothing more than the tracks of a wild animal?

THAM. Regarding mathematics, Mercury may well have investigated it and perhaps there's something in it. But with that alphabet of yours I'm afraid you're contributing absolutely nothing[35].

THEUT. But Thamus, it's that same alphabet that makes your beloved Egyptians wiser in learning and readier in memory. And I'm happy to say that this potion for memory and wisdom is *my* invention.

THAM. Love has obviously clouded your mind. What you're asserting is actually the complete opposite of what those things actually do, for neglecting the practice of memory encourages the minds of students to forget what they've just learned. Obviously, if they place their faith in the external formulæ of writing then they'll stop recalling and developing those interior formulæ by their own efforts and through a process of recollection. So you haven't discovered a potion for memory at all, but actually one for forgetfulness! And there's a second problem with another part of your proposition, and it's one that causes no small degree of inconvenience, for in those bygone days you didn't bestow upon 'my beloved Egyptians' as you call them the truth of wisdom at all, but only the *idea and appearance* of it. Since they'll have learnt a lot without a teacher they'll also give the appearance of knowing a lot, but as they're generally ignorant, as well as irritating and tiresome in their manners and conversation, they're all imbued – thanks to your patronage of them – with the conviction that they're wise – but what they're *not* imbued with is wisdom itself. I recall that, once upon a time, in that Upper Egyptian town they usually call 'Egyptian Thebes', I responded to you in the same way. Your embarrassment on that occasion made it abundantly clear that I was right to take you to task. But that was back in the days when people would, as it were, 'write in their mind'[36], with genuine knowledge of what they were writing, since the mind is alive and can remedy injustices, and since it has acquired an understanding of what should and what should not be said to people[37]. But your progeny, having been brought up abusively and injuriously by ignorant people, and being in any case idle and apathetic, are always in need of some fatherly help, for they are incapable of either remedying the injustices they've suffered or of helping themselves. So what you've actually been selling people is a quack potion for the memory, since by reasoning illogically you've disinherited the whole of posterity of this most praiseworthy study. But where are you going, my good man? Are that staff, and the power that goes with it, really the hallmarks of a god, or are they just the signs of a savage beast, as I suggested at the outset?

END OF THE FIRST PROSOPOPŒIA

ALEXANDER DICSONE OF ERROL

A PROSOPOPŒIA ON THE SHADOW OF REASON

DRAMATIS PERSONÆ: SOCRATES, THAMUS

SOCRATES. Let me put it to the test, Thamus. I heard from the old folk – and they certainly knew what they were talking about – that near Naucratis in Egypt there lived one of the old gods, Theutates by name, to whom the bird they call the ibis was sacred. They also told me that you, as King of Upper and Lower Egypt, had many discussions with Theutates about some of his discoveries. I understand that all the various pro's and con's of these discoveries were given an airing, but that when you came to the subject of the alphabet you tried to argue, without any supporting evidence, that people who rely upon writing would be inclined to neglect their memories.

THAMUS. What are you driving at?

SOC. Well, doesn't that help explain why I myself have never written anything?

THAM. Well, maybe it does. But who *are* you?

SOC. I am Socrates[38], judged by Apollo to be the wisest of mankind[39].

THAM. Oh I see, so you're that Sophist that mankind would have been better off without! But I suppose you'll say that the oracle[40] was wrong, but actually he described you just as the citizens, after they'd had a chance to get to know you, subsequently adjudged you to be. So when you say 'But Apollo examined me!', you're actually saying nothing meaningful. But I'll come back to that point in a moment. Anyway, what about what the poet said:

Qualia docuisti rudes,
Heu insania tua, civitatisque
Quæ tu nutriit
Corrumpentem adolescentulos!
'What things you have taught these idiots... Alas, how foolish you are, and how foolish also is the city that has fed you – you of all people, the corrupter of our youth!'[41]

SOC. But those are the words of Aristophanes, and in that passage his good faith is suspect, and with good reason.

THAM. Alright, let's not trust anything he says. Instead we'll deal with you ourselves. Surely, Socrates, it's possible in this world for a deceiver to be sometimes mistaken for a man of his word or *vice versa*?

SOC. Just in case you're not aware of the fact, it's actually *my* job to ask the questions. Indeed, I've always laid claim to that role as if it were mine by right. But since I fear the Trojans[42], and especially Diogenes[43], who's a real Polydamas[44], I'll answer your question, as I don't want to give the impression of being evasive. Yes, it is possible.

THAM. So, for example, you can have a medical doctor whose only real skill is turning minor illnesses into major ones and yet is buoyed up by popular approval, while another one has hardly any patients who are willing to place their trust in him?

SOC. Yes, that's also true.

THAM. And so in these cases, and others also, those who achieve something by merit that they have earned usually owe a debt to mendacity?

SOC. Perhaps.

THAM. And is it not also true, as the poet says,

Falsus honos iuvat, et mendax infamia terret?
Quem nisi mendosum, et mendacem?
'...that no one benefits from a word of false praise or is frightened by an infamous lie except the deceitful and those who are full of faults?'[45]

while another tells us that:

Fortis et ignavus parili afficiuntur honore?
'equal honour is bestowed on the brave man and the coward.'[46]

And do we not also find judges to be guilty of this fault, even though nothing should be less corrupt than the sentence handed down by a court of law?

SOC. Certainly, for the Athenians sentenced me to death even though I was innocent.

THAM. And may not a virtuous man be suspected of being a rascal and a villain, so that he is harassed, discredited, rejected and reduced to poverty, while on the other hand a wicked man may be praised and cherished, and perhaps has every honour and high office heaped upon him?

SOC. Yes, perhaps.

THAM. And although such a man may be completely ignorant, doesn't he win popular acclaim and approval?

SOC. Yes, even though I know who the intended target of this discussion is.

THAM. Good. And are not these and similar things harmful to the human race?

SOC. They are.

THAM. But what is their origin?

SOC. Deceit perhaps.

THAM. So deceit is a most pernicious thing, as it's responsible for this Earth of ours being known as the home of vanity?

SOC. Yes, it is indeed a most pernicious thing.

THAM. And yet, son of Sophroniscus[47], aren't you yourself the father of lies and a most definite charlatan?

SOC. What are you driving at?

THAM. What? Once you've checked all the counting-tokens individually do you not usually then check the total that they add up to[48]? Do you want me, if you're not happy with the result, to do the calculation all over again[49]?

SOC. You may think you've caught me in a trap and forced me to admit to something I'd rather not admit to, but that's simply not the case. But why are we going round in circles[50] like this?

THAM. What is it you've been hiding?

SOC. I don't know what you're talking about.

THAM. Tell me: were you really wise, or not?

SOC. And what if I wasn't?

THAM. Then why did Apollo praise you? Why did you debate with intellectuals? And why did you mock all of them? They debated, while you just argued. They made statements, while you just denied them. Whence the saying,

Verbulis novis ipsum,
Et sententiis sagittabo.
'I'll riddle that man through and through with new maxims and opinions.'[51]

But please don't waste your time here if you don't want to, for I understand you enjoy talking nonsense with Nestor and Palamedes[52]. SOC. But what if I *am* wise?

THAM. If you're wise then why have you dispensed with every criterion of truth? Why were you so fond of boasting that you knew nothing? On the basis of that assumption you could reasonably have asserted that all children are wise.

SOC. But I was judged to be the wisest of them all!

THAM. So there has been some dissembling, and we've established what we wanted to establish. But I'm getting off the point: you were actually the most cunning of men, and in discussion a schemer and a crafty old fox.

SOC. But I was only human, and it is human to err!

THAM. No, there was more to it than that: you were *habitually* deceitful. Don't try dissembling. Around these parts you won't find any way of leading people astray with your misrepresentations. Not even Apollo would make any bones about that, and he is the supreme interpreter of his own oracles. It is generally agreed that you were not imbued with any genuine skills or learning. If you deny that, then can you tell me what the properties of numbers are? Show me, for example, by what reasoning the circle can be squared, and the cube doubled. Describe, if you can, the movements of the planets, and the ways of the heavens. In fact, tell me about anything you like. What do you think about God for example? Who divided the light from the darkness[53]? Is God knowable or unknowable? Does He exist in the Father, in the intellect, in love? What is the divine essence? What are its accomplishments? What are the rays of God[54]? What are the signs of His existence? And what are His shadows[55]?

SOC. If you could be a god then what kind of god would you like to be?

THAM. I must admit, Socrates, that that question has left me dumbfounded. But let's move on to more relevant things. Tell me, if you can, about eternity, about the world, about time, about the generative process. What ultimately is the soul of the world-soul[56]? What is the origin of things, and what keeps them in existence? How is the world constructed? What is its form? How is it organised? What gives it motion? What is life? What is death? Finally, what of resurrection on the Day of Judgement? Tell me, what do you think of the belief that the virtuous will enjoy a better fate, given that they have hardly any power and also have an imperfect essence? And are there really any imperfections in that essence? If so, are there many of them? Are they mixed? Are they specific to the individual? And what about the spiritual faculties[57] – what are they exactly? What can you tell me about the shape of the moon? Why do its horns sometimes seem to be growing, while at other times they seem blunter or more pointed? And tell me about the sea: if it's actually blue, then why does it look purple when it's being beaten by oars?

But now you've gone quiet, which is a sure sign of your lack of experience in such matters and a testimony to your ignorance. Therefore, my friend, you should acknowledge that:

Putabas Deum nullum, præterquam nos
Et chaos hoc, et nebulas, et linguam, tria hæc.
...you don't believe in any gods except the ones *we* believe in – the triad of Chaos, Clouds and Tongue.'[58]

That friend of yours Plato, someone whom we around here can hardly stand even when he's drenched in perfume[59], was certainly in other respects very devoted to you, and yet, when starting a discussion about Nature, he didn't even get you involved in the conversation as he almost always did on other occasions, but instead devoted his attention to the excellent Timæus of Locri[60].
SOC. But I simply didn't have the strength to ascend to heaven, so I always disdained topics like that as being mere vanities. I tried to rescue philosophy from topics of this kind – with their focus on ascending to heaven and all that sort of thing – and tried to situate it within the context of people's homes and cities.
THAM. What unbelievable folly! What ignorance of the things of God! So what is left for you, and what is left for God? You turned out to be a rogue and someone obsessed with the body, and therefore a person who is unable to appreciate the Beautiful and the Good, for a soul that doesn't understand any of the things that exist falls blindly into the physical passions.
SOC. But that's not true! Please understand that I promoted and established all these things on an ethical basis. Although I might have been contemptuous of all those 'higher things', I've always worked hard on the correct forms that we need to establish for the State and the lives of private citizens.
THAM. Yes, I appreciate that, hence those famous and brilliant

proposals about wives and children being held in common, about communal ownership of land and resources, and women performing active military service along with men[61]! A real literary masterpiece, full of artistry and morality! What light-headedness caused you to show such a lack of consideration for others by preaching things like that?

SOC. But what was disgraceful about those things, especially when they attracted such praise and renown? Surely, by that reasoning, everyone will consider universal friendship to be an admirable thing, and surely the current evils of the State seem to arise from the fact that people do not own everything in common? But what I'm really referring to here are things like perjury by witnesses, toadyism among the rich, and lawsuits and other disputes about breach of contract.

THAM. But Socrates, none of these things is due to wealth not being held in common – they're due to dishonesty. Why do I say this? Because we find that people who hold property in common are more likely to fall out with each other than those who keep their resources to themselves. But you've been led astray because you thought – after looking at the matter from every side and in all its forms – that it would be more expedient to have just one household and just one State. But that's not the case; indeed, if we pursued this line of argument then there wouldn't be a State at all. And what, in the meantime, would your Producers actually receive from your Guardians[62]? What would the magistracy get out of it? What would their prospects be, and what would their remuneration be like? It also seems absurd, after putting women on the same level as wild animals[63], to insist that they should follow the same pursuits and perform the same functions as men. What have such roles got to do with wild animals?

SOC. But I then went on to explain that the magistrates and governors of the State would be different from those who are subject to their rule, just as we see the warp arising from one kind of wool and the weft from another.

THAM. I feel really sorry for you, Socrates, for surely this is incompatible with the unity and sharing that you propose? Solve that conundrum if you can, and find just one, out of all those sophisms, that can get you out of this quandary. But we'll let those things pass. You did actually seemed to be philosophising with divine inspiration when you insisted that, in human beings, reason should prevail, and that passion and anger should be kept under control. But that was a mistake, for it is not reason that summons us to duty by issuing an order or which discourages us from an act of dishonesty by prohibition; quite the contrary, for it is reason not anger that deceives and is deceived, and unless the intellect is present and people are immersed in the cup of regeneration[64] then they are wasting their time relying on your recommendation of reason, even though there'll be some among your favourites in whom that deception cannot be dispelled. To such people however I would strongly recommend not only mastery of their passions and anger but also of their reason – indeed I would recommend that the intellect alone should be supreme. Indeed, to bring the conversation back to you, that principle should have formed the substance of the Socratic state.

SOC. And yet, as everyone knows, I lived an honest life.

THAM. You are wrong, for you chose a lazy existence, devoting no time to study, learning a trade or military service, and nor did you teach your sons the right way to live[65]. And how many philosophers have escaped being affected by your wickedness? Whom did it spare? But we'll let that pass. You didn't tolerate uncultured or dishonest Sophists either. But we'll let that pass too, though indeed the censure of the magistrate would, in such cases, have been more efficacious than the satire of someone who was a Sophist himself[66]. But tell me, what passionate frenzy was it that first got you interested in Anaxagoras[67]?

SOC. Surely moderation is worthy of praise?

THAM. Now you're wriggling. I didn't think that you'd bring up the subject of moderation.

SOC. I preferred eating light meals to being a glutton.

THAM. No you didn't. You went to every banquet you could, just to tell people your views on wisdom. We'll leave to one side for now the suspicions people had about your interest in young boys, especially Alcibiades[68]. You know the rest:

Considera adolescentule, importuna esse omnia
Quæ insunt, voluptatibus si priveris
Puerorum, mulierum, ludorum, obsoniorum,
Conviviorum, cachinnorum:
Quale hoc ipsum erit vivere, his si privatus fueris?

'Young man, just think what moderation actually involves, and what pleasures you'll deny yourself if you practise it: boys, women, drinking-games, food, banquets, laughter... Tell me, without these things, is life really worth living?'[69]

Indeed, they say you thought that young men should be ashamed if they didn't have male lovers.

SOC. But those are Aristophanes' words, as I've already said. Certainly no crime was ever committed.

THAM. Even so, those actions were not beyond criticism, were they?

SOC. But what if they were?

THAM. Well, they were certainly not beyond suspicion.

SOC. But what if they were?

THAM. Did they not at least set a bad example to others?

SOC. But what about my famous tolerance? Xanthippe[70] bears witness to that.

THAM. I don't like people who are too tolerant.

SOC. But I used to walk around in my bare feet!

THAM. Well, that was just a pointless stunt that shows how stupid you are.

SOC. But I was always sober, and I often used to stand motionless all day long.

THAM. But why all this showing-off in the first place? If a person couldn't do that then would anyone really think he was in a bad way, and if he didn't want to do it then would he immediately be seen as a fool? It would have been more praiseworthy if you'd simply refrained from indulging in vanities of that kind. So, what else?

SOC. But just a moment ago you were saying how sly and secretive I am. What could be less compatible with that sort of nature than despising human kindness or considering wealth to be a thing of no importance?

THAM. Nothing, certainly. Yet you've achieved nothing, and nor can anything to the contrary be said about Socrates.

SOC. But acknowledge my steadfastness at least, for with how many chains was I was most tightly bound after I was unjustly condemned? Go on, tell me, how many?

THAM. But, my good man, you were confident you'd be set free and given your freedom. That's why you wanted to be seen with a serene expression, like someone who had nothing at all to fear from death. But when you saw that no hope remained for you then you wept for yourself and your sons just like babies do. Then, when it was time for you to depart, you displayed a certain smugness, as if you were about to suffer willingly what, in any case, you would certainly have had to endure whether you wanted to or not.

SOC. But I drank the hemlock, as you can even see from my legs, which are still puffed up and swollen.

THAM. That was just weakness and imbecility. How much better a person was the man about whom it was said:

Nolo virum facili redimit qui sanguine vitam[71]*:*
Hunc volo, laudari qui sine morte potest.
'I do not want a man who wins fame by readily shedding his blood, but rather someone who earns praise without killing himself.'[72]

So you're simply tormenting yourself in vain. Let's face it, you can't come up with any effective counter-arguments.

SOC. But surely the integrity of my disciples is enough to protect my reputation from these wagging tongues?

THAM. I'm certainly aware of Aristippus[73], who was dissolute and a drunk, and Plato, who fawned on Dionysius[74] and was even worse than Aristippus in that he was of course considered to be a more saintly man. Haven't you heard how Plato urged Dion to murder his kinsman Dionysius? And if Plato was your enemy then why did you cosy up to him? Why did you accept money from him? If he was your friend then why plot against him? And what can I say about that chap Xenophon[75], who was so effeminate he was hardly a man at all?

SOC. Well, acknowledge Antisthenes[76] at least.

THAM. Certainly I shall. For at least he was interested in women, didn't suck up to tyrants, considered money and wealth to be of no importance, and (what is surely most pleasing to you) was the only person to encourage the Athenians to become historians of your death. He also taught moderation to Crates[77], tolerance to Zeno, and peace of mind to Diogenes[78]. But, my good fellow, it's well known that he was a learned man before he even started studying with you, and that in any case he didn't spend much time with you as you lived in Athens while he lived in the Piræus[79].

SOC. Well, you've certainly given me a good drubbing today Thamus! But how do you know all these things when you died centuries before they actually happened?

THAM. If I'm making all this up or telling lies then I'm happy to be corrected. But if these things *are* true then why are you so upset about them? How can you bear to think about what you've been responsible for? But I will not dissemble: I must certainly acknowledge Antisthenes,

Crates and Diogenes, but hardly a day goes by without me hearing something you've have said or done that's harmful to us mortals.

SOC. Other people may find fault with me if they wish, but Thamus used to have an obligation to be better-natured and more fair-minded than that. I think I can perhaps request your grace for displaying a certain consistency of judgement?

THAM. In what, Socrates?

SOC. In the fact that, thanks to your influence, I never put pen to paper in my whole life!

THAM. Now *you're* finding fault with *me*! But I didn't say that people shouldn't write at all, but only that the study of memory should be restored to the place that's currently occupied by writing[80]. Think about it: one person entrusts to writing those things that he has conceived in his mind[81]. That's one thing. Another doesn't do that and instead relies on the efforts of his memory – that's surely even better? But I didn't prove either the former or the latter proposition without sound reasoning, even though I don't consider it 'to be worthy of a philosopher to appeal to authority and witnesses, who can either tell the truth by accident or, alternatively, tell lies and allow their imaginations to run riot out of malice'[82]. We should be led to and persuaded of the rightness of our actions by argument and reasoning, not by events, especially those of a questionable credibility. 'Thamus thought that something or other was the case' – well, so what? But 'Thamus established something by means of reasoning' – well, that's something quite different. But what am I doing, expecting excellence in dialectic from Socrates, as if he was a proper philosopher!

SOC. You're certainly an awkward character, Thamus. But now you must tell me in your turn whether it is right for the same person both to seek peace in wartime and to refuse to condemn the arts of war in peacetime?[83]

THAM. Yes, certainly it is.

SOC. And surely if we are able to conceive of things that are harmful to the forms of the State then we must also have conceived of things that are of advantage to them?

THAM. Yes of course.

SOC. And is it not the duty of the same person who identifies and repeals bad laws to also enact good and advantageous ones?

THAM. Perhaps.

SOC. And surely it is also appropriate that someone who has given an account of the shadow of death should seem to be able to have sat in the shadow of light so as to lead people to that shadow?

THAM. Yes, it would seem so.

SOC. So is it not therefore the task of that same Thamus, who discovered the substance of forgetfulness, to also reveal to us the potion for a good memory? When I tried to spend some time with you discussing this matter, starting with the very basics, your long-winded explanation of my life and teachings stopped me from doing so. So come along now, since you've recognised that I must now shuffle off this mortal coil by decree of the Senate,

Tu animum magnum
Contine in pectoribus: amicitia enim est melior.
'...keep your magnanimity in your breast, for friendship is better'[84]

and, if you are happy to have me as an interlocutor, then remind me about that form of memory that formed the subject of the discoveries made by Theutates.

THAM. And I have to explain all this to a Greek? And a bag of wind to boot! Well, I'll see about that. You say 'friendship is better', but tell me what persuaded you and where you got the idea from that this is in any way relevant to the matter under discussion? If there's nothing in the way of a criterion, if there's no mechanism for passing judgement, then it follows that there's nothing that can be known or perceived, for all that remains is just rash opinionising:

Sacer est morbus, et visus mentitur.
'It is a deadly disease, and the appearance is deceptive.'[85]

And once we've got rid of opinionising and perception then all we have left is assertion. But you're blushing! But wasn't that the way you thought about things? Weren't these the wares you used to peddle? Aren't they from your workshop? So what now? Are you sticking to your way of thinking?

SOC. And if I do?

THAM. Then there's nothing further to be said about the matter.

SOC. And if I don't?

THAM. It's not for sages to change their mind – right? Isn't that your opinion also?

SOC. The least you can do is show some respect for us mortals.
THAM. But it's wicked to yield and to show pity, for a wise man never allows himself to get upset. Why are you looking so ashamed, for I always thought that was your own point of view also. But do as you wish. I shall do what I was never accustomed to do in life, seeing that I disputed about things that can only be sustained by doctrine and reason: I shall recall to mind, on this Earth of ours, that form of memory which, as you say, has been investigated for centuries, and with you as my interlocutor. If that's what you want of course. And yet:

Tua messis in herba:
'you are harvesting in the grass'.[86]

for you won't understand what is said to you until you have made your peace with Anaxagoras[87] who, I hear, has also passed on. So listen carefully!

END OF THE SECOND PROSOPOPŒIA

THE SHADOW OF REASON AND JUDGEMENT

OR

THE VIRTUE OF MEMORY

A PROSOPOPŒIA

BY

ALEXANDER DICSONE OF ERROL

CHAPTER I.
MEMORY AND FORGETFULNESS.

Forgetfulness is a defect occasioned by a weak and undisciplined mind, and is that primary material legacy that dissolves and attenuates the mind's principal powers.

From this statement it will be clear that forgetfulness does not originate in God or in Nature. I have no knowledge what part Fortune plays in this, but I do know that forgetfulness is located within us and that, of our own volition, we enter into a sort of contract with it. Sophisticated people therefore hold forgetfulness in scorn, hence the saying:

Mos est oblivisci hominibus,
neque novisse, cuius nihili sit faciunda gratia.
'It's fashionable for people to forget (and even to pretend not to recognise) those whose favour has been acquired to no purpose.'[88]

When forgetfulness is present there will be no progression from the boundary[89], nor will there be any shadows, subjects, organisation or, ultimately, animation.

In such cases the immediate inspection of an object is enough to neutralise the efficacy of our thinking process. In that situation, even if we ignore the nature and effects of time, we find ourselves plunged into a state of ignorance, and that's the very worst thing of all – indeed, it resembles a form of unjust slavery[90].

Memory is the precise opposite of forgetfulness, as it is a power, an action, a shadow, and a beating of the wings of the mind[91] unencumbered by the use of the physical body and the sensory faculties. Its primary virtue lies in the shadow of the good[92], and its secondary virtue in the shadow of judgement (hence the title of this book). By 'judgement' we mean the capacity to retain what you have learned or what you yourself have conceived, even if you do not find it congenial material for reflection.

CHAPTER II.
THE CAUSES OF MEMORY.

This section deals with what you can do with your memory, and also with what you can bring forth into action, for to understand the power underlying the causes of memory is also to understand the actions that you can perform with it. But I shall deal with the latter topic elsewhere, in its proper place.

Although everything proceeds from God and the One, we do find, if we reason further, that the power that underlies the causes of memory takes three different forms: first we must reflect upon the role of Mother Nature; second we must experience the rays from the heavens and their effects; and third we must allow the counsels of reason and learning to come to our aid.

The efficacy of this virtue, which is innate in our minds, is a perfectly natural phenomenon[93], since it is born simultaneously with the cognitive faculty.

Indeed, man was contemplating and expressing this virtue even before Theutates invented writing, and nor in those days did humanity have any need of such things as letters and alphabets. Unfortunately, being all too human, mankind – after that great and skilful sage

Theutates had invented writing – came to prefer him to the natural way of doing things and so became his followers. It therefore became necessary to protect memory from the effects of his invention. Even so, a general decline in memory ensued, and humanity became less interested in working in accordance with the laws of Nature. Ultimately, mankind acted impiously towards her, which gave rise to an actually quite spurious allegation that humanity was developing a streak of weak-mindedness.

The second power comes from the gods, but it is not shared out equally, with the result that the gods are also turned towards those people who have an inferior capacity for detachment of the mind from the body.

This gave rise to the third and final power, which is that of learning and reason, and which stimulates and invigorates Mother Nature, who is otherwise latent. Indeed, that power is called forth from her womb, and with her assistance that previous conception, which is Nature herself, starts to glow with learning and reason. Indeed, when we reflect upon this alliance with Nature she sometimes seems to be the teacher and sometimes the pupil.

It used to be thought that the Art of Memory, after remaining in the background for so many years thanks to that invention of old Theutates, first saw the light of day in your own country of Greece. Indeed, it's still widely believed that it was that fellow from Ceos[94] who was the first to discover and promulgate it. But this is not correct, as you yourself discovered, for you concluded that it originated in Egypt and was then revived in our own times. But even if we set Egypt to one side, Simonides didn't really achieve that much, for if you turn the pages of the old Celtic annals and you read the stories that are brought to life within them you'll find that, long before him, the Art of Memory was starting to thrive in the school of the Druids[95]. So much for Simonides and his Tyndarides![96]

Other people, in an effort to appear more civilised, use sarcasm to try to persuade us that this Art of Memory is completely worthless, replying that they prefer to forget what they wish to forget rather than remember it[97]. I won't deny that when they say this they're expressing a truth about mankind, and maybe it's a point of view that *is* held by some poor wretches, but it certainly has no relevance to this particular topic, where we should be asking what the best course of action is, not what this or that person would prefer to remember or forget.

Anyway, those are the origins of the Art of Memory – in other words, how it arose and how it was disseminated.

CHAPTER III.
WHAT MEMORY IS.

Surely only an impudent fellow would look for the blessing and influences of this shadow within the circuit of immortal God and within that light that surpasses human understanding?

But if memory has its underlying causes; if it is conjoined with matter, with time, with an adjunct, with the generative process, and with its opposite, namely impotence; and if it is a useful thing in itself, then surely it should be allowed to flourish, and in other domains also? But does that mean that the mind that is embedded in the planets[97] and the fixed stars must also have a memory? Does the virtue both of the world-mind[99] and of him whom we call Jupiter form a subject of remembrance? Surely, if the planetary minds do not require any understanding of those things that come to pass in their midst, then they won't need the beating wings[100] of recollection either?

But, you'll say, they do recognise and arrange, one by one, whatever comes to pass. That may well be true, but it actually happens rather differently, that is to say solely by means of the virtue they have received from the Father Creator. Nor are they deprived at any time of the opportunity to contemplate the lower world, since the rational memory[101] allows a representation of any physically remote object.

Again, if someone were to ask me whether the minds of the stars[102] and planets are aware that they've orbited the Earth during the previous day, month or year, then I would ask them to understand that, although nothing that is continuous and free from change can ever allow any variation, nonetheless certain features and traces of variation can be discerned in the day, month and year. No part of something constant can therefore ever belong to yesterday.

However, the human mind is the father of the day, the month and the year, and just as someone walking along a road leaves footprints on various parts of the ground, so we divide the individual motions that the planets make within their minds into many parts, for in the celestial world the day is all one, and there is no transition from day to night.

So the minds of the stars and planets do indeed have awareness, as you say. But they do not have awareness within a temporal framework, and we said above that time is something with which memory is conjoined. Yet you still persist in saying that the planetary minds are looking down on humans, and that it may perhaps follow from this that those minds are our rememberings, and that memory is therefore active within them.

But what kind of memory is this? They look down on us, so we conclude that they too have been participating in memory, but the opposite is in fact the case, for we do not go over in our mind what we are looking at in a process of recollection, but instead recognise it comprehensively.

It will be apparent from this, after making a comparison with our own characteristics, that what you're insisting upon cannot possibly be the case. Even if a comparison may be made with that light that surpasses human understanding, the situation will be no different for the reasons that we've also outlined. From these facts we can simultaneously conclude that the minds of individuals do not have the functions of a rational memory when they have risen to a memory-locus[103] that is known to them, nor any capacity for acquiring such functions, unless perhaps:

Ad Troiam magnus mittetur Achilles.
'a great Achilles be sent to Troy.'[104]

So let's accept that a rational memory *is* present in other things, but since we've assumed that its function is conjoined with the body, and that rational memory itself is conjoined with time, then it certainly remains the case that the powers of this virtue are only present in animate beings and, indeed, only in those animate beings that have a sense of time. And if time is a number[105], and if only human beings were made by Nature to perform calculations with numbers, then why waste any more time on dumb animals?

CHAPTER IV.
THE ART OF MEMORY.

So there *is* an Art of Memory. Let that art be a power of the intellect such that it is not dependent upon any other powers, for if its home is located on the periphery then how can it ensure rest and action at the centre, and even if it is at the centre then by what reasoning might it have crossed over from the boundary?

But this is perhaps a more general topic and one that I'll examine in greater detail elsewhere.

So, my friend, now Anaxagoras can assess your powers of foreknowledge[106] and deliver judgment on you while I – and, come on now, you should remember this! – will teach you the secrets of how to remember things.

Since we have three things in Nature – namely foresight, insight and hindsight – then who would dare to claim that, if you removed either or both of the first two, he would still have hindsight of something that, I think it's fair to say, would not actually exist and would be lacking in any sort of organisation?

You would certainly be deceiving yourself and working in vain if you thought that what we're discussing and forming an idea of here is keenness of invention, and skill in judging how things need to be arranged, for in the act of hindsight you're not handing over to the mind the prudence[107] of Nature and of reason but rather the shadow of its object and, indeed, a shadow that cannot be grasped at all unless its body be disencumbered.

I have a good reason for saying this, because there's a certain kind of person who would immediately say to you, if they heard about the status of our art, 'But surely I can go over in my mind, at my leisure, by a process of recollection, whatever I read or happen to hear from other people?' But such people need not just to learn such things but to acquire an insight into them as well.

CHAPTER V.
DIVISIONS OF THE ART.

In the light of what we've just said I think we're justified in calling the Art of Memory the 'art of hindsight'.

The Art is divided into two parts: foreknowledge and discrimination. Just as someone who neither plants a tree nor looks after it properly after it has put out its first shoots ever gets any oil, figs, apples or whatever so, in the same way, unless you satisfy the art's initial needs and also cultivate what comes forth you'll wait in vain for its 'oil' to be produced, and will work to no purpose and end up empty-handed.

Once we've decided what it is we wish to remember we must first, as it were, choose where to pitch our camp. We then, to continue our analogy, have to raise our troops. You may well ask, 'After our line of battle has been drawn up and we've motivated our soldiers, what more do we need? But, you will say, is that what memory is? Surely foreknowledge and, perhaps, discrimination in the art of judgment have already been banished? What more do you want?'

But if that's your response then you're dealing in superficialities, for the two things are not exactly the same: even if foreknowledge or the invention of objects has been banished to the Island of Reason, and foreknowledge of flight and pursuit have also perhaps been banished to the city, we are still permitted to remain among the shadows, something that, by the same token, is also true of discrimination.

Foreknowledge is therefore the prior part of the mechanism, but it lies within the subjects and shadows. Indeed, since forgetfulness and memory are polar opposites – the former corresponding to darkness and, as it were, death, and the latter, by analogy, corresponding to light – and since between darkness and light there is nothing except a progression by means of interposed shadows (if Nature allows), then we have reason to believe that the same is true in this instance, and that everything that is retrieved from forgetfulness and placed in the memory may be brought there by means of intermediary shadows, which act like female messengers[108], tempering the representations of the retrieved objects and then presenting them to the soul[109].

This is why shadows are useful, and why they should lead you to the conclusion that there must be subjects from which these shadows are extracted.

First therefore I need to talk about the nature and essence of a subject, and then about how it is selected, and the principle by which it is governed. Finally, and in a similar manner, I will need to talk about shadows.

CHAPTER VI.
SUBJECTS.

A subject is therefore a sort of pocket or receptacle into which the shadows are placed. This arrangement will enable you to recite from memory whatever you might have learned, but only those things that you have visualised. So we are not concerned here with logical extremes, nor with the actual *hyle*[110], nor with something made by Nature and related specifically to her, nor with things made by an art and related to an art. Instead we are wrestling, in various contexts, with things that have been made using the shadows of a construction that needs to be disencumbered, just as marks and seals need to be[111].

CHAPTER VII.
THE ABSOLUTE SUBJECT.

One kind of subject is absolute and primary, while the other is an adjuvant (assisting) subject which acts as a sort of companion to the former.

Whereas absolute subjects are always complete in themselves either by nature or design, adjuvant subjects are generally contained by the efficacy of the vision.

But when an adjuvant is the entire universe or the bowels of the Earth, or contains all sorts of different things, or is an entire political or economic system with all its constituent parts then absolute subjects are selected from the three categories[112] just mentioned as occasion demands. Other categories are neither useful nor perhaps even possible.

CHAPTER VIII.
THE ADJUVANT SUBJECT.

The adjuvant subject is that which is adjoined to the absolute subject. It is the latter that actually contains the shadow. The adjuvant subject is adjoined in order to increase the scope of the absolute subject and to ensure a firm perception of the shadows[113].

Since the adjuvant subject is fixed and immobile, whereas the absolute subject can be moved on a pretext provided by the shadows (though only for as long as it provides the material for the animation of those shadows), it is obviously assigned to the task of using and employing those shadows.

Let's take an example. In an intercolumnar space[114] let there be a sword. Now let Alledius[115], while he's putting down a popular uprising, make threatening gestures with that sword. And now, while he's rousing up and arming the slaves against the Republic, let him stretch out that sword. Now the Republic, while invoking that innate and, by its very nature, clearly defined law of self-defence, also stretches out a sword. Now let those who want social change atone by the sword. Now let Astræa[116] also become famous for her sword.

In each prosopopœia in this memory-locus a sword is used. In the same way, if at any time a shadow that has been previously imagined doesn't immediately spring to the mind of the person trying to recall it on the basis of its effects and contingencies then the sword will point towards it, just as a finger might do.

CHAPTER IX.
IN PROLEPSIS.[117]

But situations will perhaps arise in which something in the material of the adjuvants, as a result of it only coming into existence after the animation, does not provide or signify anything of any additional value, and does, indeed, seem purely mathematical and, as a result, proves unsatisfactory. Why it may be unsatisfactory I shall explain elsewhere. For the time being I'm content to make the point that all adjuvant subjects strike me as being mathematical, not because they're separated from the concretion of matter[118] but because, apart from their role as a companion to the absolute subject, they also indicate the number and sequence of the subjects. Indeed, if they failed to do so then, in this instance, they would seem to have been adopted to no purpose. You should be able to decide for yourself whether this feature should be added to the description we have already given[119].

CHAPTER X.
THE SELECTION OF SUBJECTS.

Now we've discussed the nature and essence of subjects I'll provide some supplementary material on how they are selected and the principles they should follow.

To begin with, let's deal with sensory objects. Every object should assume a perceptible form (whether innate or assumed) even if it may not always have been moved from the boundary by the sensory faculties, otherwise you will waste your time trying to recall things you cannot even represent or construct.

The object should then be moulded to suit the visual strength of the boundary, for just as a shadow is neither light nor darkness, so its seat is located neither in the latter nor in the former. Subjects should not therefore be too bright lest they dazzle and hurt the eyes, but nor should they be too dark.

What's more, since they are to serve as containers for the shadows, let them be of a moderate and reasonable size, and make sure they maintain that size. If however anything should interfere with this process you can allow the subjects to be modified in accordance with the rules of Nature, for if they're too voluminous they can scarcely be considered images at all, whereas if they're too small they may look as if they're trying to keep the observer at arm's length.

Spaces between subjects should also be moderate in size and must be kept parallel. In this task you'll need to use the cognitive apparatus to achieve satisfactory results. The central areas however need to be, as it were, effaced and erased[120].

Next, eliminate any dissimilarities of form as well as of essential character. Even so, you should use all your skill to ensure that the infinite variety of Nature is respected.

Arrange the subjects in their own natural sequence (if they have one), but take care not to make any mistakes in any ordering that you yourself might specify, however many places the subjects might occupy.

Let everything be secondary to and be determined by the shadows. To ensure this, let all the absolute subjects be characterised by their companion adjuvant subjects, which should serve as their guards. Next, ensure that those objects that will be entrusted to the confidence of those guards are also guarded, and release those objects if the thinking process obtrudes. Do not allow them to stray into neighbouring territory, but always distribute them, as it were, among their decans[121]. The commanders and princes of the decans should be selected from among the images of the lunar mansions. A permanent decemvirate[122] should take responsibility for the administration, and golden chains[123] should be provided for them in the individual stations. But make sure you keep all these things under careful observation, so that those that wish to can remain in position and stand fast.

Great care and meticulousness must be brought to this task to ensure satisfactory results.

CHAPTER XI.
SHADOWS.

So that's how subjects should be dimensioned and delineated. Now let's move on to discussing shadows using a similar plan.

A shadow is defined as the representation of an object assigned to a subject and so selected as to ensure a firm perception[124] of that object, but it's not a representation such as we find in the First Mind[125], for that is Light and is always the same, whereas what we are seeking is a shadow of a kind that is brought forth. Nor is it something that can be found in the heavens and those everlasting fires,[126] or in the celestial circuit[127], nor is it a thing in itself[128] or a thing in something that procreates[129], or something produced by procreation. Finally, it is not something that is moved within the boundary of this virtue, but is, as it were, polished by the sensory faculties and by the file of the mind[130].

The object – the thing itself – is therefore entrusted to the subject. The result of that prior entrustment, as Mercury once explained to me, is understanding. The position of the antecedent[131] gives rise to a connection in the prudence of both Nature and wisdom; in the same way, the virtue of the shadows gives rise to a firm and expanded retention of a memory-activity.

What we've just said may make acquiring this skill sound difficult and even pointless, or perhaps vain and laborious, but whereas those who adhere to the former opinion claim that memory is a wild and uncontrollable gift of nature, those who support the latter view see it as something knavish, and have concluded that if you don't understand something when it's made patent then it should remain abstruse.

CHAPTER XII.
SIMPLE SHADOWS.

Some shadows are simple, whereas others are modified.

Simple shadows are processed by the sensory apparatus, modified shadows by the conceptual apparatus.

Simple shadows are moved from and adopted from the boundary, whereas modified shadows are brought forth and represented within the sensory apparatus.

Consequently, when we are dealing with a memory-activity that involves an object that is moderately sensory then, whatever its exact nature, that object will also be a shadow: hence, a man designates a man, Alledius stands for Alledius[132], and a wild animal for a wild animal. Everything that can be identified from its very nature as visual and can only be identified as such is therefore handed over to the cognitive faculties in the form of shadows of this kind.

I said 'from its very nature', since those objects that are perceived by the hearing and the cognitive faculties but which elude the vision and are *per se* intellectual are also handed over with the approval of the eyes[133], but in the form of modified shadows. This is so that the construction may record these as invisible and, by their very nature, removed from the judgement of vision[134], which means that you won't be able to grasp them by reflecting upon them, just as you *can* grasp them by inspecting them. But take care, for there are other objects that are knowable by the senses that refuse to serve as simple subjects – indeed, perhaps none of them does.

CHAPTER XIII.
MODIFIED SHADOWS.

If an object doesn't have its own shadow then necessity demands that you must obtain what you do not have from somewhere else. If no simple shadows are available then you should consider using imitative and representative simulacra[135], or things that are similar in some way.

This is what's known as a construction[136]: these *modified shadows* as they're known are not employed to provide amusement and a pleasurable stimulus as is usually the case with metaphors but to solve problems that have arisen and meet the urgent needs to which they have given rise, as the eyes of the intellect[137] are, as it were, drawn more readily to related abstractions. For what else can you do if necessity compels you to do something?

CHAPTER XIV.
SUBDIVISION OF MODIFIED SHADOWS.

Modified shadows can be further subdivided into those that involve a modification of objects and those that involve verbal constructions[138]. The former are sometimes encountered in absolute subjects and also in mathematical ones.

Absolute shadows are all those that do not involve any difference of number. They may be either simple or conjoined. I shall not dwell on this distinction here, provided that you remember throughout this discussion that we are dealing with abstractions that elude the judgements of the senses[139].

If objects are knowable by the senses then they have a simple formation, and just as we see in those cases that the shadows are emanating from external forms so perhaps in this instance the modified shadows need to be evoked from internal forms. Certainly, if we had the true forms of objects then every construction would need to be evoked from those forms, but if this is not the case then the construction needs to be sought out from events, subjects and the rest of the family of reason[140], just as you might seek out a potion to cure an illness or a guard to protect you.

CHAPTER XV.
MODIFIED ABSOLUTE SHADOWS.

We can fairly refer to this inflection[141] or modification of absolute shadows as a form of metaphor, not because it involves a word having to be substituted and used figuratively to add a certain lustre to an oration (which is essentially what your philosophy[142] consists of), but because it involves, as it were, a *borrowing* of objects, since an object which eludes the sensory faculties is assigned to the care of something different that *does* fall within the scope of those faculties[143]. So we don't select these shadows (which assume the role of changing these objects) in order to put them forward as strict replacements for the ineffective ones (which would be the sole cause of your selection as long as you put forward those inflected and modified shadows as replacements for the characteristic shadows) but so that, with the help of these shadows, which are latent in the cognitive apparatus, you can recall to mind those objects which they have been selected to represent and which you would otherwise not be able to retain in the memory. That's why you won't find here any of the excessively daring metaphors you were warning us about[144]. Indeed, we strenuously avoid them.

The efficient cause[145] of the created object undergoes certain changes, so that the 'father' of something is followed by his 'progeny'. So Theutates can stand for mathematics and writing, Vulcan for pyromancy[146], Nereus for hydromancy[147], Apollo for the sunrise and sunset, Chiron[148] for what's known as surgery, Minerva for wars and enterprise, Prometheus for foreknowledge[149], and Epimetheus[150] for repentance.

This shouldn't cause you any problems, because not even these hand down any judgements of vision[151], for whether they are material or immaterial, connected or unconnected, due regard must still be paid to those objects that the ancients assigned to them. So, for example, tools made of iron and other metals, and things like crowbars, will stand for building and construction, while quotations, writings and actions of any kind will be recalled to mind by thinking about the people who were responsible for them.

Now what about matter? In this context the work itself, the end-result, is perhaps more familiar to us than how it is to be produced. So the form is disregarded, and you'll find out why in due course. Instead, the efficient cause is recalled from certain *acts*. Who was it who designed the universals? Who ordained the motion of the celestial bodies? Who created everything, and who now keeps that creation in existence? Who fashioned our eyes? Who made the holes to create our nostrils? Who stretched out and joined our sinews? Who constructed our ribs? Who made our heart in the shape of a pyramid?[152] What kind of Mother is there? And what kind of Father, apart from God, and He is invisible to us. Just look at the ways in which, on the basis solely of *acts*, God is shown to be infinite and incomprehensible. There is an infinite number of such examples from which you can effectively recollect, as if from traces and seals[153], God Himself, and eternity, and the world, and time, and procreation, and also those deities whom we call the Gods of the Heathens, and anything in general which might ever have brought anything into existence.

But apart from this primary use of effects[154], you should also recognise the general role that *acts* play in the construction of all forms of shadow.

First of all the core value[155] of the shadow is conveyed to those adjuncts that you need to insert. To take an example, if you are investigating forms of government then the construction will favour the general welfare[156] rather than tyrannical inclinations. A construction involving a few people (but more than one person) who are blessed with virtue will therefore give us Aristocracy or, if they are not thus gifted, Oligarchy, while a popular conspiracy in favour of the general welfare will give us a Polity or, when it involves some sort of confrontation with the patricians, Democracy. These are the distinctions that you yourself make[157].

Virtues, diseases, strength, wealth, beauty as well as the opposites of all those things are therefore expressed on the basis of their subjects, while the properties and accidentals of all those things that are of natural origin[158] are accordingly expressed by those same things, which serve as heralds.

Approval of the subject depends upon the adjuncts and the accidentals, e.g. springtime is derived from the swallow, the planting of beans, and similar things, while in the same way the toga is used to represent peace, and armour and spears stand for war[159]. We should also mention here that, irrespective of the nature of the subject, you can evoke common accidents[160] in sequence on the basis of the inclinations and sentiments of your will. This may remind you of what we have already had to say about the association of events[161]. We can even draw inspiration from subjects that are quite different to the objects they represent. These include, in the first instance, those things that differ by virtue of reasoning alone, e.g. a badge of honour will inspire a search for victory, while the figure of a bandit will lead you to a search for treachery.

Then again you may have overlooked those examples in which, by the same reasoning, one object is set against many objects, e.g. a group of heirs might recall the memory of someone making a will; someone who has inflicted some injury or other might lead you to think of the victim; a wife might remind you of her husband; a father-in-law might call to mind his son-in-law; and a tenant his landlord.

If, for example, you recall to mind the memory of Pericles[162] you'll recognise Anaxagoras, while Hippolytus[163] can stand for an adulterer, and a slave for a freedman. Similarly, something that gives off heat may stand for something that is cold, a spendthrift for a miser, a sensible man for a fool, someone who's enjoying his wealth for someone who's been ruined financially, a blind man for a sighted one, and a sober man for a drunkard. All this is based on the effective use in the Art of Memory of material that makes you smile or which causes surprise.

In the case of those objects that are distinguished from one another by means of comparison we can imagine infinity being inspired by a multitude, a wind by Ibycus[164], Mercury by Æsculapius[165], something of moderate size by something larger, and *vice versa*, for who doesn't understand how analogy works? Certainly there's nothing in Nature that cannot be illuminated at some time by the light of resemblance. Hence someone who is

> *os humerosque Deo similis,*
> 'God-like in face and shoulders'[166]

can stand for God, somebody's mistress for Venus, and a tree made secure by its deep roots, which no force can shake, for virtue. And that ship where

> *Nudum remigio latus,*
> *et malus celeri saucius africo,*
> *antennæque gemant,*
> 'the side has lost its oars, and the yardarms and the mast, damaged by the bitter south-westerly, are groaning'[167]

will recall to mind a badly affected and struggling republic, while whirlwinds and gales will stand for dangers and calamities. Thus

> *Fulvum fingatur in ignibus aurum,*
> 'tawny gold is shaped in the flames'[168]

will stand for the idea that loyalty is often to be proved in time of misfortune.

So numerous are the allegories that can be derived from various narratives that, generally speaking, you can achieve anything you wish by using your reasoning, especially if you're employing maxims and other types of saying.

As examples of differences in quality we can use Neoptolemus[169] to help us recall the idea of Achilles, while Socrates will serve the same purpose for Anaxagoras.

So you see Socrates, we owe you a debt of gratitude for supplying us with a future example – thank you!

Finally, to exemplify the principle of distribution: wedding-flutes can stand for marriage; a single squadron for cavalry; and a roof, walls, ramparts and the individual parts of those things for a house or city. So your Mercuries, your Æsculapiuses, Prometheuses and Chirons can stand for sages, and Calatinuses[170] for distinguished citizens (even impoverished ones), while, all in all, *species* are taken to represent their *genera*[171].

So those are in general the things that seemed to me to be worth saying about the inflection of absolutes. But this puts me in mind of the constructions that relate to those objects that we've referred to as *mathematical*.

CHAPTER XVI.
MATHEMATICAL MODIFICATION.

Since mathematical objects are abstractions and are separate from any concretion of matter they are unable to project simple shadows, nor can they project those shadows that have been modified by the higher reason[172].

Since a great deficiency of this kind can usually be remedied by skilful explanation, let me try to provide a numerical example, something regarding which not even the slightest suspicion could have arisen from what I have already said.

Since we're dealing with matters numerical, let the first division be into tenths[173], calculated according to the order of the signs of the Zodiac. The individual signs of this circle determine the individual tenths in order. All the signs should therefore be distinguished and divided into ten parts according to numbers to be inserted into those tenth-parts[174]. There will now be 120 divisions. If this number appears insufficient then add to this arrangement the wandering planets and the image of the Lunar Dragon[175]. That should make 200[176].

It may seem incredible that we can use these images to memorise entire books, individual chapters and other similar material, and with a firm perception too, but we do, and with minimal inconvenience.

'But what sort of perception is that?' I hear you cry. 'Taking the signs of the Zodiac and then separating them into tenths in order! Who can find ten clear and distinct parts in the sign of Cancer or some of the others, as if I wanted a crab to stand for Cancer and some fishes to represent Pisces!'

But this is just simple-mindedness, for who would dare to be taken seriously as a mathematician if the shadows of the zodiacal signs had to be created on the basis of what we have just said? Let the shadows of these signs be constructed therefore not in the form that such critics imagine but in accordance with images appropriate to those things. Again, lest this form of comparison cause you any difficulty, we recommend that you adopt not just some of the images of the individual signs but all of them for the sake of variety. You will already know these images and how many there are, just as you know the images of the wandering planets and the Lunar Dragon.

Let that suffice as an outline of this topic.

CHAPTER XVII.
VERBAL INFLECTION.

As long as we carefully notate the forms and shadows we can easily retrieve from our memory anything we wish to remember.

But what we still need to discuss is the modification of *words*, in which regard, even if

Cui lecta potenter erit res,
nec facundia deseret hunc, nec lucidis ordo:
'he who has chosen a subject suited to his ability will be deficient neither in eloquence nor in clarity of organisation'[177]

and

Verbaque provisam rem non invita sequantur.
'the words come without effort when the subject-matter is well-digested'[178]

we still need to pay close attention to this facet of our subject even if it seems to be a matter of opinion rather than of knowledge.

First we need to understand that words will also inevitably arise from most objects in the genera of both sensory objects and non-sensory objects due to the very nature of those genera. In this respect therefore, what we have already said about objects may also be considered to apply to words.

In situations where the approval of objects proves futile, recourse is made to every kind of analogy in verbal expression, especially etymological relationship and the derivation of words.

The general arrangements for this form of modification seem to require some explanation. First therefore, let 30 letters of the alphabet, without any encumbrance[179], be assigned to a group of 30 completely different people. The same arrangement should be used to handle the distinctive effects of single objects as well as of adjuncts.

Now that the necessary preparations have been made in such a way that even Alledius[180] may promptly and expeditiously assign as many letters of such a kind, along with their effects and adjuncts, and do the same for the remaining ones, you should surely not be in any doubt that we can perform any matchings that might be required by borrowing both from the letters and the effects/adjuncts.

What reasoning should we apply to the selection of the fourth and fifth letters of these matchings? Whether the letters are finals, medials or intermediates they should always be selected with a view to creating subtle contrasts of gesture. For these same letters also certain bodies are separately constituted which furnish, from the reason, all of these five aspirates[181] with the addition of stops[182], and the effects and adjuncts of those stops for the liquids[183] and finals[184]. What else, I ask, could anyone need apart from borrowings?

You can arrange these people, bodies, effects and adjuncts – everything – to suit your own convenience.

CHAPTER XVIII.
THE PRINCIPLE OF THE SHADOWS.

So that is how the shadows are 'composed' as it were. Now let's deal with the principle of the shadows and the topic of adjuncts.

Since, with a bit of imagination, multiple shadows can be produced from any individual object (just as happens with bodies that can be seen with the naked eye) we seem to be presented with an opportunity to, as we expressed it above, 'levy some troops'[185].

First therefore you should ensure that all the shadows, both simple and inflected, meet with the approval of the eyes[186]. If an object will permit it, allow it to retain its dimensional characteristics; if it will not, then modify it by using adjuncts.

Make sure also that the shadows are bright and sharp. To do this, make them distinctive by imparting to them some novel or even amusing characteristic. Have them display some outstanding kind of beauty or even ugliness in order to stimulate the thinking, but always ensure that the subjects in which they are deposited are represented perfectly, accurately, and distinctly, and always have something that makes an impression upon the subjects and urges action on them.

If the cognitive faculties have increased then allow the subjects to escape[187] and then return by a process of revocation.

In addition, make sure that the subjects are dissimilar to one another in form and variety. Even if the sense receives similar forms from the sensory faculties, or has itself created them, always re-examine the workings and functioning of the vision.

As for foreknowledge, we have already said quite enough about that topic.

CHAPTER XIX.
DISCRIMINATION.

Let's assume that we now have all the subjects, shadows and everything else we need. What happens next?

It remains for me to say something about discrimination, using similar reasoning to that which we deployed above, but it's difficult for me to speak unequivocally on this matter since here there's a problem of coherence, for sometimes discrimination is seen as a rule and a canon of how to live one's life, while at other times it's viewed as a yardstick of the truth. Again, the latter can be variously seen as something that judges; something by which judgement is made; or something according to which that judgement has been made.

In fact, this is the very point that has given rise to every distinction that your Sages have made, with some saying that there *is* such a thing as judgement and that there is accordingly a Truth that can be discovered (a view supported by Parmenides[188], Anaxagoras, Dionysodorus[189], and many others) while others contend that nothing can be known or perceived (whence has arisen your own idle dissembling), while there are still others, such as Heraclitus[190], Xenophanes[191], Homer, Pyrrho[192], and Democritus[193], who are in doubt about the whole thing, hence the question,

Quis novit autem, an hoc vivere sit emori:
An emori sit hoc quod vocamus vivere?
'But who has ever known whether this living may be dying, or whether dying is what we call living?'[194]

But passing over both 'that which judges' and 'that according to which judgment exists', let's take up the remaining question of *that by which one judges that which judges*. Some have located this faculty in the senses, hence the saying:

πάντων χρημάτων μέτρον
'Man is the measure of all things,[195]

while others have located it in the reason alone, hence the statements:

Opinioque sacer est morbus et visus mentitur.
'Opinion is a deadly disease, and appearance is deceptive'[196]

and

Oportet vero te omnia nosse,
Tum quidem veritatis suasu facilis accuratam sententiam,
Tum vero mortalium opiniones quarum non iam vera fides: 'It is appropriate that you should learn all things, not just the unshaken heart of persuasive truth but also the opinions of mortals in which there is no true belief at all'[197]

and similarly

Ne te Deus ancipitem iuxta hanc viam cogat,
Iudicare inconsiderato visu, et resonante auditu:
Sed iudices ratione accuratam sententiam.
'Lest God force you, undecided, down this path of judging with heedless vision and with a clamour in your ears, always express an opinion that has been carefully prepared by reason.'[198]

Others still have accepted the instrumentality of both the senses *and* the reason, but in this present context we ourselves subordinate discrimination to the virtue and function of both vision and thought, for it is through the visual and cognitive apparatus that whatever is perceived as a result of the impulse of the faculties or which was fashioned by the work of the senses is insinuated into the memory by a regular stimulus, since the brain has its own sphere and its distinct orbs, namely the senses, vision, thinking and memory. The memory is at the centre, for the sensory faculties are on the boundary, and nothing can be moved to the centre except by means of all the intermediate orbs. That is why, when the faculties are stimulated, there is not an immediate folding-together[199] of our senses and our memory.

So that should be enough to make clear the value and contribution of our topic of enquiry, namely discrimination.

CHAPTER XX.
THE METHOD.

But we also encounter discrimination in both the method and in the process of animation. Vision provides the method, while the cognitive faculties provide the animation. When the faculties have received a stimulus and that sensation has been projected into the subjects and shadows, then what does this vision do? Certainly the whole of the vision is expended in judging the arrangement, but since we set up the subjects like pockets or receptacles we shall first need to explain the rationale behind our organisation of the subjects, whatever form that organisation may take.

First therefore, you should if possible establish just one prevailing idea in the subjects. This idea may soon need to be divided into common parts, which will themselves be divided into other less common parts, which are then divided into particulars[200]. Finally, the particulars are divided into third-parts. Although this may perhaps seem to be at odds with the character of the memory-locus, in what way does it interfere with the task of naming?

So trust therefore in the idea of the idea, and observe closely the common parts of the common parts, the particulars of the particulars and the third-parts of the third-parts! You can add new third-parts and tenths too, and (if it's any use) some 'veilings'[201] which may be constructed for the purposes of the adjuvants and for the support and convenience of the Golden Chain[202]. Indeed, there is nothing in this entire discourse from which you are more likely to reap greater rewards than this.

Now it remains for us to discuss the role that thinking plays in the animation process.

CHAPTER XXI.
ANIMATION OR STIMULUS OF THOUGHT.

But perhaps I'm mistaken, and you don't actually need any additional material on thinking, since someone who intrinsically grasps this method can do as much as he likes, whereas someone who does not will toil in vain and achieve nothing at all?

It would be a mistake to think that in the task we have set ourselves, as in everything else in life, good organisation can achieve just about anything. What it can do will always depend upon our skill, and I would strongly deny that our skill can do anything, as you may recall from the controversy surrounding the hypothesis of planetary motion[203].

But now let's move on to the topic of animation. First of all, don't spoil the work you do with the shadows by being lazy. Make sure the subjects in which the shadows are placed are clearly and distinctly identified. Use exaggeration to produce sharply-delineated events and striking circumstances, but do not judge in accordance with the rules of Nature, and do not judge rashly either, but rather by using your skill on the basis purely of the instruction you have received, for then the results will accurately reflect the stimulus and your strong feelings.

From this process there follows negation and, most certainly, a dual transformation[204], namely of you into the object, and of the object into itself. This is what we mean by 'animation'. It is something that is perfected by the thinking process: an (as yet unformed) thought process[205], that of the shadows, forsakes matter and time and grasps the ideas and rationales, since it has a natural propensity for such an understanding.

Every skill is something to be admired, but this, which causes inanimate objects to appear as if they are living and breathing, is especially worthy of our admiration.

CHAPTER XXII.
CONCLUSION.

So, son of Sophroniscus, now you've heard what I have to say about memory. What happens next is up to you. It all depends on your intensive study, careful reflection and hard work to ensure that nothing escapes your attention and that everything sinks in. This is a subject that requires especial dedication, and you must always abide by its rules. There is nothing that cannot be achieved with it. But since you're here on Earth, remember to give satisfaction to Anaxagoras, even though you couldn't stand him. Although I must admit that I find this whole change of outlook of yours quite suspicious, and get the impression that there may perhaps be some hidden motive behind it[206].

The End.

1   Latin *umbra rationis*. See Nicholas of Cusa, *De Beryllo*, 31: *Quare Isaac dicebat quod ratio oritur in umbra intelligentiæ et sensus in umbra rationis, ubi occumbit cognitio. Unde anima vegetabilis oritur in umbra sensus et non participat de radio cognoscitivo, ita quod possit recipere speciem et ab appendiciis materiæ separare, ut fiat simplex cognoscibile,* 'Accordingly, Isaac used to say that reason arises in the shadow of the understanding and the senses in the shadow of reason, whereby the cognition ceases to exist. Hence the vegetable soul arises in the shadow of the senses and does not participate in the ray that has the power of knowing, as it becomes a simple thing that is knowable'. The 'Isaac' referred to is Isaac Israeli ben Solomon (*c.*832 – *c.*932), also known as Isaac Israeli the Elder or Isaac Judæus, an Egyptian Jew who wrote in Arabic and who is considered to be the father of Jewish Neoplatonism. He was also a famous physician, specialising as an oculist. His works were translated in Toledo into Latin and Spanish among other languages and enjoyed a wide influence in Christian Europe. Gerard of Cremona was responsible for the Latin translations of his Book of Definitions (*Liber de Definitionibus*) and his Book on the Elements (*Liber Elementorum*). These two works were widely quoted and paraphrased by Christian thinkers such as Albert the Great and Thomas Aquinas besides Nicholas of Cusa. Indeed, Isaac's emanationism may have been at the root of Albert the Great's ideas about light and shadow. We know that Nicholas of Cusa was influenced by Albert the Great's *Super Dionysium* in his writing of his *De Beryllo* (1458), a treatise in which a beryl is used as 'intellectual spectacles to reveal the invisible realm as the coincidence of opposites' (Nicholas of Cusa and the Making of the Early Modern World, *Studies in the History of Christian Traditions*, Volume: 190, Brill, 2019, p. 429). Cusa was also influenced by esotericism and quotes Hermes Trismegistus in the *De Beryllo*. For translations of and commentaries on Isaac Israeli's works, see Altmann and Stern, *Isaac Israeli: a Neoplatonic philosopher of the early tenth century,* Chicago, 1958 & 2009. See also Colette Siret, *A History of Jewish Philosophy in the Middle Ages,* CUP 1990, Ch. 3; and Jozef Matula, *Thomas Aguinas [sic] and his Reading of Isaac ben Solomon Israeli,* at https://www.academia.edu/10100256/ 30._Thomas_Aquinas_and_his_Readi ng_of_Isaac_ben_Solomon_Israeli Cusa's *De Beryllo* has been translated by Jasper Hopkins for the Arthur J. Banning Press, 1998, as part of *Nicholas of Cusa: Metaphysical Speculations*. Dicsone may well have been indirectly influenced by Isaac via his reading in Aquinas and other Catholic writers.

2   A type of narrative in which an author communicates with his or her audience by speaking as a different person or as an object.

3   Latin *Arelii*. This use of the genitive is a most unusual way of indicating a person's origins. Normally one would expect *Areliensis*, but it is hard to see what else it could mean other than a person from the village of Errol (now in Perth and Kinross). Errol's location on the River Tay would help explain Dicsone's fascination with the ship of William Wallace (see footnote 19).

4   Robert Dudley, 1st Earl of Leicester (1532-1588), was an English statesman as well as the favourite (and, according to legend, the lover or even the secret husband) of Elizabeth I from her accession until his death. As a youth he had been tutored by Dr.

John Dee, and he was known to have an interest in esoteric subjects, allegedly asking Dee to cast a horoscope to find the best day for Elizabeth's coronation as well as employing the 'astrological physician' Richard Forester. The intimate and jesting character of the Preface suggests that Dicsone's relationship with him was a very close one.

5   *Sub umbra illius, quam desideraveram sedi*, from the Song of Solomon 2.3: 'As the apple tree among the trees of the wood, so is my beloved among the sons. I sat down under his shadow with great delight, and his fruit was sweet to my taste.' This was a favourite quotation of Giordano Bruno (see, for example, the opening of his *Triginta Intentiones Umbrarum*, Intention I A).

6   Presumably inspired by Hebrews 6.19: 'Which hope we have as an anchor of the soul, both sure and stedfast [sic], and which entereth into that within the veil.'

7   Thomas Vautrollier (or Vautroullier). Arrived in England in the late 1550s as a Huguenot refugee. Became a *denizen* (i.e. a permanent resident with some rights of citizenship) 1562. Brother of the Stationers' Company 1564. Established his first press in Blackfriars 1570. Published an unlicensed English translation of some of Luther's sermons and was fined 10 shillings for it in 1578, and then again in 1579. Worked in Edinburgh as a bookseller and then as a printer from 1584 after publishing Giordano Bruno's *Last Tromp* (dedicated to Sir Philip Sidney), which seems to have landed him in trouble with the Star Chamber. James VI became his patron, and Vautrollier printed the first of the King's published works, *The Essayes of a Prentise in the Divine Art of Poesie*, in 1584, followed by an English translation, at the King's

request, of the *History of Judith* of Guillaume de Salluste du Bartas (1584). Returned to London 1586. Died 1587.

8   A quotation from Terence, *Heauton Timorumenos* ('The Self-Tormentor'), Act V, Scene I, line 23, which is why the corresponding words are italicised in the original text.

9   Greek οὐδὲν ὁρίζω ('ooden horidzo'), one of the three great maxims of the Greek Sceptics. See Sextus Empiricus, *Outlines of Pyrrhonism*, I 197. Dicsone may have been familiar with the ideas of Sextus through the work of Gianfrancesco Pico della Mirandola, nephew of the famous humanist Giovanni Pico della Mirandola; see Arthur Oosthout, *(Un)orthodox Scepticism: the Reception of Sextus Empiricus' Pyrrhonism in the Examen vanitatis (1520) of Gianfrancesco Pico della Mirandola*. Also, one of the 54 quotations that Michel de Montaigne (1533 – 1592), with whose essays Dicsone may have been familiar (see footnote 16), was said to have had inscribed above the frieze in his library was 'I determine nothing. I do not comprehend things. I suspend judgement. I examine.'

10   Possibly a reference to the passage in Plato's *Symposium* (212c et seq.) where a drunken Alcibiades, the lover of Socrates, gate-crashes the party. Alternatively, Dicsone's may have been trying to flatter Dudley's classical scholarship by referring to the *Frogs* of Aristophanes, in which the god of the wine-harvest, Dionysus, makes ludicrous appearances at the doors of the homes of Hercules and Pluto.

11   Theutates. See footnote 22.

12   Latin *horizon*. Though this is a Brunonian term, Dicsone seems to be using it here to signify a part of his model of the human mind based on his

reading in natural philosophy. See footnote 199.

13　See Giordano Bruno, *De Umbra Idearum*, the Fourth Intention: 'In the 'fourth intention', Bruno explains the ambivalent character of the shadow. All shadow is indeed double, participating in light and in darkness; it can be said to be both 'shadow of darkness' and 'shadow of light'... Through shadow, any reality can be defined in relation to two extremes, or as Bruno says later on, in relation to two 'horizons'. The intermediary space – that of images and intelligibles – is not contradictorily opposed to truth: it is neither true nor false, being a mixture of the two. This double participation characterises the place of the shadow as dynamically oriented' (from *Renaissance Scepticisms*, ed. Paganini and Neto, Chapter 10, 'Giordano Bruno on Scepticism', Springer 2008, p. 246). Dicsone's sudden jump in this passage from talking about shadows to talking about memory is one of the things that suggests to us that the *De Umbra* is a heavily edited version of a much longer and more detailed work.

14　This is line 20 of *Baptistes*, one of the two Latin tragedies by the Scottish humanist George Buchanan, who died in 1582, shortly before the publication of *De Umbra*.

15　The 'correspondence bias' or 'fundamental attribution error' of modern psychology.

16　Or, in Hazlitt's translation, 'Olus, what is't to thee/What with themselves does he or she?' These lines are from the opening of the 10th Epigram of Martial's Seventh Book, which is about a slanderer and gossip called Olus. Dicsone misquotes this passage (*faciat* instead of *faciant*), as does Michel de Montaigne in his *Essay on Vanity* from his Third Book of Essays, which was published in March 1580

and from which, given the error and the date, Dicsone may well have drawn the quotation.

17　Zoilus (400 – 320 BC) was a Greek grammarian, Cynic philosopher, and Homer scholar whose works have not survived. His *Homeric Questions* seem to have accused the great poet of inaccuracy and indecency, and he accordingly became synonymous with harsh and unreasonable criticism. 'Every poet has his Zoilus' was once a popular saying.

18　Horace, *Art of Poetry*, lines 114-116. Davus is a name commonly held by slaves in Roman comedy.

19　Or Adams, or even Adamson. We have not been able to discover the identity of this person. At a pinch, *Lincolniensis* could refer to Lincoln's Inn, one of the Inns of Court, rather than the town, in which case he may be the John Adams of Lincoln's Inn mentioned in the *Visitation of Norfolk in the Year 1563*. Or perhaps he was a relative of Henry Adamson (1581-1637), whose poem *The Muses Threnodie*, which is famous for its references to Masonry and Roscrucianism, makes flattering reference to 'Master Dickeson [sic]' as the finder and salvager of William Wallace's ship, scuttled in the Tay to stop the English fleet reaching the Scottish hero's fastness. Whether Dicsone's salvaging of the ship had a magical or other esoteric motive we do not know.

　　See Paul Ferguson, '*Where is the Ship of William Wallace?*': https://www.academia.edu/37917652/ WHERE_IS_THE_SHIP_OF_WILLI AM_WALLACE

20　This is closely based on a similar passage in Plato's *Phædrus* 274C-275B, in which Socrates recounts the interview between Thamus, King of Egypt, and Theuth (here: Theutates), who has just invented the art of writing.

21 i.e. Hermes.

22 For Theutates see, for example, William Reeves, *The Apologies of Justin Martyr, Tertullian, and Minutius Felix* (1716): 'And in his 3d Book de Divinat[ione], he [Cicero] mentions five Mercuries, and makes Mercury Theutates the fifth, who slew Argos, and for that flew into Egypt, and there instructed the Ægyptians in Laws and Letters, from which Theutates the first Month of their Year, that is September, was called Theuth. This was the Mercury the Gauls sacrifice to, and which Lucan in his First Book refers to: *Ex quibus immitis placatur sanguine diro/Theutates, horrensque feris altaribus Hesus,* 'And they for whom the ruthless Teutates is appeased with bloodshed horrible, and Hesus awful with his cruel altars' (Lucan, *Pharsalia*, Book I, lines 444-5). Note the reference to the Gauls, which helps underline the Celtic character of Theutates.

23 Latin *vas*, a vase, vessel or dish. This is reminiscent of the *sinus* (pocket) or *receptaculum* (receptacle) whereby the subject acts as a container for the shadow (see Ch. VI).

24 See Aristotle, *On the Heavens*, Book 3, Section 8: 'Earth, again, they call a cube because it is stable and at rest. But it rests only in its own place, not anywhere; from any other it moves if nothing hinders, and fire and the other bodies do the same. The obvious inference, therefore, is that fire and each several element is in a foreign place a sphere or a pyramid, but in its own a cube...Again, combustion of a body produces fire, and fire is a sphere or a pyramid. The body, then, is turned into spheres or pyramids.'

25 See the *Corpus Hermeticum*, Book VII (VIII), 1: 'Whither stumble ye, sots, who have sopped up the wine of ignorance unmixed, and can so far not

carry it that ye already even spew it forth?' (G. R. S. Mead's translation).

26 It is hard to know what is meant here, unless it is a reference to the importance that the Ancient Egyptians and Greeks attached to the washing of the hands before religious ceremonies associated with the Mysteries, or perhaps it refers to the passage in Book II (III), 8 of the *Corpus Hermeticum*: 'Regard the animals down here, a man, for instance, swimming! The water moves, yet the resistance of his hands and feet give him stability, so that he is not borne along with it, nor sunk thereby.' (G. R. S. Mead's translation).

27 See the *Corpus Hermeticum*, Book VII (VIII), 2-3: 'But first thou must tear off from thee the cloak which thou dost wear, the web of ignorance, the ground of bad, corruption's chain, the carapace of darkness, the living death, sensation's corpse, the tomb thou carriest with thee, the robber in thy house, who through the things he loveth, hateth thee, and through the things he hateth, bears thee malice. Such is the hateful cloak thou wearest, that throttles thee [and holds thee] down to it, in order that thou may'st not gaze above, and, having seen the Beauty of the Truth, and Good that dwells therein, detest the bad of it; having found out the plot that it hath schemed against thee, by making void of sense those seeming things which men think senses' (G. R. S. Mead's translation).

28 See the *Corpus Hermeticum* XVI, *The Perfect Sermon* or the *Asclepius*, VII.1: 'Asclepius: Are not the senses of all men, Thrice-greatest one, the same? Trismegistus: Nay, [my] Asclepius, all have not won true reason; but wildly rushing in pursuit of [reason's] counterfeit, they never see the thing itself, and are deceived. And this breeds evil in their minds, and

[thus] transforms the best of animals into the nature of a beast and manners of the brutes' (G.R.S. Mead's translation).

29 Latin *materiæ vindices*. In the *Art of Memory* (Routledge 1999), p. 269, Frances Yates translates this phrase as 'punishments of matter', but *vindex* means someone who takes revenge or who defends something.

30 The atmosphere of this passage is strongly reminiscent of Book IV of the *Consolation of Philosophy* by Boethius, another Latin author with whom Dicsone seems to have been familiar: '...whence it comes to pass that the bad cease to be what they are, while only the outward aspect is still left to show they have been men. Wherefore, by their perversion to badness, they have lost their true human nature. Further, since righteousness alone can raise men above the level of humanity, it must needs be that unrighteousness degrades below man's level those whom it has cast out of man's estate. It results, then, that thou canst not consider him human whom thou seest transformed by vice. The violent despoiler of other men's goods, enflamed with covetousness, surely resembles a wolf. A bold and restless spirit, ever wrangling in law-courts, is like some yelping cur. The secret schemer, taking pleasure in fraud and stealth, is own brother to the fox. The passionate man, frenzied with rage, we might believe to be animated with the soul of a lion. The coward and runaway, afraid where no fear is, may be likened to the timid deer. He who is sunk in ignorance and stupidity lives like a dull ass. He who is light and inconstant, never holding long to one thing, is for all the world like a bird. He who wallows in foul and unclean lusts is sunk in the pleasures of a filthy hog. So it comes to pass that he who

by forsaking righteousness ceases to be a man cannot pass into a Godlike condition, but actually turns into a brute beast' (Book IV, Section III, in H. R. James' translation).

31 Explained by Yates in the *Art of Memory*, p. 270 , as follows: 'This is a reference to the thirteenth treatise of the *Corpus Hermeticum* where is described the Hermetic regenerative experience in which the soul escapes from the domination of matter, described as twelve 'punishments' or vices, and becomes filled with ten powers or virtues. The experience is an ascent through the spheres in which the soul casts off the bad or material influences reaching it from the zodiac (the duodenarius), and ascends to the stars in their pure form, without the contamination of material influences, where it is filled with the powers or virtues (the denarius) and sings the hymn of regeneration. This is what Mercurius means in Dic[k]son's dialogue when he says that the 'duodenarius' of immersion in matter and in beast-like forms is to be driven out by the 'denarius' when the soul becomes filled with divine powers in the Hermetic regenerative experience.'

32 Along with Minos and Rhadamanthus, one of the three judges of the dead in the Underworld.

33 Possibly a reference to the story found in the Greek satirical writer Lucian's *The Tyrant*, in which Hermes (sometimes identified with Theutates) manages to 'lose' one of the dead mortals he is supposed to be presenting before the three judges of the Underworld.

34 Naucratis (or Naukratis) was a city of Ancient Egypt on the Canopic branch of the Nile. It was the first and, for a long time, the only permanent Greek colony in Egypt, and was a meeting-point for Greek and Egyptian culture. See Plato, *Phædrus*, 274, where

Socrates says, 'Well, I heard that in the neighbourhood of Naucratis, in Egypt, there lived one of the ancient gods of that country; the same to whom that holy bird is consecrate which they call, as you know, Ibis, and whose own name was Theuth.' See also the start of the second prosopopœia in this present work.

35   This is a rehearsal of the argument about the discovery and value of writing in Plato's *Phædrus*, p. 274-275.

36   Latin *in animo...scriberent*. Cf. Seneca the Elder, *Controversiæ*, Book I, pr. 18, referring to the remarkable memory of his friend Marcus Porcius Latro (died 4 BC), a celebrated Roman rhetorician considered to be one of the founders of scholastic rhetoric: *aiebat se in animo scribere*, 'He used to say that he wrote his meditations in his soul.' Earlier in that same book Seneca boasts about his own astonishing memory, claiming to have been able in his youth to memorise 2000 names at random and repeat them in the correct sequence, as well as 200 lines of poetry which he would then repeat to his school-chums in reverse order. See Patricia Fairweather, *Seneca the Elder* (Cambridge University Press 2007), chapter on '*Memoria*', p. 228ff.

37   An allusion to Bruno's contention that the Art of Memory was designed to teach ethics as well as train the mind.

38   Frances Yates (*Art of Memory*, p. 269ff.) follows John Durkan ('Alexander Dickson and S.T.C. 6823', *The Bibliothek*, 3 (1962)) in stating that the Socrates portrayed here is intended as a satirical portrait of Petrus Ramus.

39   See Plato's *Apology* 21. 'You are doubtless familiar with the name of Chærephon... Upon the occasion of his having visited [the temple dedicated to Apollo in] Delphi once he ventured upon inquiring of the oracle, and do not express displeasure at what I say my friends, for he asked if there was any one wiser than me? Upon this the Pythian priestess announced, that there was none wiser.' (Charles Stuart Stanford's translation). To be fair to Socrates he subsequently devoted a great deal of energy to trying to prove the oracle wrong.

40   Latin *metaposcopus* or, more correctly, *metoposcopus*, from the Greek μέτωπον (métōpon, 'forehead') and σκοπέω (skopéō, 'examine'), i.e someone who read character or told fortunes by examining people's foreheads, a form of phrenology.

41   This and the later quotations in this dialogue seem to be based on the 1538 Latin translation by Andreas Divus of Aristophanes' *Clouds* (lines 926ff.), in which the Greek playwright lampooned the fashionable intellectual movements of contemporary Athens. The trial and execution of Socrates may have been an indirect result of the play's unflattering portrait of him.

42   One of Cicero's favourite expressions (see, for example, its use in his *Epistulæ ad Atticum* 8.16). It is taken from Homer's *Iliad* 6.442. Cicero used it to mean 'a fear of public opinion'.

43   One of the founders of the Cynic school of philosophy and a noted ascetic. Once described by Plato as 'a Socrates gone mad'.

44   A lieutenant and friend of Hector during the Trojan War who was blessed with second sight.

45   More correctly, *Falsus honor juvat, et mendax infamia terret,/Quem? nisi mendosum et mendacem?* Horace, *Epistles*, Book I, XVI, lines 39-40, *Ad Quintum*.

46   This is a translation of line 319 from Book IX of Homer's *Iliad*. Thomas Aquinas quotes it in his unfinished commentary on Aristotle (though the translation may not be by him) and so does Denis Lambin in his 1567

translation of Aristotle's *Politics*, which may be where Dicsone got it from. Lambin, Professor of Latin (from early 1561) and then of Classical Greek (from later in 1561) at the Collège de France in Paris, is an interesting figure in the present context as he was both a close friend of Ramus (Lambin is alleged to have died of shock on hearing of the death of his friend in the anti-Protestant Massacre of St. Bartholomew) and also the target of allegations of heresy and paganising tendencies by the Italian Catholics. In the Introduction to his famous annotated edition of the Roman poet Lucretius (1563) Lambin set out his stall: 'Should we really ignore a poet who not only delights our minds but who also unravels the most obscure problems of natural philosophy in the most beautiful poetry?'

47   The father of Socrates and, according to some (e.g. Timon of Philius, as quoted in Diogenes Laertius, *Lives of the Eminent Philosophers*, Book II, Ch. XIX), a mason by profession, as indeed Socrates may have been in early life.

48   A quotation from a work by Cicero, *Hortensius*, which was largely lost in the 6th century. Fragments are known to us through the work of writers such as the late Roman lexicographer Nonius Marcellus, who compiled a 20-volume compendium of Latin literature. In the *Hortensius*, Cicero, Hortensius, Quintus Lutatius Catulus and Lucius Licinius Lucullus discuss the best use of one's leisure. Hortensius argues that oratory is the greatest art, but Cicero appeals strongly for the study of philosophy. St. Augustine attributed his own interest in philosophy to reading this work.

49   *Calculum reducam*. A *calculus* was a counting-stone. Another quotation

from Cicero courtesy of Nonius Marcellus.

50   Latin *complexio*, a rhetorical figure by which one constantly refers to something that has recently been said.

51   Another quotation from Divus' translation of Aristophanes' *Clouds* (line 946).

52   Another reference to Plato's *Phædrus* (261), where Socrates refers to the 'arts of speaking' compiled by Nestor, Odysseus and Palamedes in their leisure-time at Troy.

53   *Genesis* I.4.

54   Latin *radii [Dei]*. This phrase has a distinctly Hermetic ring to it. Dicsone may have been reading the recently-published *Traité de la vérité de la religion chrétienne contre les athées, épicuriens, payens, juifs, mahométans et autres infidèles* (Antwerp, 1581) by Philippe de Mornay (1549-1623). In this much-translated publishing sensation De Mornay, a Protestant open to esoteric ideas, quotes extensively from the *Divine Pimander* of Hermes to demonstrate the essential truth of Christianity, e.g. in Chapter II he writes: 'But, says Hermes, the rays of God are actions, the rays of the world are the rays of Nature, and the rays of man are the arts and sciences'. See Florian Ebeling, *The Secret History of Hermes Trismegistus: Hermeticism from Ancient to Modern Times*, Cornell University Press, 2007, pp. 84ff.

55   See Marsilio Ficino, *De raptu Pauli ad tertium cælum et animi immortalitate*, Ch. XXVIII, *Corpora sunt umbræ Dei, animæ vero Dei imagines immortales*, 'Bodies are the shadows of God; indeed they are the immortal images of the soul of God.'

56   Latin *anima mundi*, dealt with extensively in Plato's *Timæus*.

57   See, especially, Aristotle, *De Anima*, II.4.

58   Another paraphrase from the Divus

translation of Aristophanes' *Clouds*.

59 Presumably a sarcastic reference to Plato's analogy in the *Timæus* of the Receptacle (the material or spatial substratum of the universe) as an ointment that serves as a neutral base for various fragrances (50e5–8).

60 Timæus of Locri is a character in two of Plato's dialogues, *Timæus* and *Critias*, where he appears as a philosopher of the Pythagorean school. He may not have been a historical figure but simply a creation of Plato's.

61 See Plato's *Republic*, respectively Book IV 423e and Book V 457c-d; Book III 415e-416e; and Book V 457b-c.

62 Plato divides his Just Society into three classes: Producers (all professions other than warrior or guardian), Auxiliaries (warriors), and Guardians (or philosopher-kings, chosen from among the auxiliaries). In a Just Society the Producers have no share in ruling but simply obey the Guardians.

63 i.e. as chattels held in common by men.

64 Latin *regenerationis crater*, a phrase that seems to be Dicsone's own. See the *Corpus Hermeticum*, IV (V), 3-4 (G. R. S. Mead's translation) for the conversation between Tat and Hermes: Tat. Why then did God, father, not on all bestow a share of Mind? Her. He willed, my son, to have it set up in the midst for souls, just as it were a prize. Tat. And where hath He had it set up? Her. He filled a mighty Cup with it, and sent it down, joining a Herald [to it], to whom He gave command to make this proclamation to the hearts of men: Baptize thyself with this Cup's baptism, what heart can do so, thou that hast faith thou canst ascend to Him that hath sent down the Cup, thou that dost know for what thou didst come into being! As many then as understood the Herald's tidings and doused themselves in Mind, became partakers in the Gnosis; and when they had 'received the Mind' they were made 'perfect men'.' See also Plato, *Timæus*, 41d: 'Thus spake he [the Creator]; and again into the same bowl wherein he mingled and blended the universal soul he poured what was left of the former, mingling it somewhat after the same manner, yet no longer so pure as before but second and third in pureness', and 49a: 'Our new exposition of the universe then must be founded on a fuller classification than the former. Then we distinguished two forms, but now a third kind must be disclosed. The two were indeed enough for our former discussion, when we laid down one form as the pattern, intelligible and changeless, the second as a copy of the pattern, which comes into being and is visible. A third we did not then distinguish, deeming that the two would suffice: but now, it seems, by constraint of our discourse we must try to express and make manifest a form obscure and dim. What power then must we conceive *that nature has given it? Something like this. It is the receptacle, and as it were the nurse, of all becoming'* (Archer-Hind's translation in both cases). But G. R. S. Mead, in *Thrice-Greatest Hermes*, vol. I, Ch. XV, argues, from the nonchalant way in which Plato introduces this theme, that it must already have been familiar to his audience, and that it must date back to Pythagoras (the reformer of Orphism to form Pythagoreanism) and, beyond him, to Orpheus (the reformer of the possibly Minoan cult of Dionysus to form Orphism). Whatever its origins, later echoes of a magic cup whose contents bring enlightenment and never need replenishment are to be found in pagan Celtic mythology, e.g. the tale of

Branwen in the second branch of the Mabinogi where the Pair Dadeni ('Cauldron of Rebirth') is a magical cauldron in which dead warriors could be placed and then be returned to life, save that they lacked the power of speech, and also in some recensions of the Christianised Grail legends, such as that of Chrétien de Troyes where the Grail is a salver containing a single Mass-wafer sufficient to sustain life, or that of Robert de Boron where it is the chalice of the Last Supper in which Joseph of Arimathea collected Christ's blood upon his removal from the cross. The latter may be an echo of the alleged human sacrifices of the Druids, where the blood of the victim, collected in a bowl, was deemed to contain the *numen* of the god or goddess to whom he had just been sacrificed. But Dicsone may also have intended the reader to draw parallels between the regenerative Grail cup and his memory-system. The Grail legends would have been fresh in the minds of Dicsone's contemporaries, thanks partly to Edmund Spenser's *Faerie Queen*, which had been published, seven years before the *Thamus*, in 1590 and which James VI ordered to be banned in Scotland for its unflattering portrayal of his mother Mary Queen of Scots as the character Duessa. A. E. Waite, in his *Hidden Church of the Holy Graal*, p. 100, describes how one Arthurian text, the 'Longer Prose Perceval', 'has two cryptic descriptions of the Graal Vessel... It is said concerning Gawain, when he looked at the Graal in his wonder, that it seemed to him a chalice was therein, 'albeit there was none at this time'. It was, therefore, an ark or a tabernacle which was designed to contain a cup, but when the latter was removed it still held the shadow or semblance thereof. In the course of the same episode a change was performed

in the aspect of the external object, and it appeared to be 'all in flesh', meaning that it was transformed into a vision of Christ crucified.' (Our underlining). This seems to closely mirror the process in which the Magus engages in Dicsone's magical memory system. Besides the Cup of Regeneration we also find a Cup of *Forgetfulness* in the 3rd or 4th century Gnostic text known as the *Pistis Sophia*: 'Mary answered and said unto the Saviour: 'My Lord, surely the rulers do not come down to the world and compel the man until he sinneth?' The Saviour answered and said unto Mary: 'They do not come down in this manner into the world. But the rulers of the Fate, when an old soul is about to come down through them, then the rulers of that great Fate who [are] in the regions of the head of the æons, which is that region which is called the region of the kingdom of Adamas, and which is that region which is in face of the Virgin of Light, then the rulers of the region of that head give the old soul a cup of forgetfulness out of the seed of wickedness, filled with all the different desires and all forgetfulness. And straightway, when that soul shall drink out of the cup, it forgetteth all the regions to which it hath gone, and all the chastisements in which it hath travelled. And that cup of the water of forgetfulness becometh body outside the soul, and it resembleth the soul in all [its] figures and maketh [itself] like it, which is what is called the counterfeiting spirit.' In Greek legend, the dipping of the infant Achilles in the River Styx by his mother Thetis in an attempt to ensure his immortality may be a reflection of this concept. Socrates and Xanthippe had three sons: Lamprocles, Sophroniscus and Menexenus. Aristotle had a low opinion of all of them, calling them 'silly and dull' (*Rhetoric* 1390b30–

65

32).

66 A paraphrase of a line from Cicero, *De Republica*, Book IV, Ch. 10, referring to the criticism, on the stage, of politicians: *Patiamur, inquit, etsi eiusmodi cives a censore melius est quam a poeta notari*, 'We may tolerate that, though indeed the censure of the magistrate would, in these cases, have been more efficacious than the satire of the poet.'

67 Anaxagoras of Clazomenæ (born *c.*500 – 480 BCE) was the first of the Presocratic philosophers to live in Athens. He propounded a physical theory of 'everything-in-everything', and claimed that *nous* (intellect or mind) was the motive cause of the cosmos. See Plato, *Phædo* 46 and *Apology* 14.

68 Alcibiades, son of Cleinias (*c.*450 – 404 BC), from the *deme* of Scambonidæ, was a prominent Athenian statesman, orator, and general. Xenophon attempted to clear Socrates' name at trial by relaying information that Alcibiades was always corrupt and that Socrates merely failed in attempting to teach him morality.

69 Another quotation from Divus' translation of Aristophanes' *Clouds*, lines 1071ff.

70 The wife of Socrates, a notorious nagger and shrew.

71 More correctly: *sanguine famam*.

72 Or, as an anonymous 17th century translator expressed it, 'I like no squanderers of life for fame:/Give me the man that living makes a name!' Martial, *Epigrams*, Book I, IX, *To Decianus*.

73 Aristippus of Cyrene (*c.*435 – *c.*356 BCE) founded the Cyrenaic school of philosophy. A pupil of Socrates, he adopted a very different outlook, teaching an ethical hedonism.

74 Dionysius the Younger (c. 397 BCE – 343 BCE), also known as Dionysius II, ruled Syracuse from 367 BCE to 357 BCE and from 346 BCE to 344 BCE. When his father died in 367 BCE Dionysius, still in his twenties, inherited supreme power and ruled under the guidance of his uncle Dion, who became increasingly concerned about his nephew's dissoluteness and so summoned his old teacher Plato to Syracuse. Dion and Plato tried to restructure the government and establish Dionysius as the archetypal 'philosopher-king', but without success. See Plato, *Seventh Letter*.

75 Xenophon of Athens (*c.* 430 – 354 BCE) was a philosopher, historian and student of Socrates. He was also probably the greatest military commander of his time. Diogenes Laertius reports how Xenophon met Socrates: 'They say that Socrates met him in a narrow lane, and put his stick across it and prevented him from passing by, asking him where all kinds of necessary things were sold. And when he had answered him, he asked him again where men were made good and virtuous. And as he did not know, he said, 'Follow me, then, and learn.' And from this time forth, Xenophon became a follower of Socrates.'

76 Antisthenes (*c.*445 – *c.*365 BCE) was an ardent disciple of Socrates, developing the ethical side of his teaching and recommending an ascetic life conducted in accordance with virtue. Later writers saw him as the founder of the Cynic philosophy. He was present when Socrates was executed and never forgave his master's persecutors.

77 Crates of Thebes (*c.*365 – *c.*285 BCE) was a Cynic philosopher who gave away his personal fortune to live on the streets of Athens.

78 The links between these philosophers and Socrates may have been fabricated by the later Stoics to establish a line of succession from Socrates to Zeno, the

founder of the Stoic school.

79 Quite true, but according to Diogenes Laertius in his *Lives of the Eminent Philosophers* Antisthenes walked from the Piræus to Athens every day to converse with Socrates, a distance of some five miles.

80 *Reponendum* carries the idea of something being revived or restored, as the Art of Memory was a partial revival of previous habits of humanity in pre-literate times, rather than something entirely new.

81 *Sensa*, nominative plural of *sensum*, a rare word. Literally 'something sensed', or an unelaborated elementary awareness of stimulation (www.memidex.com).

82 A quotation from Cicero, *De Divinatione*, Book II, Ch. 11.

83 Another quotation from Petrus Ramus. See his *Præfatio Tertia, Rami de Cæsaris Militia* (1559), where, referring to Cæsar, he remarks that 'it is fitting for a great prince both to seek peace in wartime and to refuse to condemn the arts of war in peacetime'.

84 This is a Latin version of lines from Homer, *Iliad*, Book IX, lines 257ff. They seem to be a paraphrase drawn from the marginal Latin translation in Henri Estienne's famous 1566 edition of the *Iliad*. In this passage Odysseus reminds Achilles how his father Peleus must have taught him to be kind to his friends and to control his fearsome temper.

85 This seems to be a splicing of phrases from Ramus and Bruno; see *P. Rami Scholæ in liberales artes*, Book I, Ch. 2, *De Logica Mathematicorum*, Basel 1569 for a similar phrase, *Sacer est morbus, et aspectus fallitur*, which means more or less the same thing, and Giordano Bruno, *De Immenso et Innumeralibus*, Book 3, Ch. 1 for *visus mentitur*.

86 A Latin expression for someone who is acting rashly. From Ovid, *Heroides*,

XVI, line 263: 'But you are in too much of a hurry, for your harvest is only just starting to sprout.'

87 Socrates was initially strongly attracted to and then repelled by the view of Anaxagoras that the cosmos is controlled by *nous*, i.e. mind or intelligence (see Plato, *Phædo*, 97b8ff.).

88 Plautus, *Captives*, Act V, Scene 3, line 8.

89 As we explain in the section entitled *Dicsone Decoded*, Dicsone's microcosmic model of the intellect seems to hypothesise memory as being located at the centre of the mental 'universe', with the sensory and cognitive apparatuses, which contribute material to the memory, located at the boundary that surrounds it.

90 Cf. Cicero, *De Republica*, Book III, 25: 'For I consider it to be a form of unjust slavery when someone who is capable of being his own master is enslaved to another, but not when that person is unable to govern himself.'

91 Latin *remigium alarum animi*, literally 'a rowing with the wings [of the mind]', but *remigium* was also used by Virgil and others to mean *flying*. This expression occurs on page 7 of the 1567 Latin translation of a work by the Middle Platonist philosopher Alcinous called Ἐπιτομὴ τῶν Πλάτωνος δογμάτων *(An Epitome of Plato's Doctrine)*. The translation, entitled *Alcinoi ... Elementa atque initia, quibus quis imbutus, ad Platonis decretorum penetralia facilè introire, ac pervenire possit*, was by Denis Lambin, whom we have already met (see footnote 46) and with whose work Dicsone seems to have been familiar. Marsilio Ficino also translated this work by Alcinous into Latin as *Alcinoi philosophi Platonici de doctrina Platonis liber*. An English translation by George

Burges of the Greek original will be found in volume 6 of the *Works of Plato* in Bohn's Classical Library: Chapter IV deals with perception and memory.

92 See Giordano Bruno, *Triginta Intentiones Umbrarum (The Thirty Intentions)*, Intention I A: *Qui autem fieri potest ut ipsum cuius esse non est proprie verum, & cuius essentia non est proprie veritas; efficaciam & actum habeat veritatis? Sufficiens ergo est illi atque multum: ut sub umbra boni, verique sedeat. Non inquam sub umbra veri bonique naturalis atque rationalis (hinc enim falsum diceretur atque malum) sed Methaphysici, Idealis, & supersubstantialis,* 'But how is it possible that what is not strictly true and whose essence is not strictly the truth still has the effectiveness and action of truth? In that case it is enough...to sit in the shadow of the good and the true, i.e. in the shadow not of the natural and the rational (for this should be defined from this perspective as false and evil) but of the metaphysical, the ideal and the super-substantial.'

93 See Cicero (attrib.), *Ad Herennium*, Book III, xvi, 28: *Sunt igitur duæ memoriæ: una naturalis, altera artificiosa. Naturalis est ea quæ nostris animis insita est et simul cum cogitatione nata; artificiosa est ea quam confirmat inductio quædam et ratio præceptionis,* 'There are, then, two kinds of memory: one natural, and the other the product of art. The natural memory is that memory which is embedded in our minds, born simultaneously with thought. The artificial memory is that which is strengthened by a kind of training and system of discipline' – Caplan's translation for Loeb, slightly adapted.

94 Simonides of Ceos (*c.*556 – 468 BCE) was a Greek lyric poet born at Ioulis. According to legend, during the

excavation of a collapsed dining-hall from which Simonides had luckily escaped the poet was asked to identify the body of each guest, which he accomplished by correlating them with their places at the dining-table. He later used this experience to develop the mnemonic system of the 'memory theatre' or 'memory palace'.

95 See, for example, Cæsar, *De Bello Gallico*, Book VI, 14: 'Report says that in the schools of the Druids they learn by heart a great number of verses, and therefore some persons remain twenty years under training. And they do not think it proper to commit these utterances to writing, although in almost all other matters, and in their public and private accounts, they make use of Greek letters. I believe that they have adopted the practice for two reasons – that they do not wish the rule to become common property, nor those who learn the rule to rely on writing and so neglect the cultivation of the memory; and, in fact, it does usually happen that the assistance of writing tends to relax the diligence of the student and the action of the memory' (translation for Loeb by H. J. Edwards).

96 i.e. the sons of King Tyndareus, Castor and Pollux, who, according to legend, saved Simonides from certain death in the collapsing dining-hall (see footnote 94) by asking him to step outside.

97 See Cicero, *De Oratore*, Book II, lxxiv, 299: '...we are told that the famous Athenian Themistocles was endowed with wisdom and genius on a scale quite surpassing belief, and it is said that a certain learned and highly accomplished person went to him and offered to impart to him the science of mnemonics, which was then being introduced for the first time; and that when Themistocles asked what precise

result that science was capable of achieving, the professor asserted that it would enable him to remember everything; and Themistocles replied that he would be doing him a greater kindness if he taught him to forget what he wanted to forget rather than teaching him to remember' (E. W. Sutton's translation for Loeb 1967, slightly adapted).

98   The known planets in Dicsone's day were Mercury, Mars, Venus, Jupiter and Saturn.

99   Latin *communis animus*. Dicsone probably encountered this term in the 1571 Latin paraphrase of the fourteen books mistakenly attributed to Aristotle on the secret wisdom of Ancient Egypt, *Libri quattuordecim qui Aristotelis esse dicuntur, De secretiore parte divinæ sapientiæ secundum Aegyptios*, by Jacques Charpentier (Jacobus Carpentarius, 1524 – 1574), a professor at the Collège Royal and an arch-enemy of Petrus Ramus. The work is now known to be a mediæval Arabic redaction of parts of Plotinus's *Enneads*. After a copy was discovered in Damascus in the early sixteenth century it was translated into Latin and published in 1519. Given the date of publication of Charpentier's paraphrase of it and the rarity of the term we think we can conclude that Dicsone was familiar with it.

100 See footnote 91.

101 Latin *ratiocinans memoria*. Another term from Jacques Charpentier's edition (Book IX this time) of the pseudo-Aristotelian *Libri quattuordecim qui Aristotelis: esse dicuntur, de secretiore parto divinæ sapientiæ secundum Ægyptios* (see footnote 99). It was a book much drawn on in later times by, among others, Emanuel Swedenborg. Cf. Swedenborg's *Hieroglyphic Key to natural and spiritual mysteries, by*

way of representations and correspondences translated from the Latin by J. J. G. Wilkinson, 1847, p. 26: 'It follows then, that there is a correspondence and harmony between all things, namely, of natural with spiritual, and vice versa; and that in universal nature we have nothing but types, images and likenesses of particular things in the spiritual sphere, which is the region of exemplars or antitypes. Were it not so, it would be permanently impossible for a spiritual intelligence of any description to comprehend the objects of a lower sphere, which yet spirits do comprehend spontaneously and instinctively, *ex se* and *in se*. The Egyptians appear to have cultivated this branch of learning, and to have signified these correspondences by a vast number of different hieroglyphics, not merely expressive of natural, but also at the same time of spiritual things. Respecting this science of the Egyptians we have an entire treatise by Aristotle.'

102 Latin *stellarum animi*. Another term from Charpentier's Aristotle paraphrase (see footnote 99).

103 See Cicero (attrib.), *Ad Herennium*, III, 17: *Constat igitur artificiosa memoria ex locis et imaginibus. Locos appellamus eos qui breviter, perfecte, insignite aut natura aut manu sunt absoluti, ut eos facile naturali memoria conprehendere et amplecti queamus: ut ædes, intercolumnium, angulum, fornicem, et alia quæ his similia sunt*, 'The artificial memory is therefore established on the basis of memory-loci and images. By memory-loci I mean those things that are naturally or artificially complete in themselves concisely, perfectly and distinctively, so that we can easily understand and grasp them with the natural memory, e.g. a building, an intercolumnar space, a recess, an arch,

or something similar.'
104 Virgil, *Eclogues*, IV, line 36. Virgil's *Fourth Eclogue* is one of the most famous of all Latin poems. Probably written around 42 BCE, it describes the birth of a boy who will eventually become divine and rule the whole world. In the Christian era it began to be seen as a prediction of the birth of Jesus Christ, an interpretation in which Constantine the Great, St. Augustine, Dante and Alexander Pope, among others, all believed. This was one of the roots of the mediæval idea that Virgil was a prophet and even a magician. See *Vergil* [sic] *in the Middle Ages* by Domenico Comparetti, translated by E. F. M. Benecke. Lines 34-36 of the poem, from which this line is taken, describe the two conditions for the return of the Golden Age: war, and a second Argo, the ship in which the Argonauts sailed in search of the Golden Fleece. This quotation can therefore be interpreted as 'when the Golden Age returns'. It will also be found in Giordano Bruno's *Expulsion of the Triumphant Beast*, 1st Dialogue, 1st Part.
105 See Aristotle, *Physics*, Book IV, 219b 1-2. For a detailed treatment of this subject see Ursula Coope, *Time for Aristotle*, Oxford University Press, 2005, ISBN 0199247900.
106 Possibly a reference to the alleged predictive powers of Anaxagoras, who is said to have foretold the landing of meteorites, including one at Aegospotami in 467 BCE. This is mentioned by a number of classical authors, including Diogenes Laertius (with whose *Lives of the Eminent Philosophers* Dicsone seems to have been very familiar), Plutarch and Pliny, as well as by Eusebius of Cæsarea. Meteors were also a very popular subject in Dicsone's time (see Arianna Borelli, *'The Weatherglass and its Observers'*, in *Philosophies of*

Knowledge: Francis Bacon and his Contemporaries, volume 1, Brill 2008). Pliny describes the Anaxagoras predictions thus: 'The Greeks boast that Anaxagoras, the Clazomenian, in the second year of the 78th Olympiad, from his knowledge of what relates to the heavens, had predicted, that at a certain time, a stone would fall from the sun. And the thing accordingly happened, in the daytime, in a part of Thrace, at the river Ægos. The stone is now to be seen, a wagonload in size and of a burnt appearance... There is a stone, a small one indeed, at this time, in the Gymnasium of Abydos, which on this account is held in veneration, and which the same Anaxagoras predicted would fall in the middle of the earth' (Pliny, *Natural History*, Book II, Ch. 59, Bostock and Riley's translation).
107 Latin *prudentia*. See Cicero, *De Inventione*, Book II, Ch. liii: *Prudentia est rerum bonarum et malarum neutrarumque scientia. partes eius: memoria, intellegentia, providentia. Memoria est, per quam animus repetit illa, quæ fuerunt; intellegentia, per quam ea perspicit, quæ sunt; providentia, per quam futurum aliquid videtur ante quam factum est,* 'Prudence is the knowledge of good and bad things and of things that are neither good nor bad. Its parts are memory, intelligence and foreknowledge. Memory is that through which the mind repeats those things which have been, intelligence that through which it perceives those things that are, and foreknowledge that through which something is seen before it has occurred.' See also Spencer Pearce, 'Dante and the Art of Memory', *The Italianist* 16, 1996, p. 22: 'The renewal of interest in the art of local memory was instigated...by Albert the Great and his pupil Thomas Aquinas... It is highly significant...

that the context in which St. Augustine and St. Thomas offer their mnemonic device is not a treatise of rhetoric but of ethics: for both writers memory is a fundamental aspect of the virtue of prudence.'

108 Latin *nuncias*, specifically female messengers or, perhaps, eagles (*nuncia fulva Iovis*, 'Jupiter's tawny messengers').

109 Latin *anima*, the soul considered as the vivifying substance of every human being, though perhaps used loosely by Dicsone here to mean simply 'mind'.

110 Greek ὕλη, defined by Aristotle as 'matter' but in the sense of 'the substratum which is receptive of coming-to-be and passing-away: but the substratum of the remaining kinds of change is also, in a certain sense, 'matter', because all these substrata are receptive of 'contrarieties' of some kind' (*On Generation and Corruption*, Book I, Ch. 4, in Harold Joachim's translation).

111 Latin *notæ* and *sigilla* respectively. These and some related Brunonian terms are ably explained by Johann Gottlieb Buhle in Volume II Part II pp. 762ff. of his *Geschichte der neuern Philosophie seit der Epoche der Wiederherstellung der Wissenschaften* (Göttingen 1801):

'In Book II of his *De imaginum, signorum et idearum compositione*, Bruno depicts Nature as a sort of living mirror in which we perceive the images of natural things, the shadows and the Divinity. This mirror contains the idea (the form) which is its causal principle, just as the image of the object in the mind of the artist is the cause that determines the work that he or she produces. But Nature contains the idea as the substance itself, for matter is nothing other than this substance, which draws forth from itself an incalculable number of forms

subject to an infinite number of variations, i.e. it is nothing other than the idea (the form). But the idea of Nature can be shared in twelve different categories which make it knowable by the spirit: 1. the idea (*idea*), which is the metaphysical principle, the absolute form, the cause of which is supernatural; 2. the trace (*vestigium*), the form of the physical world, 3. the shadow (*umbra*), the form of the universe in the intelligence; 4. the mark (*nota*), everything that indicates something medially or immediately through a proximate or remote cause; 5. the character (*character*), which indicates something by a series of lines and points, e.g. the alphabet; 6. the sign (*signum*), which encompasses everything by which something is designated; 7. the seal (*sigillum*), which designates an object according to one of its more remarkable parts or qualities; 8. the token (*indicium*), which does not express the thing in itself but serves only to announce it and draw our attention to it; 9. the figure (*figura*), which indicates not the interior, like the idea, trace and shadow do, but the exterior, and contains a space through which the figure is distinguished from the character; 10. the resemblance (*simile*), a form perceived by the senses and conserved in the imagination and corresponding to an object; 11. the analogy (*proportio*), which expresses a relationship between several things; and finally 12. the image (*imago*), which denotes a more or less perfect identity with its object, and consequently plays upon an expressive force that is greater than simple resemblance. However, all the forms of nature which are knowable by the intelligence, however they might be expressed, must be related to the visual sense, i.e. they must be images.' (Our own free translation).

It should be mentioned in passing that Buhle had interesting views on the origins of Freemasonry, arguing that speculative Freemasonry arose in England between 1629 and 1635 through the work of Robert Fludd, who had earlier been introduced to Rosicrucianism by Michael Maier. For more on the Brunonian terms, see Manuel Mertens, *Magic and Memory in Giordano Bruno: The Art of a Heroic Spirit*, Brill 2018, p. 107ff.

112   We take this to mean the three categories of universals; subjects that contain many other subjects; and entire systems.

113   See Cicero (attrib.), *Rhetorica ad Herennium*, Book I, ii.3: *Memoria est firma animi rerum et verborum et dispositionis perceptio*, 'Memory is the firm perception by the mind of things and words and their arrangement.'.

114   See footnote 103.

115   It is difficult to know who is being referred to here. Titus Alledius Severus is mentioned in Book XII of the *Annals* of Tacitus as marrying his niece (which was perfectly legal at that time and place). There was also a famous glutton called Alledius who is mentioned in Juvenal's *Fifth Satire*: 'Before Virro is put a huge goose's liver; a capon as big as a goose, and a boar, piping hot, worthy of yellow-haired Meleager's steel. Then will come truffles, if it be spring-time and the longed-for thunder have enlarged our dinners. 'Keep your corn to yourself, O Libya!' says Alledius; 'unyoke your oxen, if only you send us truffles!' (G. G. Ramsay's translation). Cicero's *Letters to Atticus*, Book XII, Letter IV, also mentions someone of this name, but Dicsone makes him sound like a leader in the Servile Wars, though no one of that name seems to have been

involved in them. Perhaps it is a satirical reference by Dicsone to a famous glutton of his time with radical sympathies who was known by that nickname or, perhaps, to Petrus Ramus.

116   According to legend, Astræa, the virgin goddess of justice, innocence and purity, was the last of the immortals to live among mankind during the Golden Age, and will one day return to Earth to restore it to its former glory. We find a possible reference to her in Virgil's *Fourth Eclogue*, line 6 (see footnote 104): *Iam redit et virgo, redeunt Saturnia Regna*, ('Now the virgin returns, and the Saturnian powers return with her'). In Dicsone's time Astræa was identified with Elizabeth I, the virgin queen presiding over a Golden Age. See Frances Yates, *Astræa: The Imperial Theme in the Sixteenth Century* (1975).

117   A rhetorical figure whereby a speaker anticipates possible objections to his argument and then immediately answers them.

118   Latin *materiæ concretio*, a phrase Dicsone may have picked up from Jean Fernel's *Physiologia*. See footnotes 182 and 185 of the *Thamus*.

119   This phrase is made clearer in the *Thamus* as 'added to the existing utilities provided by the adjuvants'.

120   We take this to mean that the spaces between subjects should not be allowed to intrude on the mind's eye.

121   Latin *tribus*, 'third-parts'.

122   The *decemviri* ('ten men') were Roman magistrates with absolute authority, originally appointed in 451 BCE to protect the interests of the lower classes from the predations of the patricians. After a promising start, including the enactment of the Laws of the Twelve Tables, the *decemviri* fell into bad ways and the consular system was reintroduced.

123 Presumably a reference to the decemvirs' chains of office, but also to one of the most famous of all esoteric images, the Golden Chain of Homer. The tradition is too long and complex to trace in detail here. Suffice it to say that in the opening of the 15th book of his *Iliad* Homer portrays Zeus awakening after being seduced by Hera to find the Trojans in retreat. He scolds Hera with the words, 'Do you not remember how once upon a time I had you hanged? I fastened two anvils on to your feet, and bound your hands in a chain of gold which none might break, and you hung in mid-air among the clouds.' Plato and Kircher, among others, took this literally to be a reference to the Sun, but a more esoteric interpretation can be traced via the commentaries by Favonius Eulogius and Macrobius (both 5th century CE) on the 'Dream of Scipio' to be found in the 6th Book of Cicero's *De Republica*, in which the disembodied soul of the Roman general Scipio Æmilianus has a vision of the nine celestial spheres of the universe. In Book I Ch. 44 of his commentary Macrobius argues that the Golden Chain is an uninterrupted connection of causes that bind themselves together by mutual bonds and run from God to the vilest dregs of matter. Petrus Ramus, however, saw it as a chain of dialectic, e.g. in his *Aristotelicæ animadversiones*, Paris, 1543, pp. 2 recto-3 verso, and his 1549 edition of Euclid, page 1: *Hic enim prima mediis, media postremis, omniaque inter se, velut aurea quadam Homeri catena sic vincta, colligataque sunt* ('For here the first are thus bound and connected to the middles, and the middles to the finals, and everything to each other, just like that Golden Chain of Homer'). According to Plotinus it is possible to ascend to the world of ideal forms by moving up the Golden Chain, and the image became an essential component of the strictly contemplative systems of Pseudo-Dionysius, Aquinas, Cusa and Ficino and eventually of Giordano Bruno's hermetic memory system. See Joshua Ramey, *The Hermetic Deleuze: Philosophy and Spiritual Ordeal*, Duke University Press 2012, Chapter II; Leo Catana, *The Concept of Contraction in Giordano Bruno's Philosophy*, Routledge 2005; Robert Lamberton, *Homer the Theologian: Neoplatonist Allegorical Reading and the Growth of the Epic Tradition*, Univ. of California Press 1989; and Pierre Lévêque: *Aurea catena Homeri: une étude sur l'allégorie grecque*, Paris: Les Belles Lettres 1959. But the Golden Chain almost certainly pre-dates even Homer, e.g. Proclus, in Book II of his commentary on Plato's *Timæus*, tells us that Orpheus made use of this image.

124 See footnote 113.

125 Or Primal Mind, Latin *mens prima*. A term from Giordano Bruno (found in his *Summa terminorum physicorum. Intellectus. Seu Idea*), who may have obtained it from Dante's *Convivio*, Book II, 3.8-12: 'And tranquil and peaceful is the place of that supreme Deity which alone completely sees itself. This is the place of the blessed spirits, according to the Holy Church, which cannot tell lies; and Aristotle also seems to hold this view, to anyone who follows what he is saying, in the first book of *On Heaven and Earth*. This heaven is the overarching edifice of the universe, in which all the universe is enclosed, and outside of which nothing exists; and it is not in any place but was formed alone in the First Mind *(ma formato fu solo ne la prima Mente)*, which the Greeks call *Protonoe*. This is the magnificence of which the Psalmist spoke, when he says to God: 'Elevated above the

heavens is your magnificence'.'
Dicsone may also have been reading
Marcantonio Flaminio's paraphrase of
Book XII Aristotle's *Metaphysics*,
published in 1536, in which the term
occurs.

126 See Cicero's *Dream of Scipio* (see
footnote 123): 'For men were created
subject to this law, to keep to that
globe, which you see in the centre of
this region and which is called the
Earth; and to them a soul was given
formed from those everlasting fires,
which you mortals call constellations
and stars, that, round and spherical in
form, alive with divine intelligences,
complete their orbits and circles with
marvellous swiftness' (Pearman's
translation).

127 Latin *periodus cœli*. See Giordano
Bruno, *De Umbris Idearum*,
Conceptus VI.F: *Rerum formœ sunt in
ideis, sunt quodammodo in se ipsis;
sunt in coelo; sunt in periodo cœli*,
'The forms of things are in ideas; they
are, in a certain way, in themselves;
they are in the heavens; they are in a
circuit of the heavens.'

128 See footnote 127.

129 Presumably he means 'in an animate
being.'

130 Latin *lima mentis*. Cf. the mediæval
hymn to St. Catherine: *Tandem ista
margarita/Lima mentis expolita/Et
fracturis carnis trita/Paradisum adiit*,
'At last that pearl/Polished by the file
of the mind/And burnished by the
breaking of the flesh/Has entered
Paradise.'

131 A term from syllogistic logic: the
position (i.e. positing or assertion) of
an antecedent leads naturally to the
position (positing) of the consequent,
e.g. If a man has feeling then he is an
animal/But a man has
feeling/Therefore he is an animal.

132 See footnote 115.

133 Cf. Cicero, *De Oratore*, Book II, 87:
Vidit enim hoc prudenter sive

*Simonides sive alius quis invenit ea
maxime animis affigi nostris, quœ
essent a sensu tradita atque impressa;
acerrimum autem ex omnibus nostris
sensibus esse sensum videndi; quare
facillime animo teneri posse ea, quœ
perciperentur auribus aut cogitatione,
si etiam oculorum commendatione
animis traderentur*, 'For Simonides or
whoever it was who discovered it was
wise enough to see that those things
are most likely to stick in our minds
are those which are communicated to
or impressed by the senses. But the
keenest of all our senses is that of
seeing, which means that those things
which can most readily be retained in
our minds are those that are perceived
with the ears or cognition if they are
also conveyed to our minds with the
approval of the eyes.'

134 Latin *aspectus iudicium*. Cf. Carl von
Morgenstern, *Commentatio de Arte
Veterum Mnemonica*, Dorpat (Tartu)
1835: *Imago autem, quœ collocatur in
loco quodam, etiam perfectior esse
potest, ita ut eâ non solum
admoneamur rei, sed ut eius vi etiam
repræsentetur et in aspectus iudicium
vocetur res ipsa, cuius memoria opus
est*, 'But an image which is positioned
in a certain memory-locus can be even
more perfect, so that we are not just
reminded of the thing itself but also in
such way that the thing itself which
needs to be recalled to mind is
represented in all its vigour and is
called before the judgement of vision.'

135 Latin *imitata et efficta simulachra*, a
phrase lifted from Ch. III of Cicero's
uncompleted translation of Plato's
Timœus, known as the *De
Universitate*.

136 Latin *conformatio*. This seems to be a
term of Dicsone's devising.

137 Latin *mentis oculi*, a term used by
Cicero in his discussion of metaphor
in *De Oratore*, Book III, 163: 'for the
eyes of the intellect are drawn more

readily to things we have seen than to things we have heard of'.

138 Latin *conformatio verborum.* See Cicero, *De Oratore,* Book III, Ch. 52.

139 Latin *sensuum iudicia.* See Cicero, *De Finibus Bonorum et Malorum,* Book I, 64: *Nisi autem Rerum Natura perspecta erit, nullo modo poterimus autem sensuum iudicia defendere,* 'On the other hand, without a full understanding of Nature it is impossible to defend the judgements of our senses.'

140 Latin *rationis familia,* a strange expression which seems to mean all those possible sources of a shadow which are not to be found either in the internal or external forms of objects.

141 Latin *inflexio.* Dicsone seems to use this term synonymously with *modificatio.*

142 i.e. the Sophistic philosophy.

143 Cf. Cicero, *De Oratore,* Book III, 156: 'Metaphors are therefore a kind of borrowing, since you take from something else that which you have not of your own. Those that display a slightly greater audacity are the ones that...add a certain lustre to an oration.'

144 Cf. Cicero, *De Oratore,* Book III, 165: 'A metaphor ought not to be too daring, but should be of such a nature that it may appear to have been substituted for another expression rather than have leapt into its place, to have entered by entreaty, and not by violence.'

145 Latin *efficiens,* one of Cicero's favourite words (see, for example, the *Topica* 14, *De Divinatione,* I, 55, etc.). According to Aristotle the efficient (or moving) cause of a process of change consists of things apart from the thing being changed or moved which interact so as to be an agency of the change or movement. So, to take one of Aristotle's own examples, the efficient cause of a boy is his father.

146 Fortune-telling using fire. Like hydromancy (see footnote 147) it was one of the seven *artes magicæ* or *artes prohibitæ* (practices forbidden by canon law, and mirroring the seven 'respectable' arts of the trivium and quadrivium). Others included necromancy (divination by contacting the dead), geomancy (divination using markings on the ground, tossed stones or earth, or specially-constructed domino-like figures), aeromancy (divination from weather phenomena, comets etc.), chiromancy (palmistry) and scapulimancy (divination from animal bones, especially shoulder-blades).

147 Fortune-telling using water, more specifically by dropping pebbles into a pool.

148 A Centaur, born in Thessaly.

149 It has been claimed that his name means 'foresight', just as his brother's name Epimetheus seems to denote 'hindsight'.

150 The foolish brother of Prometheus: his lack of foresight led to regret, which he was able to experience thanks to his gift of hindsight.

151 See footnote 134.

152 See *The Divine Pimander,* Book V (VI), 6: 'If thou would'st see Him too through things that suffer death, both on the earth and in the deep, think of a man's being fashioned in the womb, my son, and strictly scrutinize the art of Him who fashions him, and learn who fashioneth this fair and godly image of the Man... Who [then] is He who traceth out the circles of the eyes; who He who boreth out the nostrils and the ears; who He who openeth [the portal of] the mouth; who He who doth stretch out and tie the nerves; who He who channels out the veins; who He who hardeneth the bones; who He who covereth the flesh with skin; who He who separates the fingers and the joints; who He who widens out a

treading for the feet; who He who diggeth out the ducts; who He who spreadeth out the spleen; who He who shapeth heart like to a pyramid; who He who setteth ribs together; who He who wideneth the liver out; who He who maketh lungs like to a sponge; who He who maketh belly stretch so much; who He who doth make prominent the parts most honourable, so that they may be seen, while hiding out of sight those of least honour?' (G. R. S. Mead's translation).

153 See footnote 111.

154 Latin *effectum*, the result of an efficient cause.

155 Latin *id quod subest*, literally 'that which lies underneath.' I take this to mean that you should choose a general underlying expression of the shadow concerned rather than something extreme or partial.

156 Latin *communis utilitas*, a concept much discussed by Cicero, especially in his *De Officiis*, e.g. Book III, section 52: 'What say you? comes Antipater's argument on the other side; 'it is your duty to consider the interests of your fellow-men and to serve society; you were brought into the world under these conditions and have these inborn principles which you are in duty bound to obey and follow, that your interest shall be the interest of the community and conversely that the interest of the community shall be your interest as well; will you, in view of all these facts, conceal from your fellow-men what relief in plenteous supplies is close at hand for them?' (Walter Miller's translation for Loeb). Aquinas also examined it extensively in his commentary on Aristotle, *In Libros Politicorum Aristotelis Expositio*.

157 See Book VIII of Plato's *Republic* for the discussion between Socrates and Plato's brother Glaucon about the various forms of government.

158 Latin *natura constant*. See Lucretius, Book II, line 378.

159 A phrase from Cicero, *De Oratore*, Book III, 42.

160 'Property is an accident that is proper; or, it belongs to its subject; hence its name, property. It differs from accident that is common, in this: property belongs to the species of the object; i.e., agrees with an object on account of its specific nature or form, the *common accident* agrees with an object or individual in virtue of its matter, or quasi matter; e.g., 'Man limps, because Peter is lame; Peter laughs, because man is a laughing being.' Lameness is an accident that is common to individuals of many species of animals that walk; laughter, strictly so-called, is peculiar or proper only to man' (Rev. W. H. Hill S.J., *Elements of Philosophy*, 1873).

161 In the previous Chapter. Cf. William Brown, *Lectures on the Philosophy of the Human Mind* (Edinburgh 1828), Lecture XXXVII, *Of Nearness in Place or Time:* 'Even with those who are more accustomed to use, on great occasions, the stricter dates of months and years, this association of events, as near to each other, forms the great bond for uniting in the memory those multitudes of scattered facts which form the whole history of domestic life, and which it would have been impossible to remember by their separate relation to some insulated point of time. It is the same with nearness in place. To think of one part of a familiar landscape is to recall the whole. The hill, the grove, the church, the river, the bridge, and all the walks which lead to them, rise before us in immediate succession. On this species of local relation chiefly have been founded those systems of artificial memory which at different periods have been submitted to the world, and which, whatever perfections or

imperfections they may possess in other respects, certainly demonstrate very powerfully, by the facilities of remembrance which they afford, the influence that is exercised by mere order in place, on the trains of our suggestion.'

162 The great Greek statesman, patron of the arts and promoter of democratic principles was a great admirer of Anaxagoras, and may have spoken up for him at his trial for impiety.

163 In Greek mythology Hippolytus was a son of Theseus and was killed after rejecting the amorous advances of his step-mother.

164 Presumably a reference to the Greek erotic poet of that name (6th century BCE), who once compared falling in love to a down-rush of the Thracian north-wind armed with lightning (Fragment 286).

165 Presumably because of the similarity between the caduceus of Mercury and the rod of Æsculapius.

166 Virgil, *Aeneid*, Book I, line 589. A description of Aeneas as he meets Dido for the first time in Carthage.

167 Horace, *Odes*, Book I, 14, lines 4-6.

168 A paraphrase of Ovid's *Tristia*, Book I, V, lines 25-26. Ovid has: *Scilicet ut fulvum spectatur in ignibus aurum, tempore sic duro est inspicienda fides*, 'It is clear that just as tawny gold is *tested* in the flames so loyalty must be proved in times of stress'. I wonder if this (presumably deliberate) misquotation is an alchemical reference by Dicsone?

169 The son of Achilles by Deidamia.

170 Presumably a reference to Aulus Atilius Calatinus, a distinguished Roman general in the first Punic war, who was twice consul (BCE 258 and 254) and once a dictator (and the first to wage war outside of Italy). Cicero mentions him admiringly in, among other places, his *De Finibus Bonorum et Malorum*, Book II, 116: 'You will

not find anyone extolled for his skill and cunning in procuring pleasures. This is not the purport of laudatory epitaphs, like that one near the city gate:
HERE LYETH ONE WHOM ALL MANKIND AGREE ROME'S FIRST AND GREATEST CITIZEN TO BE.
Do we suppose that all mankind agreed that Calatinus was Rome's greatest citizen because of his surpassing eminence in the acquisition of pleasures?'

171 In the Aristotelian sense, whereby the genus is a larger group of which the species is merely one proper subset, see Aristotle, *Categories*, V, 2b.

172 Latin *superior ratio*, a term that has its *locus classicus* in St. Augustine's *De Trinitate* XII 3:3, where he argues that the human reason is superior insofar as it contemplates spiritual things, and inferior insofar as it contemplates the mundane: they are not separate powers, but are distinguished only in terms of function. This debate was taken further by the Scholastics, and especially by Thomas Aquinas (*Summa Theologica* Ia, q. 79).

173 Latin *decuria*, literally 'a group of ten', i.e. ten degrees or a decan, which is what the word is taken to mean in astrological works from Dicsone's time, e.g. in the *Astrologica* (1532) of Joachim Camerarius the Elder, but this would not give us the 120 divisions which Dicsone's system requires, so we must assume he means 'a tenth part'.

174 The terminology used here is similar to that of Dialogue II, Part II.IV.IV of Bruno's *Cantus Circæus* ('The Song of Circe').

175 Dicsone may have in mind the image of the Lunar Dragon at the end of Bruno's *De Umbris Idearum*, described thus: *Homo rex habens in dextra draconem; super regis caput flamma*

ignis, et caput draconis simile est capiti accipitris, 'A king-like man holding a dragon in his right hand. On the king's head is a flame of fire, and the dragon's head is like the head of a hawk.' This seems to have been taken, in slightly adapted form, from the astral images to be found in Heinrich Cornelius Agrippa's *De Occulta Philosophia*, Book II, 45 (see illustration). As Yates says in her *Art of Memory*, p. 215: 'We have to see all these astral images in the context of the *De Occulta Philosophia* to realise what Bruno is trying to do. In Agrippa's text-book of magic, such image-lists occur in the second book, the one on celestial magic which is concerned with operating on the middle world of the stars... One of the chief ways of operating (according to this kind of magical thought) with the celestial world is through the magic or talismanic images of the stars. Bruno is transferring such operations within, applying them to memory by using celestial images as memory images, as it were harnessing the inner world of the imagination to the stars, or reproducing the celestial world within.' But Dicsone seems to follow Agrippa's procedure more closely than Bruno's.

176 Presumably by dividing the five wandering planets into tenths, plus the Sun, Moon and Lunar Dragon similarly divided in order to make 80 (plus 120 equals 200).

177 Horace, *De Arte Poetica*, lines 40-41.

178 Horace, *De Arte Poetica*, line 311.

179 By this I assume he means 'without any accents or diacritics', such as would be used in Latin.

180 See footnote 115.

181 The sounds made 'with the whispering breath', e.g. in English the letters or letter-combinations *f, h, k, p, s, sh, t, th, wh,* in, for example, the words *fame, hut, kite, pit, sin, shade, tin, thin, what.*

182 I assume that is what Dicsone means by a *consistens*. A 'stop' is a consonant in which the vocal tract is blocked so that all airflow ceases. Consonant sounds such as the English voiceless stops *p, t,* and *k* at the beginning of words like *pat, top* and *keel* are also aspirates because they are pronounced with a forceful expulsion of air. Dicsone does not use this term in the *Thamus*.

183 In English the letters *l, m, n, r, s.*

184 i.e. letters that end a word.

185 Latin *delectus habendi*, a military term used by Cæsar. This echoes the military metaphors used in Chapter V.

186 See footnote 133.

187 We take this to mean that the rational faculties should not be allowed to interfere with what is essentially an irrational (or, more correctly, non-rational) process.

188 Parmenides of Elea (*fl.* late sixth or early fifth century BCE) founded the Eleatic school of philosophy, which rejected the epistemological validity of sense experience and used logical standards of clarity and necessity as the criteria of truth. They were hostile to the early physicalist philosophers, who explained everything in terms of primary matter, and to Heraclitus, with his theory of perpetual change. Only fragments of one work by Parmenides (*On Nature*) have survived. Dicsone was familiar with it and subsequently quotes from a Latin translation of it (see footnotes 197 and 198). Dicsone would also seem to have known the work of Diogenes Laertius entitled *Lives of the Eminent Philosophers.*

189 Dionysodorus (*c.*430 BCE – late 5th century or early 4th century BCE) was an ancient Greek Sophist and teacher of the martial arts, generalship, and rhetoric. He is unflatteringly portrayed by both Plato (in his *Euthydemus*) and Xenophon (in the *Memorabilia* 3.1) as the worst kind of Sophist, using

logical fallacies to defeat arguments and taking people's hard-earned money from them in return for shoddy teaching.

190 Heraclitus of Ephesus (c.535 BCE – c.475 BCE) maintained that the fundamental principle of the universe was ever-present change ('No man ever steps into the same river twice), in contrast to Parmenides ('What is, is').

191 Xenophanes of Colophon (c.570 BCE – c.475 BCE) was more of a wandering poet with philosophical leanings than a philosopher in the true sense. His poetry reveals him to be a theist but a sceptic with regard to the Greek pantheon (which he considered to be human projections) and their ability to interfere in human affairs.

192 Pyrrho (c.360 BCE – c.270 BCE) was the founder of the Sceptic school of Greek philosophy. He travelled to India with Alexander the Great's army and was certainly influenced by the philosophers of the Indus region.

193 Democritus (c.460 BCE – c.370 BCE) was a materialist philosopher and the developer of an atomic theory.

194 A Latin translation of a fragment from a lost play by Euripides called *Phryxus*, quoted in the section on Pyrrho in Diogenes Laertius, *Lives of the Eminent Philosophers*, Book IX, Ch. XI, No. VIII.

195 A saying of Protagoras, quoted in Plato's *Theætetus*, 152a. Sextus Empiricus also quotes it directly in his *Against the Logicians*, Book I, Section 60: πάντων χρημάτων μέτρον ἐστὶν ἄνθρωπος, τῶν μὲν ὄντων ὡς ἔστιν, τῶν δὲ οὐκ ὄντων ὡς οὐκ ἔστιν, 'Of all things the measure is Man, of the things that are that they are, and of the things that are not that they are not.'

196 See footnote 85.

197 A Latin version by an unknown translator of lines from Part 1 of *On Nature* by the Greek pre-Socratic philosopher Parmenides.

198 A Latin version by an unknown translator of lines from Part 7 of *On Nature* by the Greek pre-Socratic philosopher Parmenides.

199 Latin *complicatio*. This section of the text, with its description of the brain as a microcosm, with the memory located in the solar position in the centre and the sensory faculties in orbit around it, seems to be Dicsone's clearest explanation of what he means by the 'boundary' (*horizon*). This was of course written during the time of the Copernican revolution, in which Bruno was an important figure.

200 Latin *partes communes* and *partes propriæ*, so for example the 'common parts' of an eyelid are skin, adipose tissue etc., because these are common to most of the human body, whereas the 'particular parts' are the eyelashes, which are unique to the eyelid. Dicsone's system therefore seems to allow parts or aspects of objects to be studied and memorised and not just parts of them.

201 Latin *velificationes*, literally 'sailings', or 'settings sail', but it is hard to see how this meaning could be relevant in this context. It is perhaps being used here in a very specialised sense to mean the 'veiling' used to signify deity in Roman art, whereby the god or goddess in question holds a cloak over their head so that it billows in the form of an arch, which 'recalls the vault of the firmament' (Karl Galinsky, *Augustan Culture: An Interpretive Introduction*, Princeton University Press, 1996, pp. 158 and 321). Its esoteric meaning in this context is not entirely clear.

202 See footnote 123.

203 Copernicus's ground-breaking *De Revolutionibus Orbium Cælestium* ('On the Revolutions of the Heavenly Spheres') proposing a heliocentric

model of the universe was published in 1543, just before the astronomer's death.

204 Latin *gemina transformatio*. Dicsone may have borrowed this term from Dialogue IV of the *Necyomantia* [sic] of Étienne Forcadel (Stephanus Forcatulus, 1519-1578), a famous lawyer, Neo-Latin poet and esoteric writer. Forcadel published a series of bizarre books exploring the intersection of law, satire and the occult. See Wim Decock, Law on Love's Stage: Étienne Forcadel's (1519-1578) *Cupido Jurisperitus* in Inszenierung des Rechts / Law on Stage, München: Martin Meidenbauer, 17-36: 'In his Oracle of a Jurist or Dialogues on Occult Jurisprudence (*Necyomantia iurisperiti sive de occulta jurisprudentia dialogi*) of 1544, for example, Forcadel had staged a fictitious encounter between classical Roman jurists, famous representatives of the Medieval *ius commune*, and lawyers of his own time. They discussed perennial legal issues against a magical background highly reminiscent of the fantastic setting of the witty dialogues written

in Greek by the satirist Lucian of Samosata (ca. 125-180).'

205 Latin *informata cogitatio*, a phrase used by Cicero (see *Letters to Atticus, Book I, Letter I*) to denote a thought-process that has begun but which has not yet been completed, i.e. 'a partly-baked idea'.

206 Presumably a reference to Socrates' disillusionment with the philosophy of Anaxagoras. 'Having one day,' says [Socrates], 'read a book of Anaxagoras, who said the divine mind was the cause of all things, and drew them up in their proper ranks and classes, I was ravished with joy. I perceived there was nothing more certain than this principle that mind was the cause of all things.' Socrates purchased the books of Anaxagoras, and began to read them with avidity, but he had not proceeded far till he found his hopes disappointed. The author, he said, 'makes no further use of this mind, but assigns as the cause of the order and beauty that prevailed in the world, the air, water, whirlwind, and other agencies of nature' (Rev. John Hunt, *An Essay on Pantheism*, London, 1866, p. 68).

Alexandri Dicsoni Arelii

De Umbra Rationis Et Iudicii,

Sive De Memoriæ Virtute Prosopceia.

AD ILLUSTRISSIMUM D[OMINUM] D[OMINUM] ROBERTUM
DUDLÆUM
COMITEM LICESTARÆUM, etc.

LONDINI,
Excudebat Thomas Vautrollerius
Typographus. 1583.

[Motto on printer's device:] ANCHORA SPEI.

ALEXANDRI DICSONI ARELII
PRÆFATIO.

AD ILLUSTRISSIMUM D[OMINUM] D[OMINUM] ROBERTUM
DUDLÆUM
COMITEM LICESTARÆUM, etc.

ANTUM igitur, illustrissime Comes, *abs re tua*, vel publica potius, *est otii tibi*, ut meam etiam nugantis aspicias umbram? Rides, inquis, vel insanis: Hoc etenim si nugas affers, illud, si non affers, consequi forte videatur. Οὐδὲν ὁρίζω. Sic enim, in huius causæ iudicio et æstimatione, me nihil potius definire deceat, quam efferentem alioqui, aut contra etiam dissimulantem, vanitatis aut stultitiæ suspectum iri. Si quis enim quæ sua sunt, aut laudibus efferat, aut contra etiam deprimat, ut elegantior scilicet et modestior videri possit: utrunque esse tumidi videtur. Illud simplicis et aperti: hoc esurientis et fere malitiosi. Nunc ista qualiscunque meditatio, si tua gravissima negotia reputet, resistat sane: valdeque caveto, ne si tuam ianuam pulset, ebria videatur. At si mores, si natura spectetur, quem quæso potius, quam communem literarum parentem, philosophica meditatio recognoscat? Ea si tibi ferri posse videatur, quæ sub tui nominis umbra requiescat, erit quod ipsi gratuler: valdeque contendam, ut memoriæ non ingratæ, argumentum forte uberius, aliquando feras. Vale. Cal. Ian.

ALEXANDER DICSONUS LECTORI, S[ALUTEM]

UIDNAM esse putem (inquis) in umbra, lucis? cum in huius illa quidem horizonte consistat. Certe cum duo sint in rerum natura, hinc ipsa in sua idea memoria, hinc ad eam rationis accessio: illic audentibus esse licet. omnes enim singularem esse memoriæ virtutem sine recusatione fatentur. In altero vero quæstio est. Nam et sitne rationis hic ulla potentia, et si sit, quid ipsi primum invenerimus requiri possit. Quo loco, qui duriores erunt, ipsi viderint: non laboro. Qui non erunt, aut quæ scient, profiteri volent: aut quæ nescient, a nobis fortasse petenda iudicabunt. Atque ut hominibus istis gratum fecisse videmur, sic illorum animantum genios non moramur. Ergo ut sunt leves eiusmodi homines, et minime malitiosi, e suis ingeniis, de nostro quoque coniecturam facilem esse præsumant: a medico memoriæ bonitatem petere malint: meam authoris memoriam requirant: nullam hic artem, vel operosam saltem et gravem esse contendant: denique me vanum, et macri fortasse pectoris hominem. omnia impune. Neque enim levium avicularum rostris et impetu commoveri solemus. Verum istis miseris dimissis, ut iis etiam elegantioribus amiculis nostris, qui

Priusquam noscere queant, exigunt:

Alterum occurrit genus eorum, qui nimis hæc obscure a nobis instituta queruntur. Qui, si amici sunt, e circumstantibus rebus causas eruent: si inimice insectantur, illud audiant Poëtæ:

Ole, quid ad te,
De cute quid faciat ille, vel ille sua.

Mea cutis est: mea impensa est: nihil ad Olum. postremo (si novi Zoilum) exorientur et illi, quibus in oppugnando et explicando Socratico fuco, iudicii nostri libertas insolentior esse videatur. esto. quid tum? dum suam vicissim iudicii paupertatem agnoscant. agnoscent, nisi me, propius accedere malint. Cæterum non parum interest, Lector,

Davusne loquatur, herusne,
Maturusne senex, an adhuc florente iuventa
fervidus.

Etenim si quicquam difficile est, Prosopopœia est. Ubi, et videndum, ut personis consonet oratio: et interim verendum, ne tua de conformatione soliciti, persona neglecta sit. Quo loco, quia necessaria contingit interdum ab altero declinatio: certe ad eius, quœ sit inducta, personœ decorum inclinandum potius videtur. Hic igitur si minus a nobis cautum esse reris, ad Prosopopœiœ circumstantias et exigentiam, tum vero etiam ad benevolentiam tuam provocare certum est. Vale.

IOANNES ADAMUS LINCOLNIENSIS LECTORI, S[ALUTEM]

 REBRIS sermonibus tritum est, candide Lector, probas et solidas merces, ementientis mercatoris officiis non egere: ut nec vina sincera monstrantis hæderæ prolectamenta requirunt. Hæc igitur, post varios variorum conatus, nunc tandem Dicsoni nostri diligenti et accurata solertia, de memoriæ virtute emersa idea, nullo meo commendantis et efferentis officio, nullis fucis egere videatur. Argumentum enim rarum est, et pulchrum, et utile: sed hoc omnes sine disceptatione fatentur. Forma item virilis et absoluta: forma philosophica plane. Quippe hic omnis syllaba, sui momenti: omne verbum, sui sensus: omnis sententia, sui ponderis reperietur. Quid quæris? solidum corpus, non fictam et adumbratam imaginem exhibet. Cum enim memoriæ bonitas, inductis iam olim literis extincta, nunc tandem ætate nostra cœpisset excitari: sed ita tamen, ut melancolica barbarie gravissime affecta, et monstrosa specie deformis, indigna generosis procis amica videretur: Ecce Dicsonus inventus est, qui quasi novalem terram aliquam, diuturna aratione, novatione, iteratione, omnique adeo cultu, et satione dimensam, naturæ sensusque prioris vigori restitueret. restituit, et magna mortalium utilitate vulgavit. Sed adeo late patet ætatis nostræ execrandum monstrum, invidentiæ rabies, ut nihil vel inventione rarum, vel artificio politum, in hac rerum universitate reperias, quod non petulanti petatur lingua, rodatur, et laceretur. Quibus pugiunculis, tantum abest, ut moveri possit author: ut eorum potius, plumbeum acumen miserari soleat. At, tu, amice Lector, suavem et amœnam umbram, atque operæ tuæ precio dignam, gratis, ut aiunt ulnis, amplectere, atque adeo fave. Vale.

ALEXANDRI DICSONI ARELII
DE UMBRA RATIONIS,
PROSOPOPŒIA.

THAMUS, MERCURIUS, THEUTATES.

 UNT ista vera Mercuri: nihil etenim, simile est omnibus impari, et uni, ac soli. unam habet ideam, unus, unique notam: incorpoream quidem illam, at mundi, temporis, et generationis ideas omnes, per corpora prodentem. Et poterit vas cuiusquam, quod sola mente complectimur, imaginatione prehendere? At hæc est earum rerum quæ sub ortum cadunt: et ipsa fortasse generatio: ut ne radios quidem tantæ lucis perferre possit. Ergo ignorantiæ pravitas terram alluit materiæ sarcinam baiulantem. Hæc est absoluta malitia. Hæc, ignis pyramidem in cubi speciem transformans, superioribus orbibus non sinit applicare. At non hic sistitur. O quam ridiculum! Una generatio, tempus unum, et mundus, et ævum: ipsum autem unum, quotum esse contenderint? Sed viderint: nisi potius evomere malint.

MER. At immersas habent in aquas manus. Nam, quem deferunt amictum, quando erit, ut perrumpere velint, aut etiam possint?

THAM. Amictum?

MER. an non dixisti? aut quotum est, quod non sit in imagine sepulchri?

THAM. Ignorantiæ texturam dicis, et in ambitu tenebroso furem inquilinum: sat est. Cæterum quando et otium est, et deambulandi potestas data: visne ut reliquo sermoni operam dantes, ad orci fauces et spatia contendamus: nam et hoc, tua, tradentis umbras, officia forte etiam requirant: nisi tu quid aliud malis.

MER. At me senatus, et concio iam frequens vocat: est enim, ne forte nescias, in certi generis feras, rogatio ferenda. Qua in re decernenda, solus fortasse desideror.

THAM. Quid hic ad feras? an non in terris, una cum corporibus penitus extinguuntur?

MER. Certe homines ita existimant: et solas tamen feras admittit orcus.

THAM. At quotidianum est, homines huc descendentes videre: feras autem non videmus.

MER. Nescis, o Thame, nescis: feræ sunt, humanam illæ quidem speciem ementientes.

THAM. rem incredibilem narras: sed Mercurio credendum est. quamvis hoc ad efferatos mores transferri possit. perge.

MER. nequitiæ quidem regio, terra est, et in hypocrisi natura mentitur: hominis enim veri forma, mens est: quæ ubi materiam suscepit (suscipit autem per animum, et spiritu ministrante) in lucis umbra, et horizonte sedens, ad ipsam inclinat: et ad ea quæ sub intelligentiam cadunt, et quæ revera sunt, convertitur. Non patitur hic a sensibus: sed materiæ vindicum securus, quasi ex obscuro quodam, et nocturno die, ad id quod est ascendere conatur. Qui vero suam animam corpore constrinxerint, et abiecerint, feræ sunt immanes: quibus de metamorphosi fortasse metuendum.

THAM. tenere mihi videor: sed quos vocas materiæ vindices? explicatius, quæso, hoc.

MER. duodenarius est, a denario propulsus. Sed properantem me moraris, curiose nimis interrogando.

THAM. atqui, sed abiit: et quis est iste? certe Theutates est: agnosco radium, numeros, calculos, tesseras, et ipsa etiam elementa: totus denique is est. Hoc illud fuit, o Theutates, nempe Deus etiam orcum subisti?

THEUT. utique Deus, o Thame, Theutates est, nec hoc dubitant Ægyptii tui: at ego umbra eius.

THAM. sed quid interim Æacus? elusisti in simili, nonne?

THEUT. sic est.

THAM. prorsus assentior: et is es vere.

THEUT. ergo rides, o bone? at si circa Naucratem esses, de numine nostro, absurde dubitare, desineres.

THAM. certe et nunc etiam absurde, dubitare desiero. Sed erras: homo es: non: sed fera, ut nuper Mercurium disserentem audivi.

THEUT. calumniaris, o Thame. Ergo literarum usus, ergo Mathematicæ nostra inventa, feræ tibi vestigia videntur?

THAM. de Mathematicis viderit Mercurius: et hic subesse forte aliquid possit. Cæterum de literis, nihil affers.

THEUT. at hæc, o Thame, disciplina, sapientiores Ægyptios tuos, memoriaque promptiores effecit: memoriæ enim, et sapientiæ pharmacum id inventum est meum.

THAM. at amor tibi pectus obscuravit: at contra tu quidem affirmas, quam ipsæ possint: hæ siquidem, neglecto memoriæ studio, discentium animis oblivionis materiam præbebunt: externis quippe scripturæ formulis confisi, interiores ipsas, a se ipsis recordatione repetere et excolere desinent. Non igitur memoriæ, sed oblivionis pharmacum invenisti. Accedit alterum, in altera propositi tui parte, non parvum incommodum: neque enim Ægyptiis quondam meis, veritatem sapientiæ, sed opinionem et apparentiam præbuisti. Nam cum multa sine doctore perceperint, multa quoque scire videbuntur: cum tamen vulgo ac passim ignari sint, atque in hominum congressu et consuetudine graves et importuni, ut qui sapientiæ opinione, non ipsa sapientia, tuo scilicet beneficio, sint imbuti. Atque hæc quidem, me quondam in civitate superioris loci, quam vulgo Ægyptias Thebas appellant, tibi hæc ipsa venditanti, respondisse memini: cum tu te iure perculsum, ipso pudore significares. At fuit illud tempus, cum homines in animo cum scientia scriberent: hic autem quia vivit, iniurias ulcisci potest, novitque, quæ apud quosque dicenda ac tacenda sint. Tua vero soboles, ab indoctis contumeliose et iniuriose tractata, paternum semper auxilium, inanimis illa quidem et ignava, desiderat. neque enim acceptas iniurias ulcisci, neque ipsa sibi opitulari potest. Falso ergo memoriæ pharmacum venditasti: cum contra reputando, posteros omnes, laudatissimi studii patrimonio exhæredaris. Quid tergiversaris mi homo? iste Dei radius et efficientia, an potius immanis feræ (quod initio proposui) vestigium videtur?

ALEXANDRI DICSONI ARELII
DE RATIONIS UMBRA
PROSOPOPŒIA.

SOCRATES, THAMUS.

ERUM experiar tamen. Audivi o Thame a maioribus, et ipsi verum norant, circa Ægypti Naucratem, antiquorum Deorum quendam fuisse, et ipsi Deo nomen Theutati, cui et sacra sit avis quam ibim vocant. tum vero te, universæ Ægypti regem, multa quidem in utramque partem, de quibusdam eius inventis cum eo disseruisse: cum autem ad Quæstionem de literis ventum esset, nulla ratione probasse: quod homines literis confisi, minus memoriæ studerent.

THAM. quorsum ista?

SOC. Nempe ob eandem causam nihil ipse scripsi.

THAM. Fortasse, et quis tu?

SOC. Socrates ille, sapientissimus Apolline teste iudicatus.

THAM. Ergo tu es Sophista ille quo melius mortales carere potuissent? at erravit, inquis, metaposcopus. non: sed talem descripsit, qualem cives postea cognitum iudicarunt. At Probavit Apollo. nihil affers, et postea videro. Verum

> *Qualia docuisti rudes,*
> *Heu insania tua, civitatisque*
> *Quæ tu nutriit*
> *Corrumpentem adolescentulos!*

SOC. At hæc sunt Aristophanis, cuius est hoc loco, certis de causis suspecta fides.

THAM. Nihil igitur illi credatur: ipsi tecum agamus. Nunquid igitur in terris, o Socrates, insidiator aliquando pro fido, et fidus pro insidiatore habetur?

SOC. at meæ sunt, si nescis, interrogantis vices: id mihi semper quasi meo quodam iure vendicavi. Verum quia metuo Troianos, et præsertim hunc Polidamanta Diogenem, et ne tergiversari videar, respondebo tamen: sic est.

THAM. an non medicus ille, ex levibus morbis magnos efficit, et populi tamen comprobatione iactatur: alter autem vix habet, qui se fidei suæ credere velint?

SOC. Et illud.

THAM. annon in his, et aliis quoque rebus, qui emerita virtute aliquid consequuntur, mendacio fere debere solent?

SOC. Fortasse.

THAM. annon etiam, ut ait ille,

Falsus honos iuvat, et mendax infamia terret?
Quem nisi mendosum, et mendacem?

Et ille,

Fortis et ignavus parili afficiuntur honore?

An non etiam in iudicibus suus quoque contingit error? cum nihil tam incorruptum esse debeat, quam lata sententia?

SOC. certe: nam et me, licet innocentem, Athenienses morte mulctarunt.

THAM. an non bonus ille vir, sceleratus et nefarius putatur? ut inde vexetur, damnetur, explodatur et egeat? contra autem improbus ille laudetur, colatur, omnes fortasse ad eum honores, omnia imperia conferantur?

SOC. Fortasse.

THAM. annon illi, cum sit rerum omnium ignarus, populi clamor et approbatio contingit?

SOC. assentior: quanquam et illud scio, quem hoc petat.

THAM. bene est. at hæc et talia humano generi sunt perniciosa, nonne?

SOC. sunt.

THAM. at unde orta?

SOC. a mendacio fortasse.

THAM. mendacium ergo perniciosissimum, ut quo terra vanitatis sedes esse dicatur?

SOC. perniciosissimum.

THAM. at tu, o Sophronisci fili, mendacii pater es, et ipse mendax.

SOC. unde illud?

THAM. quid? Tu si æra singula probasti, summum quæ ex his confecta est non soles probare? visne ergo, si te dati alicuius pœnitet, ut calculum reducam?

SOC. captum me, ut video, putas, et id quod nollem fateri coactum. non

sic: sed unde est inquam ista complexio?
THAM. quæ tua fuit dissimulantia?
SOC. non agnosco.
THAM. dic igitur sapiens fuisti, annon?
SOC. si non?
THAM. cur igitur laudatus ab Apolline? cur cum sapientibus disputabas?
cur omnes etiam irridebas? disputabant illi: tu contra disserebas: illi
affirmabant: tu negabas. Unde illud:

> *Verbulis novis ipsum,*
> *Et sententiis sagittabo.*

Ut ne hic quidem te contineas: etenim cum Nestore et Palamede, ut
audio, plerunque nugaris.
SOC. si sapiens?
THAM. cur igitur veritatis omne criterium sustulisti? cur igitur toties te
nihil scire iactasti? sic enim et pueros omnes, sapientes esse dixeris.
SOC. at sapientissimus tamen iudicatus.
THAM. fuit ergo dissimulantia, et habemus quod volumus. Sed erro:
vaferrimus enim fuisti, ac in disputando veterator, et malitiosus.
SOC. homo fui, errare potui.
THAM. imo amplius, et fallere consuevisti. sed ne dissimula: nullum
hic invenies divorticulum fucis: non ipse hoc dissimulat Apollo. at is
optimus interpres oraculi sui: constat enim te nulla doctrina, nullis
artibus fuisse imbutum. Quod si negas, responde mihi, quot sunt
numerorum affectiones? circuli tetragonismus, aut cubi diaplasiasmus,
qua fieri ratione possit, ostendito: distingue, si potes, corporum
cælestium motus, cælique viam. Quid vis amplius, et quid habes de Deo?
quis universa distinxit? Deus notus, an ignotus, in patre, mente, et
amore? quæ Dei essentia? efficaciæ? radii? quæ vestigia? quæ etiam
umbræ?
SOC. tu si Deus esse posses, qualem te esse velles?
THAM. iugulasti me Socrates. Sed ad citeriora veniamus. dic, si potes,
de ævo, de mundo, de tempore, de generatione. quæ est tandem anima
animæ mundi? quæ rerum origo? quæ perseverantia? quæ mundi
fabrica? quæ forma? quis ordo? motus? vita? mors? quæ tandem
restauratio? Dic, quæ bonis expectatio melior: cum potestate tantum sint,
habeantque essentiam imperfectam? Ecquonam imperfecta? multa?
mista? singularia? ipsa etiam animarum instrumenta? quid? Lunæ quæ

lineamenta sint potesne dicere? cur eius nascentis, alias hebetiora, alias acutiora cornua videntur? dic etiam de mari: si cæruleum ipsum, cur eius unda pulsa purpurascit? At hic vocem contines, indicem imperitiæ tuæ, testem ignorantiæ: Unde illud agnosce, amici:

> *Putabas Deum nullum, præterquam nos,*
> *Et chaos hoc, et nebulas, et linguam, tria hæc.*

Hinc tuus ille, quem hic etiam in unguentis vix ferimus, Plato, tibi quidem alioqui devinctissimus, de naturæ rebus sermonem instituens, non te, ut alias fere semper, sed Timæum Locrum disserentem inducit.

SOC. at in cœlum scandere non valebam: proinde illa, ut vana semper contempsi: proinde philosophiam eiusmodi rebus intentam, et hoc ipso in cœlum ascendere meditantem, revocavi, et in domos, civitatesque deduxi.

THAM. O dementiam incredibilem, et eorum quæ Dei sunt ignorantiam! quid igitur tibi et Deo? Nihil ergo eorum quæ pulchra, et bona sunt percipere potuisti, corporis cultor, ac nequam existens. Anima enim nihil intelligens eorum quæ sunt, cæcutiens in passiones corporis impingit.

SOC. At non ita est: quin potius quæ de moribus a me profecta sunt, et instituta cognosce. quamvis enim superiora illa contempserim: in Reipublicæ tamen administrandæ formis, et privatorum vita recte instituenda, sedulo laboravi.

THAM. agnosco: et inde fuit præclara illa, et speciosa rogatio, de uxorum et liberorum communione: de fundo et facultatibus communicandis: tum etiam de mulieribus, ut una cum viris belli munus sustineant. O Literas! o artes! o mores! quæ te vertigo capitis impulit, ut ista tam inconsiderate præciperes?

SOC. verum quid ista probra, probra præsertim laudis et gloriæ plena? annon erit, ista ratione admirabilis omnibus inter omnes amicitia? malaque quæ nunc sunt in Reipublicæ administrandæ formis, ex eo certe nasci videantur, quod non sint omnium omnia communia. dico autem falsorum testimoniorum iudicia, divitum assentationes, tum etiam lites et controversias de rerum contractarum fide.

THAM. at nihil horum, o Socrates, propterea quod non sit bonorum communicatio, sed id ex improbitate contingit. Quid? quod eos qui bona communicant, magis inter se dissidere videmus, quam qui seorsim facultates habent? Tibi vero fraudis originem dedit, quod omni ex parte, atque omnibus modis, unam esse domum et unam civitatem expedire existimasti. At non ita est: imo vero isto modo longius progressa, ne civitas quidem erit. Quid interim opifices a custodibus? Quid præmii qui Magistratum gerent? Qua spe? Quo precio? Absurdum autem esse videatur, facta cum brutis comparatione, eadem studia, eademque munera, cum viris obire mulieres. quid hic ad beluas?

SOC. Præterea Magistratus et Reipublicæ præfectos, ab iis qui imperio subiecti sunt, differre oportere disserui: quemadmodum ex alia lana stamen, ex alia subtemen fieri videmus.

THAM. Equidem me miseret tui. Annon hoc positæ a te unitati, et communioni repugnat? dic igitur si quid potes, et e tot sophismatis, unum quod te hinc expediat adhibeto. Sed ista transeant. Insuper, divine tibi philosophari videbaris, cum, hominibus rationis imperium, cupiditatis et iræ obtemperantiam inculcares. At falsum. neque enim ratio est, quæ vocet ad officium iubendo, aut vetando a fraude deterreat. Imo vero contra, ratio est, non ira, quæ decipit, quæque decipitur: et nisi mens adsit, et in regenerationis craterem homines immergantur, frustra rationis commendationi nitentur. Quamvis erunt e nepotibus tuis, quibus fucus ille non possit avelli. quibus tamen, non modo cupiditatis et iræ, sed et rationis etiam obtemperantiam, solius vero mentis imperium, valde suaderem. Ac talis quidem, ut ad te revertar, Socraticæ politeiæ materia fuerit.

SOC. at fuit, quod omnes norunt, vita proba.

THAM. erras: nam et otiosam delegisti, non studiis, non arti vacans, non militiæ: nec filiis etiam rectam vivendi rationem demonstrasti: Tum quotum quemque Philosophum, non attigit tua malitia? cui pepercit? esto: populares homines, improbos Sophistas non tulisti: et hoc: (etsi huiusmodi a Censore melius est, quam ab ipso etiam Sophista notari:) sed quis te furor in Anaxagoram commovit?

SOC. an non tamen laudanda temperantia est?

THAM. tergiversaris: at ego, te temperantiam allaturum non putabam.

SOC. victum tenuem prætuli copioso.

THAM. non: verum conviviis omnibus, ut sapientiæ opinionem dares, affuisti. Omitto nunc suspiciones de puerorum, præsertim Alcibiadis: nosti cœtera,

Unde illud,

Considera adolescentule, importuna esse omnia
Quæ insunt, voluptatibus si priveris
Puerorum, mulierum, ludorum, obsoniorum,
Conviviorum, cachinnorum:

Quale hoc ipsum erit vivere, his si privatus fueris?

Imo vero opprobrio adolescentibus te iudice fuisse dicitur, si amatores non haberent.

SOC. At hæc sunt Aristophanis, ut dixi: et crimen abfuisse certum est.

THAM. At non carent ista reprehensione.

SOC. si reprehensione?

THAM. At non suspicione.

SOC. si illa?

THAM. at non saltem exemplo malo.

SOC. At patientiæ nostræ, testis est Xantippe.

THAM. non amo nimium patientes.

SOC. At nudis pedibus incedere solebam.

THAM. stultitiæ vana fuit ostentatio.

SOC. at sobrius fui, et tota sæpe die, immobilis stare consuevi.

THAM. Quorsum hæc primum ostentatio? an si quis hoc non possit, malus: si nolit, continuo stultus erit? imo vero, laudabilius fuisset ab huiusmodi vanitate temperare. quid deinde?

SOC. At, ubi me occultum et astutum paulo ante finxisti, quid est quod minus cadere in eiusmodi naturam possit, quam aut hominum aspernari benevolentiam, aut opes nullius esse ducere?

THAM. certe nihil: sed nihil effeceris: nec repugnantia de Socrate dici queant.

SOC. At constantiam agnosce. quanta enim illa vincula, quibus quidem constantissime, me iniuste damnatum, astringi ferebam, quanta sunt?

THAM. solutionem, o bone, et libertatem sperasti; unde interrito vultu videri voluisti, ut qui mortem nihil omnino formidares. Verum ubi spem nullam reliquam esse videres, infantium ritu, te tuosque liberos deplorasti. Cæterum cum emigrandi tempus adesset, confidentiam quandam præ te ferebas: quasi volens id esses passurus, quod alioqui nolenti, volenti, omnino fuerat ferendum.

SOC. At venenum hausi: quod vel ex inflatis, et tumidis adhuc cruribus, videri potest.

THAM. Hæc revera mollities fuit, et imbecillitas: At quanto melius ille,

Nolo virum facili redimit qui sanguine vitam:
Hunc volo, laudari qui sine morte potest.

Frustra ergo te crucias: nihil quod in hæc valeat, afferre queas.

SOC. At discipulorum meorum integritas, mei nominis famam a malevolorum iniuriis vindicabit.

THAM. Agnosco Aristippum, dissolutum illum et ebrium: et Platonem, Dyonisio quoque blandum, tanto priore illo deteriorem, quanto sanctior scilicet habebatur. An non audisti, ut Dionem, ad Dyonysii, coniuncti sui cædem invitarit? si inimicus ille, cur adis? cur pecunias accipis? si amicus, cur insidias paras? Nam quid ego de Xenophonte dicam, molli illo quidem, atque etiam vix viro.

SOC. At Antisthenem saltem agnosce.

THAM. certe: nam et fœminas amavit ille: nullis etiam tyrannis blandus: pecunias et opes, nullius esse ducebat: solusque (quod tibi gratissimum est) Athenienses in tuæ necis authores incitavit. Idemque Crati, continentiæ: Zenoni, tolerantiæ: Diogeni tranquillitatis author fuit. At hic prius o bone, doctor fuisse scitur, quam tuus discipulus: nec tecum etiam commorari solebat: tu Athenis: ille in Pyræeo.

SOC. Utique me hodie perculisti, o Thame: cæterum quomodo ista omnia, sic esse nosti, cum multis ante seculis e vita discesseris?

THAM. si fingo, si mentior, cupio refelli: sin autem ista vera sunt, quid præterea sollicite labores? aut qui potes interim intueri quæ gesseris? Verum nec hoc etiam dissimulabo: Antisthenem igitur hunc ipsum, Cratetem illum et Diogenem recognosce. Quamvis præterea quotidianum est, aliquid audire de te, quod in mortalium perniciem dixeris, aut feceris.

SOC. at, ut alii calumnientur, Thamus tamen facilior, et æquior esse debebat: tuamque fortasse gratiam, pro meo quodam et certo iudicio repetere possem.

THAM. Unde hoc o Socrates?

SOC. nempe tua authoritate inductus, nihil in vita scripsi.

THAM. calumnia est: neque enim absolute non scribendum, sed in literarum locum memoriæ studium reponendum esse contenderam. Hic igitur, sua sensa literis commendat: aliquid est: non commendat, sed memoriæ studiis incumbit: Hoc etiam maius. At qui nec hoc, nec illud, nulla hunc ratione probaverim. Quamvis interim, hoc ego Philosophi non arbitror, authoritate et testibus uti: qui aut casu veri, aut malitia falsi fictique esse possunt. Argumentis et rationibus oportet, ad facienda impelli et adduci, non eventis, iis præsertim, quibus non credere liceat. Thamus censuit: quid tum? ratione firmavit: hoc aliud est. quanquam quid ago, qui a Socrate dialectici dignitatem, ut a Philosopho requiro?

SOC. utique difficilis es, o Thame. Verum dic vicissim iam nunc tu. An non eiusdem est, et bello pacem quærere, et hic illius artes non contemnere.

THAM. certe.

SOC. annon, si ea quæ sunt Reipublicæ administrandæ formis perniciosa, animo teneamus: et ea quoque quæ salutaria, tenuerimus?

THAM. sic est.

SOC. Et eiusdem, qui leges malas deprehenderit, et abrogarit, bonas et salutares condere?

THAM. fortasse.

SOC. annon etiam, eius qui mortis umbram demonstrarit; in lucis etiam umbra sedisse, ad eamque ducere posse videatur?

THAM. videtur.

SOC. an non igitur, eiusdem Thami est qui oblivionis materiam deprehenderit, memoriæ quoque pharmacum exhibere? Atque hoc quidem, me tecum ab initio agere conantem, impediit tua nostræ disciplinæ ac vitæ expositio. Ergo age, et quoniam ex senatus consulto mihi transeundum esse nosti,

Tu animum magnum
Contine in pectoribus: amicitia enim est melior.

Et me, si placet internuncio, Theutatis inventis exactæ memoriæ, memoriam excitato.

THAM. Egone ut homini græco, et vano? sed videro. Nunc esto ut inquis amicitia melior: Cæterum unde tibi persuasum est, unde obsecro succurrit, de re proposita dici posse? Si nihil est criterii, si nihil est quod iudicat, nihil etiam sciri, nihil percipi posse consequitur. Nam reliqua illa opinandi temeritas,

Sacer est morbus, et visus mentitur.

Ergo opinatione, ergo perceptione sublata, assertio retinenda sit. sed erubescis: Hæc tua fuit sententia? istæ tuæ merces? ex tua inquam officina, nonne? Quid iam est, manes in sententia?

SOC. si maneo?

THAM. nihil igitur de re proposita dici potest.

SOC. si non maneo?

THAM. at non est sapientis mutare sententiam. quid? an et hoc etiam tuum?

SOC. at tu saltem respice mortales.

THAM. sed flecti et misereri nefarium est: nulla enim in sapientem cadit perturbatio. Quis est iste pudor? hoc tuum etiam ut video fuit. Verum fiat sane quod exigis: faciamque, quod ne in vita quidem facere solebam, ut iis de rebus, quæ doctrina et ratione contineantur, disputarem: memoriæque memoriam, tot, ut inquis, seculis exactæ, te etiam internuncio (siquidem hoc ita vis) in terra excitemus. At erit interim

Tua messis in herba:

Nec prius quæ dicentur intelliges, quam cum Anaxagora, quem transisse etiam audio, in gratiam redieris. Sic igitur accipe.

ALEXANDRI DICSONI ARELII
DE UMBRA IUDICII SIVE
DE MEMORIÆ VIRTUTE
PROSOPOPŒIA.

CAP. I.
OBLIVIO, MEMORIA.

 BLIVIO nequitia est impotentis animi, atque demissi: eademque materiæ soboles prima, potentias animi principes dissolventis et attenuantis. Ex quo apparet, non divinitus, non a natura contingere: (nescio fortunam) sed in nobis sitam, et nostra sponte contractam. Nunc enim a cognoscente res ipsa contemnitur: Unde,

Mos est oblivisci hominibus,
Neque novisse, cuius nihili sit faciunda gratia.

Unde, nulla sequitur ab horizonte progressio, nulla umbra, subiectum nullum, nullus ordo, nulla tandem animatio. Nunc ipsa rei præsens inspectio, cogitationis respuit efficientiam. Nunc etiam, ut temporis essentiam et efficacias omittam, quod omnium pessimum est, in ignoratione versamur. ut servitutis iniustæ genus quoddam esse videatur. Huic contraria memoria, potentia quidem illa, et actus, et umbra, remigium est alarum animi, corporis ministerio, et sensuum instrumentis expeditum. Huius virtus prima est in umbra boni: altera, iudicii (quæ causa etiam præscripti tituli fuit) tenere quæ didiceris, quæ ipse etiam non accepta cogitando conceperis.

CAP. II.
DE MEMORIÆ CAUSIS.

Est hic quod possis, est hic etiam quod in actum educas. potentiam ergo in causis agnosce, agnosce et actum. de hoc alias, et suo loco. Illa, si longius progrediare, licet omnis a Deo et uno procedat: in triplici tamen nunc esto varietate. Nunc enim naturæ parentis reputamus officium: Nunc superum radios, et efficacias sentimus: Nunc rationis et doctrinæ consilia succurrunt. Etenim naturalis est, animis nostris insita virtutis huius efficientia, eaque simul cum cogitatione nata. Quam cum ante Theutatis inventum homines intuerentur, expresserunt illi quidem: nec erat, ut literas et elementa requirerent. postea vero, quam doctoris illius artibus effectum esset, ut illum quam naturam, homines esse mallent quem sequerentur, et a quo memoriæ præsidium petendum esset: secuta declinatio est, defuitque naturæ industria humana. unde nata tandem in matrem impietas, et falsa de impotenti vena querimonia. Proxima est a superis potentia, sed in impari communione: sicut ad illos et impari animi solutione homines convertuntur. Ex quo tertia et reliqua, doctrinæ rationisque potentia secuta videatur: quæ latentem alioqui naturam, evocet atque confirmet: ex illius etiam utero et ipsa evocata. Illius igitur ope, præceptio, illa, doctrina et ratione nitescit. ut coniurationem istam reputanti, illius, hæc quodamtenus discipula, quodam alio modo tenus magistra esse videatur. Quæ cum multis annis, senis illius invento latuisset, in Græcia primum vestra emersisse putatur. Imo Chius ille, primus eam invenisse et protulisse creditur. At falsum: quod et ipse vidisti, dum ab Ægipto, et nostra ætate repetendam esse iudicares. Quod si separetur etiam Ægiptus, nihil tamen effecerit ille. Etenim si Celtarum replicentur annales, et excitentur historiæ, multo ante in Druidum schola viguisse reperias. valeat igitur, cum suis Tindaridis ille. Alii autem, ut elegantiores scilicet videantur, et artem hic nullam esse, ridendo persuadeant: malle se, quæ vellent oblivisci, quam meminisse respondent. De homine dicunt aliquid: non repugno: et ista est fortasse digna misero, et afflicto sententia. at de re certe nihil: in qua, quid optimum sit quæritur: non quid hic aut ille meminisse, aut oblivisci maluerit. Ac istæ quidem memoriæ causæ fuerint, is ortus, ea propagatio.

CAP. III.
DE MEMORIÆ SUBIECTO.

Et non sit impudens, qui in immortalis Dei circo, et ipsa, captum humanum superante luce, umbræ huius bonitatem et momenta quærat? Etenim si suas causas habet: si cum materia: si cum tempore: si cum appendice: si cum generatione et imbecillitate coniuncta: si utilis et ipsa: valeat, et in aliis esto. Ergo animus ille, qui in syderibus errantibus, et inerrantibus inest, memoriam habet? aut communis animi virtus, eiusque qui Iovis est recordatur? An, quia rerum earum quæ in medio geruntur, cognitione non indigent orbium animi: idcirco ne recordationis etiam remigiis egebunt? At cognoscunt, inquis, quæque geruntur a singulis dispensant. Verum fortasse, sed alio modo: sola quippe virtute, quam a patre effectore tulerunt. Nec unquam inferioris orbis contemplatione privantur: cum sit absentium, ratiocinantis memoriæ præsentatio. Porro si quis hoc quoque percontetur: annum stellarum et orbium animi, die vel mense, vel anno superiore, se terram circuisse agnoscant: Sic accipito. Nihil continuum et commutationis expers declinationem admittit: In die autem, mense, et anno, declinationis quædam extrema et vestigia cernuntur. Nihil igitur in eo quod constans est, hesternum esse possit. Verum animus humanus, diei pater est, et mensis, et anni. Atque quemadmodum qui in itinere est, pedis eiusdem vestigia, variis terræ partibus imprimit: sic orbium motus in suis animis uni a nobis quidem in multas partes distinguuntur. etenim in cœlesti mundo dies unus est, nullæ noctis vices. Quare stellarum et orbium animi, cognoscunt illi quidem quæ dicis: at non in tempore: et memoriam cum tempore coniunctam supra dictum est. Verum pergis adhuc, et orbium, inquis, animi in homines intuentur: ex quo fortasse eosdem nostri memores esse sequi possit: proindeque in iis memoriam vigere. At quale est hoc? intuentur: ergo etiam memoriæ participes erunt. imo contra est: neque enim quæ intuemur, recordatione recolimus: sed absolute cognoscimus. Ex quo apparet, facta nobiscum comparatione, quod agis contingere nullo modo posse. Quod si fiat autem cum ipsa etiam luce contentio, tale erit eodem modo, propter eas quas fere etiam diximus causas. Ex quibus et illud simul intelligi potest, nec singulorum animos, ubi ad locum sibi cognatum ascenderint, ratiocinantis memoriæ functiones habere: nec ullam etiam ad eam rem facultatem: nisi forte iterum

Ad Troiam magnus mittetur Achilles:

In aliis igitur esto. Quando autem eius munus cum corpore, ipsamque cum tempore coniunctam esse posuerimus: Relinquitur quidem certe, in solis animantibus, atque iis quidem animantibus, quæ temporis sensum habent, virtutis huius potentias inesse. Atqui si tempus numerus est: et solus homo natura factus ad numeros subducendos: quid moror amplius in brutis?

CAP. IIII.
DE ARTE.

Ars igitur memoriæ: ars igitur mentis potentia talis esto: nulli tamen reliquarum addicta. Etenim si in peripheria sedes eius, ecquonam modo requiem et actum in centro, ipsa præstaret? Si in hoc, ecquanam ratione ex horizonte transmitteret? Sed hoc est forte generalius, et alias a nobis accuratius excutietur. Nunc tuam, o bone, providentiam expendat Anaxagoras: nunc tibi iudicium dirigat idem (et hoc age memineris) ego te memorem dabo. Nam cum tria sint in rerum natura, prospexisse, perspexisse, et hæc ipsa respicere: quis est, qui sublato aut altero, aut utroque, id quod non est, credo, quodque indigestum est, respicere se audeat dicere? Hic igitur si inventionis acumen, si disponendi in iudicando solertiam, proponi et informari existimas, te certe nequicquam fallis. Neque enim naturæ rationisque prudentiam, sed eius rei umbram, in respicientia tradere est animo: et eam quidem umbram, quæ, nisi expedito suo corpore apprehendi nullo modo possit. Neque hoc sine causa dictum existimari velim: est enim quoddam genus eorum, qui si artificii nostri statum audierint, nonne tibi protinus videris audire: ergone quæcunque legere, quæcunque ab aliis etiam audire contigerit, in promptu mihi sit recordatione recolere? quos tamen, hæc ipsa percepisse præterea, atque etiam perspexisse decebat.

CAP. V.
DE PARTIBUS ARTIS.

Ex quibus etiam si placet, ars hæc respicientia vocetur. Eius partes duæ sunt, providentia et criterium. Ut enim qui neque serit vitem, neque quæ sata est diligenter colit: oleum, ficus, poma non habet: Ita nisi res necessarias provideas primum, et provisas etiam colas: frustra hic oleum sperabis, et vacuus operam ludes. Posito ergo eo quod recolendum sit, primo quasi castra quæruntur, et delectus habentur: tum vero acie instructa, militibusque confirmatis et animatis, quid præterea quispiam requirat? Sed hoc est, inquis, memorem esse? annon providentia, annon fortasse criterium in iudicandi solertia iam ante relegatum est? Quid igitur affers? At ludis in superficie: nec idem utrinque est. Etenim rerum sive providentia, sive inventio in rationis insulam relegata est: et potuit fugiendi et persequendi quoque providentia, in civitatem etiam relegari. at nobis interim in umbris esse liceat. Quod de criterio verum est eodem modo. Ergo providentia prior est pars in apparatu: est autem in subiectis et umbris. Etenim cum oblivio et memoria extrema sint: et illa tenebris et quasi morti, hæc vero luci ex proportione respondeat: certe ut a tenebris ad lucem, nulla est, nisi per interiectas umbras patiente natura progressio: idem etiam hoc loco credere par est. Omne igitur quod ab oblivione in memoriam fertur, per medias umbras, quasi nuncias, quæ rerum species temperent et animæ propinent, feratur oportet. Sunt igitur opus umbræ. unde et subiecta etiam, e quibus ipsæ exprimantur agnosce. Primum ergo de subiecti natura et essentia: tum vero etiam de delectu et lege: postremo de umbris simili modo dicendum erit.

CAP. VI.
DE SUBIECTIS.

Est ergo subiectum sinus et receptaculum umbrarum. Hinc poteris quæ audieris, sed sola tamen quæ videris memoriter pronunciare. Non sumus ergo in enunciati extremis: non in ipsa Hyle: non in re natura facta et ad ipsam: non in arte facta et ad artem relata: verum in hac et illa, facta cum expediendæ conformationis umbris, quasi notis et sigillis, contentione versamur.

CAP. VII.
DE SUBIECTO ABSOLUTO.

Est autem subiectum aliud absolutum et principale, aliud adiuvans et quasi socium. illud natura semper, aut manu absolutum est: hoc est autem visionis efficientia plerunque contentum. Cum sit autem ipsum universum, et ima tellus, et continens hæc aut illa, et politeia, et œconomica dimensio, et partes eius: e proximis quidem tribus generibus, absoluta subiecta pro occasione assumuntur: reliqua illa nec sunt opus, nec usuvenire etiam fortasse queant.

CAP. VIII.
DE ADIUVANTE.

Adiuvans est, quod absoluto et continenti adiungitur: ad eius illud quidem multiplicationem, et umbrarum etiam firmam perceptionem assumptum: Et cum illud immotum sit et fixum: hoc tamen, dum umbrarum animationis materiam præstat, pro earum occasione movetur: quippe quod earum usibus et ministerio sit addictum. Esto igitur in intercolumnio gladius. nunc hic, seditiosos dum reprimit ille, gladio minax esto. nunc in Rempublicam dum servos ciet et armat Alledius, gladium porrigat. nunc innatam, et ex ipsa natura expressam sui defendendi legem, insinuans illa, gladium etiam porrigat. nunc novis rebus studentes, gladio luant. nunc etiam Astræa, gladio insignis esto. omnisque adeo hoc loco prosopopœia gladii ministerium admittat. Idemque si quando credita, repetenti non protinus occurrat umbra, ab effectis et contingentibus, quasi digito demonstrat.

CAP. IX.
IN PROLEPSI.

Sed exorientur fortasse, quibus adiuvantium aliud, in materia, ex eo quod post animationis materiam, nihil hic præterea præstet, et designet: aliud vero mathematicum esse videatur. non placet: cur non placeat alias ostendemus: id nunc admonuisse contenti, omnia quidem adiuvantia, mathematica   nobis   videri: non quod a materiæ concretione separata sint: verum quia præter positi ministerii societatem, subiectorum etiam numerum et ordinem designent: et ni designent, frustra hic assumi videantur. Videris ergo, an et hoc etiam allatæ finitioni sit adiiciendum.

CAP. X.
DE DELECTU SUBIECTORUM.

Sic fuit subiecti natura et essentia: adiuncta sequuntur, in delectu et lege. Sunto igitur primum e genere rerum earum, quæ sub sensum cadunt: inhærentem inquam, vel extrinsecus assumptam, sed utramque sensibilem formam admittunto: quamvis interim non semper ab instrumentis, et horizonte moveantur. Nam frustra alioqui repetas, quæ ne effingere quidem et collocare potueris. Tum ad horizontis in aspectu potentiam conformantor. Ut enim nec est umbra lux, neque etiam tenebræ: ita nec in his, nec illa sedes eius. Hic igitur nec nimis illustria, ne præfulgenti splendore offendant: nec vehementer etiam obscura sunto. Cæterum, cum sint umbrarum receptacula, mediocri et modica magnitudine providentor ac definiuntor. Si quid autem prohibessit, ex naturæ præscribentis arbitratu modificantor. Nam si præter modum ampla, vix umbræ statum impetrassint: angusta vero, fortasse etiam repellere videantur. Porro intervalla mediocria, et parallela sunto: idque ut opportune succedat, cogitationis apparatum adhibento. Mediæ autem areæ, quasi abolitæ, deletæque sunto. Tum dissimili forma, dissimili etiam natura, similitudinis insolentiam amovento: naturæ autem in varietate solertiam exprimunto. Ex ordine (si quid aliud,) assumuntor: is autem ordo, quo secius, quoto quoque loco, quicque positum sit provideas, vitio careto. Ab umbris omnia patiuntor, et afficiuntor: idque ut fiat, absoluta omnia, sociis illis, et adiuvantibus, quasi custodiis, insignita sunto. Quæ autem illorum fidei credentur, hæc ipsa custodiunto: si cogitatio creverit dimittunto. In viciniam ne digrediuntor. At in suas quasi tribus distribuuntor. Tribuum autem præfecti et principes, ex lunæ mansionum imaginibus assumuntor. decemviratum perpetuum exercento. suas in singulis stationibus cathenas aureas providento. Hæc autem omnia ut maneant, et hærere possint, qui volent observanto. Qui operæ suæ præcium requirent, diligenter et accurate censento.

CAP. XI.
DE UMBRIS.

Sic igitur subiecta dimensa atque descripta sunto: nunc autem ad umbras simili ratione transeamus. Est igitur umbra, efficta rei species credita subiecto, ad firmam illa quidem perceptionem assumpta. Et species quidem, non qua in mente prima, hæc etenim lux est, atque eadem semper: nos quærimus umbram, eamque quæ gignitur. Non qua in cœlo et sempiternis ignibus illis, aut periodo cœli: non qua in se, eove quod procreat, aut ipso etiam eventu. Postremo, neque qua in virtutis huius horizonte movetur. sed qua sensus apparatu, et cogitationis lima polita est. Huius fidei res ipsa creditur, hæc ipsa, subiecti. Atque quemadmodum ex antecedente fide (ut Mercurium hunc aliquando disserentem audivi) consequitur intelligentia: et in naturæ rationisque prudentia, ex antecedentis positione, complexio: sic ex umbrarum etiam virtute, negotii sequitur firma et explicata retentio. Nunc quibus hæc ardua et desperata videtur, aut vana et operosa fortasse solertia: impotentem illi quidem venam, hi malitiosam agnoscant: norintque quod explicatum non capias, vel involutum esse tenendum.

CAP. XII.
DE SIMPLICIBUS UMBRIS.

Sunt autem umbrarum aliæ simplices, aliæ modificatæ: simplices quidem, rerum earum quæ sub sensum cadunt: modificatæ conceptuum. Illæ ab horizonte moventur et accipiuntur: Hæ vero in ipso sensu gignuntur et effinguntur. Itaque cum de re sub sensum mediocriter cadente negotium est: qualis sit illa, talis erit et umbra. Hic homo hominem, Alledius Alledium, et beluam belua designat. omnesque adeo res quæ sua natura sub aspectum, et isto modo cadere possint, sub huius generis umbris cogitationi traduntur. sua natura dico, quia et ea quoque quæ percipiuntur auribus, et cogitatione, quæque ab aspectu abhorrent, et sub intelligentiam per se cadunt, aspectus etiam commendatione, sed modificata, traduntur. ut cæca hæc, et ab aspectus iudicio sua natura remota, ita notet conformatio, ut quæ cogitando complecti nequieris, quasi intuendo tenere possis. At heus tu, sunt et sensibilia forte aliqua, quæ subiectorum in simplici forma recusent officium. Et forte nulla.

CAP. XIII.
DE UMBRIS MODIFICATIS.

Hic igitur, si res suam umbram et propriam non habeat, necessitas cogit, quod non habeas aliunde assumere. Ergo cum simplices non occurrent umbræ, bene agi existima, si imitata et efficta simulachra aut quoquo modo similia afferentur. Hæc est illa conformatio: hæ umbræ modificatæ: non quidem voluptatis et delectationis causa inductæ: (quod in translationibus usuvenire solet) sed angustiis et necessitate premente: ut ad ea quoque quæ abstracta, quæque coniuncta sint, quasi facilius mentis oculi ferantur. Quid enim aliud restet, si necessitate cogaris?

CAP. XIIII.
DE MODIFICATARUM DIVISIONE.

Porro modificatio alia rerum est, alia vero in verborum conformatione cernitur. Illa, nunc in absolutis est, nunc vero etiam in Mathematicis. Absoluta sint, quæcunque nullam numeri differentiam secum afferunt: simplicia sint, coniuncta sint, nihil moror: dum illud in omni hoc sermone memineris, rerum quidem abstractarum, et a sensuum iudiciis abhorrentium, negotium agi. Siquidem earum rerum quæ sub sensum cadunt, efformatio simplex est. Atque quemadmodum in illis, a formis externis, umbras emanare videmus: Sic hic ab internis peti modificatæ fortasse debeant. Et certe si rerum formas veras haberemus, omnis esset inde evocanda conformatio. nunc cum non habeas, a factis, subiectis, et reliqua rationis familia, quasi pharmacum et præsidium petendum erit.

CAP. XV.
DE MODIFICATIS ABSOLUTIS.

Atque hæc quidem rerum absolutarum, sive inflexio sive modificatio, tropus sane vocetur: non quidem immutandi et transferendi verbi, quod orationi splendoris aliquid arcessat: (quæ vestra philosophia est)[.] Sed quo rerum quasi mutationes adhibentur: cum quod a sensuum instrumentis abhorret, alterius sub hæc ipsa cadentis officio creditur. Quæ tamen, non ideo a nobis assumuntur, ut pro impotentibus illis, hæc quidem, quæ rerum earum vicem subeunt, proferantur: (quæ vestræ assumptionis causa sola est: dum pro propriis, inflexa illa et modificata profertis.) sed ut horum in cogitationis apparatu latentium adiumentis, illa ipsa pro quibus assumpta sint, quæque alioqui complecti nequeas, pronunciare possis. Ob eamque causam, quod a vobis de verecunda translatione præcipitur, a nobis quidem negotio flagitante negligitur. Nunc igitur, efficiens rei factæ vices subit: hinc patrem sequitur sua proles. Hinc mathematicas et elementa, Theutates: Pyromantiam, Vulcanus: Hydromantiam, Nereus: ortum et occasum, Apollo: eamque quæ chirurgia dicitur, Chiron: hinc bella et molitiones, Minerva: providentiam, Prometheus: Epimetheus pœnitentiam præstare possit. Nec illud interim te conturbet, quod ne hæc quidem aspectus iudicium ferant. sive enim corpora sint, sive corporum expertia: et sive cohæreant, sive non: ad ea tamen corpora respiciendum est, quæ sunt ipsis a veteribus tributa. Hinc etiam ferramenta, ministri, et vectes, molitionem et fabricam designabunt. sic dicta, scripta, omninoque facta omnia, a suis authoribus repetuntur. Nam quid ego de materia dicam? cuius in eo quod agimus, ut finis etiam fortasse, notior opera est, quam ut afferenda sit. At forma præterita est. certe: sed unde, videris. Nunc a factis, efficiens et causa repetitur. Quis universa distinxit? quis cœlestium corporum motus ordinavit? quis omnia procreat, eademque conservat? quis oculos tornavit? quis nares perfodit? quis nervos produxit et alligavit? quis costas compegit? quis cor pyramidatum effecit? qualis mater? quis pater, nisi qui non videtur Deus? ecce ut ipsum infinitum, incomprehensum, ab effectis ostenditur. Infinita sunt huius generis exempla, unde, quasi ex vestigiis et sigillis, Deum ipsum, et ævum, et mundum, et tempus, et generationem, gentium etiam quos diximus deos, omniaque omnino, quæ quidvis effecerint, oportune repetere possis. Verum præter hunc primarium effectorum usum, in omnium omnino umbrarum conformatione, factorum, si intelligis, officium recognosce. Nunc id quod subest, ad adiuncta insinuanda traducitur. Sic huius in principatu, communi utilitati consulentis conformatio regnum dabit: non consulentis vero tyrannidem. horum autem paucorum quidem, sed plurium uno, eorumque virtute præditorum, conformatio, Aristocratiam: non præditorum, Oligarchiam affert: sic populi, ad communem utilitatem conspiratio, Politeiam: ad patriciorum vero contumeliam, Democratiam (ut vos quidem distinguitis) significabit. sic virtutes, morbi, firmitas, opes, pulchritudo: eaque quæ his contraria, e suis illa quidem subiectis exprimuntur. Sic rerum omnium earum quæ natura constant, proprietates et accidentiæ, ab ipsis quasi præconibus enuntiantur. Nunc a rebus adiunctis et accidentiis, subiecti commendatio dependet. sic ab hirundine, a fabæ satione, cæterisque similibus, ver habetur. sic toga pro pace: sic arma ac tela pro bello ponuntur. Quo loco et illud etiam observa, communes quidem accidentias, ex alio atque alio subiecto, alia atque alia, ex voluntatis tuæ sententia et arbitratu, posse proferre. Ut illud interim hic etiam agnoscas, quod de factorum communione iam ante dictum est. Nunc etiam a dissentaneo lux affertur. Hic in iis primum quæ sola ratione dissentiunt, ex insigni, victoriam: parricidam, ex latrone venaberis. Tum iis forte præteritis, quorum unum multis pari ratione videmus opponi: ecce tibi, ut ex hæredibus, testatoris: ex eo qui damnum dedit, eius qui tulit: ex coniuge, mariti: ex socero, generi: eiusque qui locat, ex conductore memoria reportatur. Hic, si Periclis memoriam repetes, Anaxagoram recognosce. Nam et adulter, Hippolytum: et servus, libertum: et quod calet, frigidum: et qui prodigus, parcum: et qui prudens, idiotam: et qui secundis rebus utitur, calamitosum: cæcus, videntem: et sobrius ebrium fortasse designet. Ex irrisionis illud quidem efficacia, vel materiam occasione præbente. Nunc in iis rebus quæ comparatione cernuntur: ex multis, infinitio: ex Ibice, ventus: ex Æsculapio, Mercurius: ex eo quod maius, id quod modicum: et ex modico, maius poterit effingi. Nam proportionis officium quis non videt? nihilque certe est in rerum natura, quod similitudinis aliquando luce non possit illustrari. hic igitur ille,

Os humerosque Deo similis,

Deum: hic amata illa, venerem dabit. sic arbor altissimis defixa radicibus, quæ nulla vi labefactari possit, virtutem: sic navis illa cuius,

Nudum remigio latus,
Et malus celeri saucius Africo,
Antennæque gemant,

Rempublicam male affectam, et laborantem animo commendabit. Sic turbines et procellæ, pericula et calamitates designabunt. Sic si,

Fulvum fingatur in ignibus aurum,

Sententiam illam (in impetu fortunæ inspicienda est fides) exhibebit. Atque hic quidem fabularum allegoriæ tanti sunt, ut ea fere sola ratione, in sententiis præsertim, quantum voles, efficere queas. Nunc in diversæ qualitatis rebus, Neoptolemus, Achillem: et Socrates, Anaxagoram excitabit. debeturque tibi gratia pro exemplo futuro. Postremo, ut distributionis etiam opportunitates exemplo ostendamus: ecce tibiæ nuptiales, matrimonium: una turma, equitatum: tectum, parietes, mœnia, earumque rerum partes, domum, et urbem intelligi volent. sic Mercurii, Æsculapii, Promethei, Chirones, pro sapientibus: sic Calatini, pro civibus ornatis, iisdemque pauperibus: atque omnino pro suis generibus species assumuntur. Ac ista fere sunt, quæ de rerum absolutarum inflexionibus dicenda videbantur. Nunc res admonet, ut ad earum quoque rerum, quas Mathematicas diximus, conformationes transeamus.

CAP. XVI.
DE MODIFICATIS MATHEMATICIS.

Res igitur Mathematicæ, cum abstractæ sint, et ab omni materiæ concretione separatæ, simplices quidem umbras proiicere nequirent: nec vero etiam superiori ratione inflexas: siquidem hic a nobis numerorum exhibitio quæritur: cuius rei, ne suspitio quidem ex iam dictis poterat oriri. Tentetur igitur et hoc etiam a nobis: tantæque nuditati, solers impositio succurrat. Et quoniam numeri negotium agitur, eius primum, in decurias, quæ ex Zodiaci signorum ordine reputentur, esto divisio. Singula autem orbis huius signa, singulas decurias, ex ordine sortiantur. Tum vero etiam, ad digitos in decuriis insinuandos, omnia quidem signa, decem partibus distincta et divisa sunto. Erunt igitur 120. quæ si minus satisfacere videantur, idem in errantibus etiam, et imagine Draconis Lunæ tentetur eodem modo: fient 200. quorum usus in librorum, capitum, cæterorumque similium censu, firmaque perceptione, incredibilis forte videatur. At occurritur nobis, et quidem a minime malitiosis. Qualis est, inquiunt, ista præceptio? Zodiaci signa vis assumi: assumpta in decem partes ex ordine distingui. At quis in Cancro, aliisque nonnullis, perspicuas decem partes et differentes inveniat. Quasi vero cancrum pro Cancro, pro Piscibus pisces effingi velim. simplicitas est. quis est enim, qui signorum umbris ex eo quod dicitur fingendis, Mathematicum se audeat dicere? horum igitur umbræ, non quidem in eo, quod isti suspicantur: sed in propriis ipsorum imaginibus conformentur. Hic etiam, ne quando similitudo fortasse conturbet, non unas modo, singulorum signorum imagines assumi, verum omnium omnes pro varietate consulimus. Quæ autem, et quot sint istæ imagines, quæ item errantium, et Draconis Lunæ: hoc omnes scitis. Ac rerum quidem adumbratio talis esto.

CAP. XVII.
DE VERBORUM INFLEXIONE.

Ergo, quotiescunque rem ipsam meminisse volemus, si formarum et umbrarum diligenti notatione utemur, facile ea quæ volemus memoria consequemur. Reliqua est verborum inflexio: quo loco etsi

Cui lecta potenter erit res,
Nec facundia deseret hunc, nec lucidus ordo:

ET

Verbaque provisam rem non invita sequantur:

Tamen et huic etiam parti prospiciatur: etsi res hæc opinionis potius, quam scientiæ vestigium videtur. Illud igitur primum intelligi par est, Plurima quidem, ex eorum genere quæ sub sensum cadunt, tum vero etiam eorum quæ non cadunt, eiusmodi esse, ut ex ipsis verba quoque necessario sequantur. Hic igitur quæ de rebus dicta sunt, de verbis etiam dicta esse putentur. Nunc ubi rerum existet inutilis commendatio, ad omnis quidem in voce proportionis, præsertim vero coniugationis et originationis, officia recurratur. Verum generalis, inflexionis huius potentia subiicienda videatur. Primum igitur, in certis et ubique variis hominibus, 30. elementorum sit expedita præsentia: idem sit in singulorum effectis propriis: idem in adiunctis. Quibus ante provisis, atque ita quidem provisis, ut prompte et expedite, tot ac talia designet elementa cum suis effectis et adiunctis Alledius: eodemque modo in reliquis: quid dubitas, ex horum, et illorum mutuationibus quascumque compositiones effingere? Nam pro quartis et quintis etiam compositionum elementis, quid ratio afferenda sit? sive enim postremo, sive medio et interiecto loco occurrant, ex gestuum solerti varietate quærenda sunt. Rursus, pro ipsis etiam elementis, certis corporibus seorsim constitutis, hisque omnibus, quinque consistentium accessione spirantibus, eorumque consistentium effectis et adiunctis pro liquidis et finalibus ex ratione providentibus: quid hic nisi mutationes, quid quæso præterea quispiam requirat? hos autem homines, hæc corpora, hæc effecta, hæc etiam adiuncta, sibi quemque suo commodo convenit apparare.

CAP. XVIII.
DE LEGE UMBRARUM.

Hæc igitur umbrarum quasi consitura fuerit: Ad legem et adiuncta veniamus. Nam cum ab unaquaque re, pro luce ingenii, multiplices umbræ produci possint, quod in opticis corporibus contingit eodem modo: delectus habendi, et opportunitas expendenda videatur. Omnes igitur umbræ simplices, omnes inflexæ, oculorum primum commendationem procuranto. Si res ita feret, in suæ dimensionis specie manento: Si non feret, ex adiunctis modificantor. Cæterum illustres et acres sunto: id autem ut expediatur, novis quidem, aut ridiculis etiam rebus, insignitæ sunto. Ergo egregiam pulchritudinis, aut turpitudinis speciem aliquam, ad cogitationis scilicet pulsum, præ se ferunto. subiecta autem in quibus reponentur, perfecte et accurate signanto. vagæ ne sunto. Semper autem in subiecta, vel in subiectis aliquid quod afficiat, et impellat agunto. Inde, si cogitatio creverit, exeunto: eademque revocante redeunto. cæterum dissimiles forma, et in varietate sunto. Quod si ab instrumentis, similes formas sensus acceperit, aut ipse creassit, visionis opera et officio retrectantor. Ac de providentia quidem satis fere dictum est.

CAP XIX.
DE CRITERIO.

Verum esto, sint provisa subiecta, umbræ provisæ, provisa omnia: Quid deinde? reliquum scilicet est, ut de criterio simili ratione dicendum sit. At hoc non uno modo dici videtur: nunc enim quo cohærentiæ quæstio disceptatur: nunc vitæ canon et idea: nunc autem veritatis mensura criterium appellatur. Hoc rursus, aliud quod iudicat, aliud vero quo iudicat, tertium secundum quod et ipsa iudicatio. Atque hinc quidem omnis vestrarum scholarum est orta distinctio: Aliis hoc esse, et verum quod esset inveniri posse dicentibus, quales, Parmenides, Anaxagoras, Dionisidorus, aliique permulti. Aliis vero nihil sciri, nihil percipi posse contendentibus, unde tua manavit ignava dissimulantia. Aliis tandem dubitantibus, Heraclito, Zenophane, Homero, Pyrrhone, Democrito: Unde illud,

Quis novit autem, an hoc vivere sit emori:

An emori sit hoc quod vocamus vivere.

Nos autem, et eo quod iudicat, et eo secundum quod existit iudicatio, prætermisso, reliquum id quo iudicat, id quod iudicat, assumamus. atque hoc quidem alii in sensu reposuerunt: ut sit ille πάντων χρημάτων μέτρον: alii vero in sola ratione: Unde illud,

Opinioque sacer est morbus et visus mentitur.

Et illud,

Oportet vero te omnia nosse,
Tum quidem veritatis suasu facilis accuratam sententiam,
Tum vero mortalium opiniones quarum non iam vera fides:

Et illud,

Ne te Deus, ancipitem iuxta hanc viam cogat,
Iudicare inconsiderato visu, et resonante auditu.
Sed iudices ratione accuratam sententiam.

Alii rursus, utrunque sensus et rationis instrumentum acceptarunt. Nos autem in eo quod agitur, visionis et cogitationis virtuti et functioni subiicimus. quarum rerum fiat apparatu, ut quæ ex instrumentorum pulsu percepta, vel sensus opera efficta fuere, iusto impulsu in memoriam insinuentur. habet etenim cerebrum suam sphæram, et distinctos orbes, sensum, visionem, cogitationem, memoriam. atque hæc quidem in centro est: in horizonte vero sensuum instrumenta. Nihil igitur ad centrum, nisi per interiectos orbes omnes moveri potest. Non igitur, ut instrumenta pulsentur, existit protinus sensus et memoriæ complicatio. ex quo criterii virtus et accessio quæsita videatur.

CAP. XX.
DE METHODO.

Est autem criterium, in methodo, et animatione: methodum visio præstat, animationem vero cogitatio. Impulsis igitur instrumentis, ipso etiam sensu in subiectis et umbris impulso: Quid hic visio? certe in dispositionis iudicatione, tota consumitur. Cum autem subiecta, quasi sinus et receptacula posita sint a nobis: certe ordinis ista quæcunque ratio, de subiectis primum demonstranda erit. Primum igitur, in subiectis, una si possit idea statuatur, quæ mox in partes communes sit distribuenda: Hæ rursus, in alias minus communes: illæ, in proprias: propriæ, tandem in tribus secernantur. Et quamvis fortasse loci natura pugnare videatur: quid est tamen quod impositionis operam possit impedire? Ideam igitur, crede ideæ: communia item, communium: propria, propriorum: et tribuum, tribus, observantiæ committe. Insuper, novas, et tertias, et decimas etiam si sit opus, velificationes adhibeto. id quod adiuvantium usibus, et aureæ catenæ ministerio et opportunitate conficitur. Atque hac quidem re, nihil est in hoc omni sermone fœcundius. Nunc reliqua est cogitationis in animatione solertia.

CAP. XXI.
DE ANIMATIONE SIVE PULSU COGITATIONIS.

Sed erro fortasse: nec est, ut cogitationis operam præterea requiras. Methodum enim qui teneat, tantum fortasse, quantum volet efficiat: qui non teneat, frustra se vexando, nihil prorsus efficere queat. At falsum. Ut enim in negotii nostri proposito, sicut in aliis rebus omnibus, plurimum possit ordo: at quod possit, artificii nostri est: et omnia tamen posse valde negavero. Quod ex orbium Hypothesi repetere licet. Nunc ad animationem. Primum igitur ne dormiatur in umbris. Tum facta acria, et circumstantias insignes, superlatio præstet. Non sit autem a natura, neque forte temere, sed ex voluntatis præscripto iudicatio. Tum vero quæ fient, impulsum et affectus vehementes præ se ferant. inde sequitur negatio: hinc, tui in rem ipsam, rei in seipsam, gemina nempe transformatio. Hoc est animare: hoc est quod cogitatione perficitur. sic enim informata cogitatio, materiam deserens atque tempus, umbrarum illa quidem ideas et rationes arripit, in ipsam intelligentiam pro facultate propensa. Ac cum omnis solertia admiranda est: tum ea præsertim, quæ efficit, ut inanima quæ sunt, quasi vivere et spirare videantur.

CAP. XXII.
PERORATIO.

Habes, o Sophronisci fili, de memoria iudicium nostrum. Reliqua sunt in cura, cogitatione, labore. Hinc est ut nihil effugiat, atque omne quod erit in re, occurrat et incidat. Hæc igitur præcipue colenda est tibi: hæc semper adhibenda: hæc nihil est quod non assequatur. At tu, cum eris in terris, Anaxagoræ, quem non tulisti, satisfacere memento. Quamvis hæc tota transitio mihi suspecta est: et hic forte aliquid subesse possit.

FINIS.

Thamus
or
The Virtue of Memory

A Preliminary Investigation

by
Alexander Dicsone of Errol[1]

'I sat down under his shadow with great delight'[2].

LEIDEN
Printed by Thomas Basson[3].
1597[4].

Preface

What, I hear you say, do I find so fascinating about the contents of the shadow that is cast by a light-source? Surely the former merely defines the boundary[5] of the latter?

It is beyond dispute that there are two movements at work here, namely Nature and reason. I am happy to leave the former topic to the brave, for everyone unconditionally agrees that the virtue of memory is both unique and innate. However, it's the latter topic that I'm concerned with in this book, for it is a legitimate subject of enquiry whether there is any virtue of reason involved in the Art of Memory and also if there is any way of mastering that art and, if so, what aspect of it we should seek out and pursue first.

And here I must indulge in a certain frankness, for I am writing only for those who wish to consider the matter objectively; I shall certainly not be wasting my time flattering the tastes of anyone else. As some in the latter category are inevitably flippant (and therefore, to an equivalent extent, of minimal importance to me) they will inevitably draw conclusions about my own personality on the basis of their own characters and their own wretched (and yet, at the same time, blissful) perception of things:

Nam satis est dives, cui sensus pauperiei nullus adest:
'for he who has no sense of poverty is wealthy enough'.[6]

So, for example, they'll prefer to ask a physician to help them develop these powers and advantages, or alternatively will seek the source of my theory of memory in the Creator. Such people consider the Art of Memory to be something rotten, or a thing of naught or, at the least, tedious. They will also say that I have sought to conceal what they could have comprehended through Nature herself. Finally, they will see me personally as vain or, perhaps, even weak-minded.

But they do all this with impunity, for I simply refuse to lose my temper when I'm pecked at by such tiny birds as these. Indeed, it is essential that creatures like these exist:

namque est in rebus inane:
Quod si non esset nulla ratione moveri
res possent,

'for there is also a void in things...for if there were not then things could not be moved by any means'.[7]

Nor is anything completely solid, just as, if there were no lightness in things, then there would be nothing that you could strictly define as being heavy, and just as, if you were unwilling to acknowledge the possibility of darkness, there would not be any areas of light or shadow, for these things are assuredly alliances of Nature.

But I occasionally encounter a second type of person, namely those who complain that I conceal too much and that what I have to say is too obscure. If, however, such people wish to be considered impartial judges then they must appreciate that clarity is not something I can provide at the drop of a hat: there were words to decline and conjugate, and there was terminology to construct, as is required in all other disciplines. Also, since I've assumed the character of that most ancient and most grave King Thamus (which I thought was the most suitable persona to adopt, seeing that Plato describes the allegations he made against Theutates with regard to memory and the invention of writing[8]*) is it not inevitable that a short and pithy speech that can also accurately reflect and portray a particular person and occasion should also be obscure? For, in any speech:*

Intererit multum Davusne loquatur, herusne,
maturusne senex, an adhuc florente iuventa
fervidus.

'it matters a great deal whether it's Davus that's speaking, or the master of the house, or an old man, or a hot-blooded fellow in the bloom of youth'[9,]

for if any literary form is difficult to make convincing then it's the prosopopœia[10]*, partly because, in this form of narrative, you need to ensure that what the characters are saying matches their personalities, while at the same time being on the alert that, in your desire to achieve conformity between character and utterance, you do not neglect the former. It's also inevitable that, from time to time, you'll fail in one respect or the other, though it certainly seems preferable to try to ensure in the first instance that the character you've just introduced to the reader justly prevails. If you can do that then nothing that follows could be simpler, even though it is difficult at first:*

Cernere nemo
se supra potis est; at voces excipere extra.
*'for no one can see through something, but they can hear voices
from beyond it.'*[11]

*I reply in the same manner to my sane and generous supporters, but to
those who have closed minds I recommend that they heed the words of
the poet:*

Ole quid ad te,
De cute quid faciat ille, vel ille sua.
*'What does it matter to you, Olus, what this man or that woman
does with their own skin?'*[12]

*Well, it's my skin, and it's my choice too, so it's certainly no business
of Olus.*

But what if:

Vitium vas efficit ipsum,
'it's the vessel itself that gives rise to the corruption'?[13]

*What if it is the vessel itself which is fragile and full of holes?
And certainly in this case it <u>is</u> the vessel that's causing the corruption,
for here the defect is not to be found in the light but in the lamp
from which it shines forth, and even that light does not cast a
glow for everyone, nor in just one particular way, for the force of the
mind is undiscriminating, and either puts up a weak struggle or none at
all.*

    *As for all those people who think I have been unfair to Socrates, and
there will certainly be some, they will surely have been slaves to his ideas
while I myself have always maintained a cautious distance. Such people
will, I hope, leave me to my own feelings, but even if I cannot secure
such a favour from them they may wish to bear in mind that it's not me
who's doing the talking here but Thamus.*

    *But whatever form that discussion may take, it certainly ponders
some very weighty matters concerning both princes and peoples, and it
may indeed outstay its welcome, so please make due allowance for the
fact that if some theory or other (and especially a threadbare one) does*

come knocking at the doors of the high and mighty then it may well appear to be drunk[14].

And indeed for those:

Cui scire est quod fama virum vulgataque fides
suggerit
'for whom knowledge is simply what men's opinion and common belief suggest it is '[15]

my argument will be neither popular nor easy to understand, and nor should it be for of course it's always more profitable to speak Platonically, in other words to experience great difficulty in understanding things and then, when you have understood them, give an incorrect account of them to the great unwashed.

But, unless I am very much mistaken, for people of that kind a little bit of love, some wings[16], *and a firm resolve will all prove useful as well as comforting and confidence-giving. My argument is certainly a sane one, and is copied from the rays and footprints of Nature*[17], *although in this case you might prefer to define me as nothing other than someone who expresses things differently, or as someone who likes to find fault, or as someone who might possibly be guilty of vanity or stupidity.*

Of course, any reasoning of this kind strikes me as excessively prideful, for it is typical either of the unsophisticated and the excessively frank or of the starveling and the incorrigibly vain. You may give the impression that you think that such actions are a token[18] *of your candour, but:*

Si cum natura sapio et sub numine,
id vere plus quam satis est.
'if I understand something with the help of Nature and under the will of God then that is more than enough for me. '[19]

THAMUS

OR

THE VIRTUE OF MEMORY

AN INTRODUCTION

BY

ALEXANDER DICSONE OF ERROL

DRAMATIS PERSONÆ: THAMUS[20], MERCURY[21], THEUTATES[22]

There is nothing like God, nor is there any foreshadowing[23] of Him.
THAMUS. But Mercury, those things *are* true, for nothing can be similar or equal to all those things which are the Odd, the One and the Single. The one idea is entirely of the One, with just one sign to indicate that it is the One. That idea is certainly incorporeal, but it injects into physical bodies all the ideas of the age, of the world, of time and of origin. But can we really use our imaginations to understand the vessel[24] of anything that we usually grasp with the intellect alone? This is true of everything that perishes beneath the rising of the sun, and perhaps it is even true of the generative process itself, given that it may not be able to endure the rays shed by such a great light. Accordingly, the perversity of ignorance has washed over the Earth, so that it now carries a huge burden of matter. This is pure evil, for a fire that transforms a pyramid into a type of cube[25] certainly does not allow any appeal to be made to the cognate spheres.

The ridiculous multitude of gods.
But that's not all. Oh how absurd this is! There's just one generative process, one time, one world, one eternity – but how many different things have the philosophers asserted that One Thing to be? But at least they did genuinely reflect upon the subject unless, of course, they preferred just to spew the whole thing forth[26].
MERCURY. But they have had their hands immersed in the waters[27], for what shall I say about the cloak, or when the time will come when

those people wish to tear that cloak asunder, or whether they are even able to do so?

THAM. Cloak?

MERC. Isn't that what you said? But how many cloaks are there which aren't fashioned in the image of the tomb!

The perniciousness of ignorance.

THAM. What you're referring to is the web of ignorance, and the robber that's a sojourner in its dark expanse[28]. But that's quite enough of all that! Besides, since it's a holiday and we've been given permission to go for a walk, would you not like, while you're listening to the rest of this conversation, to proceed to the jaws of Hell and its wide expanse? Maybe you're obliged to do this anyway as part of the duty you have to tell us about the shadows – unless you want to do something else that is.

MERC. But the Senate's already in session and has already summoned me several times! Just in case you didn't know, there's a motion before the Senate relating to wild animals of a certain kind, and my presence there may be required to enable a decision to be made upon it.

THAM. What's all this about wild animals? Surely they're entirely extinct upon the Earth, along with their bodies?

MERC. People certainly believe that, but in fact the sinister world[29] *only* welcomes wild animals.

THAM. But it's an everyday occurrence to see humans migrating to the Underworld. We certainly don't see any wild animals going down there!

Wild animals.

MERC. You are ignorant, Thamus, simply ignorant. Those *are* wild animals – they're just pretending to have the human form of the creature in question[30].

THAM. Well, what you're telling me is simply incredible, but I suppose we're obliged to believe anything that Mercury says, although I would say that this phenomenon could perhaps be attributed to people's bestial habits. But do continue.

Mankind.

MERC. The Earth is a place of sin, and Mother Nature – guilty of an evil trick and with a virgin slain[31] – deceives us, for the form of a true man is intellect. In the shadow of the light it clothes itself in matter through the soul and with the assistance of the spirit. Positioned at the boundary of the image it inclines towards matter but is driven back to those things that fall within the scope of the intelligence – the things that actually exist.

The defenders of matter.
The intellect does not suffer from the weakened senses nor is it held fast by the bonds of the body but, untroubled by the defenders of matter[32] and rendered insensible to those proud masters, it tries to rise towards that which actually exists, as if from a dark and, as it were, night-like day. The peace that this mind enjoys nothing can remove, be it the heat of desire or the coldness of fear. Those who have bound up their minds[33] within the body and have therefore cast it aside are savage beasts, who should perhaps be frightened of coming back in the next life as animals.[34]
THAM. I think I understand. But what do you mean by 'the defenders of matter'?
MERC. I'm talking about contradictions. But I'm in a hurry, and your excessive inquisitiveness is making me late.
THAM. But... Oh, he's gone. But who's this? Why, it's Theutates! I recognise his staff, his numbers, his counting-stones and tablets, and his alphabets as well. Yes indeed, it *is* him. Was what we've been talking about something you're familiar with, Theutates? Have you, as a god, also endured the Underworld?
THEUTATES. Theutates most certainly is a god, Thamus, and nor are your beloved Egyptians in any doubt that he is, but I'm just his shadow.
THAM. But what about Æacus[35]? You tricked him in a similar way, didn't you[36]?
THEUT. Yes I did.
THAM. I approve of that wholeheartedly by the way. You are most certainly a god!
THEUT. Are you laughing at me, my good man? If you'd been a member of high society in Naucratis[37] then you wouldn't have these absurd doubts about my divinity.
THAM. But I certainly would have been absurd if I'd ceased to have any doubts. But you're quite wrong: you're not a man after all, but a wild beast, as Mercury has just been explaining to me.
THEUT. You're slandering me, Thamus. Do literacy, mathematics and so many great intellectual efforts really strike you as nothing more than the tracks of a wild animal?

The uses of literacy.

THAM. Regarding mathematics, Mercury may well have investigated it and perhaps there's something in it. But with that alphabet of yours I'm afraid you're contributing absolutely nothing[38].

THEUT. But Thamus, it's that same alphabet that makes your beloved Egyptians wiser in learning and readier in memory. And I'm happy to say that this aid to memory and wisdom is *my* creation.

The curse of memory.

THAM. Love has obviously clouded your mind. What you're bragging about is the complete opposite of what those things actually do, for if the attentiveness of students is weakened then forgetfulness and neglect are the result. Obviously, if students place their faith in the external formulæ of writing then they'll stop recalling and developing those interior formulæ by their own efforts through a process of recollection. So your efforts have not been directed at achieving a mental union with memory at all but with forgetfulness, and all your cleverness is just a matter of

illa se iactet in aula.
'Æolus lording it in that particular hall.'[39]

The pretence of wisdom.

And there's a second problem with another part of your proposition, and it's one that causes no small degree of inconvenience, for in those bygone days you didn't bestow upon 'my beloved Egyptians' as you call them the truth of wisdom at all, but only the *idea and pretence* of it. Since they'll have learnt a lot without a teacher they'll also give the appearance of knowing a lot, but as they're generally ignorant, as well as irritating, annoying and tiresome in their manners and conversation, they're all imbued – thanks to your patronage of them – with the conviction that they're wise – but what they're *not* imbued with is wisdom itself. I recall that, once upon a time, in that Upper Egyptian town which the common herd usually call 'Egyptian Thebes', I responded to you in the same way. Your embarrassment on that occasion made it abundantly clear that I was right to take you to task.

The writing-tablet of Nature.

But that was back in the days when everyone would, as it were, 'write everything in their mind'[40], since the mind is alive and can remedy injustices, and since it has acquired an understanding of what should and what should not be said to people[41]. But your progeny, having been brought up abusively and injuriously by ignorant people, and being in any case idle and apathetic, are always in need of some fatherly help, for they are incapable of either remedying the injustices they've suffered or of helping themselves. So you've been pretending to produce an age of wisdom, but quite falsely, for by reasoning illogically you've disinherited the whole of posterity of this most praiseworthy study. But where are you going, my good man? Are that staff, and the power that goes with it, really the hallmarks of a god, or are they just the signs of a savage beast, as I suggested at the outset?

Socrates approaches Thamus.
SOCRATES. I heard, Thamus, from my elderly relatives – and they certainly knew what they were talking about – that near Naucratis in Egypt there lived one of the old gods, Theutates by name, to whom the bird they call the ibis was sacred. They also told me that you, as King of Upper and Lower Egypt, had many discussions with Theutates. I understand that all the various pros and cons of these discoveries were given an airing, but that when you came to the subject of the alphabet you tried to argue, without any supporting evidence, that people who rely upon writing would be inclined to neglect their memories.
THAMUS. What are you driving at?
SOC. Well, that obviously helps explain why I myself have never written anything.
THAM. Well, maybe it does. But who *are* you?
SOC. I am Socrates[42], judged by Apollo to be the wisest of mankind[43].

A Sophist and the plague of humanity.
THAM. Oh I see, so you're that Sophist they talk about who's the plague of mankind, and certainly a Greek as well?
SOC. But I'd say that Zopyrus[44] was quite wrong.
THAM. But he described you just as your fellow-citizens subsequently judged you to be, when they learned of your deceitfulness, on the basis of hard evidence.
SOC. But Apollo examined me.
THAM. You're saying nothing meaningful. But I'll come back to that point in a moment. Anyway, what about what the poet said:

Qualia docuisti rudes,
heu insania tua, civitatísque
quæ tu nutriit
corrumpentem adolescentulos!
'What things you have taught these idiots... Alas, how foolish you are, and how foolish also is the city that has fed you – you of all people, the corrupter of our youth!'[45]

SOC. But those are the words of Aristophanes, and in that passage his good faith is suspect, and with good reason.

THAM. Alright, let's not trust anything he says. Instead we'll deal with you ourselves. Surely, Socrates, it's possible in this world for a deceiver to be sometimes mistaken for a man of his word or *vice versa*?

Socratic reasoning dissected.

SOC. Just in case you're not aware of the fact, it's actually *my* job to ask the questions. Indeed, I've always laid claim to that role as if it were mine by right. But since I fear the Trojans[46], and especially Diogenes[47], who's a real Polydamas[48], I'll answer your question, as I don't want to give the impression of being evasive. Yes, it is possible.

THAM. So, for example, you can have a medical doctor whose only real skill is turning minor illnesses into major ones and yet is buoyed up by popular approval, while another one has hardly any patients who are willing to place their trust in him?

SOC. Yes, that's also true.

THAM. And so in these cases, and others also, those who achieve something by merit that they have earned usually owe a debt to mendacity?

SOC. Perhaps.

THAM. And is it not also true, as the poet says,

Falsus honos iuvat, et mendax infamia terret?
'...that no one benefits from a word of false praise or is frightened by an infamous lie except the deceitful and those who are full of faults?'[49]

while another tells us that:

Fortis et ignavus parili afficiuntur honore?

'Equal honour is bestowed on the brave man and the coward.'[50]

And do we not also find judges to be guilty of this fault, even though nothing should be less corrupt than the sentence handed down by a court of law?

SOC. Certainly, for the Athenians sentenced me to death even though I was innocent.

THAM. And may not a virtuous man be suspected of being a rascal and a villain, so that he is harassed, discredited, rejected and reduced to poverty, while on the other hand a wicked man may be praised and cherished, and perhaps has every honour, praise and high office heaped upon him?

SOC. Yes, perhaps.

THAM. And although such a man may be completely ignorant, doesn't he win popular acclaim and approval?

SOC. Yes, even though I know who the intended target of this discussion is.

THAM. Good. And are not these and similar things harmful to the human race?

SOC. They are.

THAM. But what is their origin?

SOC. Deceit perhaps.

THAM. So deceit is a most pernicious thing?

SOC. Yes, it is indeed a most pernicious thing.

Socrates, the father of lies.

THAM. And yet, son of Sophroniscus[51], aren't you yourself the father of lies and a most definite charlatan?

SOC. What are you driving at?

THAM. What? Once you've checked all the counting-tokens individually do you not usually then check the total that they add up to[52]? Do you want me, if you're not happy with the result, to do the calculation all over again[53]?

SOC. You may think you've caught me in a trap and forced me to admit to something I'd rather not admit to, but that's simply not the case. But why are we going round in circles[54] like this?

THAM. What is it you've been hiding?

SOC. I don't know what you're talking about.

THAM. Tell me: were you really wise, or not?

SOC. And what if I wasn't?

THAM. Then why did Apollo praise you? Why go to so much trouble to praise wisdom so highly? But please don't waste your time here if you don't want to, for I understand you enjoy talking nonsense with Nestor and Palamedes[55].

SOC. But what if I *am* wise?

THAM. So what if you are if there's nothing to know? If there's no such thing as perception, or understanding, if there are no rules, and no yardstick of truth, if wisdom does know know itself or what it should doubt about itself, then how can it merit the name of wisdom? That's a very strange kind of wisdom, not to know anything, or to be certain of anything, and yet to fight against that which struggles to hold high the banner of wisdom. That way you would say that every child and every idiot is wise as well.

SOC. But surely Apollo's description of me carries some weight?

An explanation of the oracle of Apollo.

THAM. So you persist in that vanity! There has been some deceit, and you have been the most cunning of men. Don't try dissembling around these parts, for you won't find either an escape-route or any way of leading people astray with your misrepresentations. Not even Apollo would make any bones about that, and he is the supreme interpreter of his own oracles. It is generally agreed that you were not imbued with any genuine skills or learning.

Socrates largely ignorant of mathematics, and of physics as well.

If you deny that, then can you tell me what the properties of numbers are? Show me, for example, by what reasoning the circle can be squared, and the cube doubled. Describe, if you can, the movements of the planets, and the ways of the heavens. In fact, tell me about anything you like. What do you think about God for example? Who divided the light from the darkness[56]? Is God knowable or unknowable? Does He exist in the Father, in the intellect, in love? What is the divine essence? What are its accomplishments? What are the rays of God[57]? What are the signs of His existence? And what are His shadows[58]?

SOC. If you could be a god then what kind of god would you like to be?

THAM. I must admit, Socrates, that that question has left me dumbfounded. But let's come to more relevant things. Tell me, if you can, about eternity, about the world, about time, about the generative process. What ultimately is the soul of the world-soul[59]? What is the origin of things, and what keeps them in existence? How is the world constructed? What is its form? How is it organised? What gives it motion? What is life? What is death? Finally, what of resurrection on the Day of Judgement? Tell me, what do you think of the belief that the virtuous will enjoy a better fate, given that they have hardly any power and also have an imperfect essence? Is it really fitting that they be released from bondage and transported to Heaven when that same region can be seen as the abode of everyone? And are there really any imperfections in that essence? If so, are there many of them? Are they mixed? Are they specific to the individual? And what about the instruments of Nature – what are they exactly? What can you tell me about the shape of the moon? Why do its horns sometimes seem to be growing, while at other times they seem blunter or more pointed? And tell me about the sea: if it's actually blue, then why does it look purple when it's being beaten by oars?

The gods of Socrates.
But now you've gone quiet, which is a sure sign of your lack of experience in such matters and a testimony to your ignorance. Therefore, my friend, you should acknowledge that:

Putabas Deum nullum, præterquam nos
Et chaos hoc, et nebulas, et linguam, tria hæc.
'...you don't believe in any gods except the ones *we* believe in – the triad of Chaos, Clouds and Tongue.'[60]

That friend of yours Plato, someone you can hardly stand even when he's rubbing in ointments and is drenched in perfume[61], was certainly in other respects very devoted to you, and yet, when starting a discussion about Nature, he didn't even get you involved in the conversation as he almost always did on other occasions, but instead devoted his attention to the excellent Timæus of Locri[62].
SOC. But I was simply unable to ascend to heaven, so I always disdained topics like that as being mere vanities. I tried to rescue philosophy from topics of this kind – with their focus on ascending to heaven and all that sort of thing – and tried to situate it within the context of people's homes and cities.

The need to engage with Nature so as to avoid erring in morals.
THAM. What unbelievable folly, latent in a sort of dissimulation![63] And what abysmal ignorance of the alliances of Nature! So what is left for you, and what is left for God? Will such folly not

hoc violare fidem primam, et convellere tota
fundamenta, quibus nixatur vita salusque?
'violate this first faith and shatter all the foundations by which life and prosperity are supported?'[64]

We must therefore, my friend, penetrate into Nature and seek to thoroughly understand its requirements[65]

nam libella aliqua si ex parte claudicat hilum,
omnia mendose fieri atque obstipa necesse est,
prodita, iudiciis fallacibus, omnia primis.
'for if the level should deviate from the true at any place than the whole structure must necessarily be faulty and crooked, with all these errors arising from the initial incorrect measurements.'[66]

For a mind that understands nothing of the things that exist goes mad and, hopelessly lost, melts away into inanition[67].
SOC. But that's not true! Please understand that I promoted and established all these things on an ethical basis. Although I might have been contemptuous of all those 'higher things', I've always worked hard on the correct forms that we need to establish for the State and the lives of private citizens.
THAM. Also, since you had doubts about the matter, what is the final or ultimate aim of good actions[68]? But so much is clear: you must establish a beginning which everyone follows when they start to do something.

What Socrates envisaged in ethics and politics.
But who would dare to undertake something or actually do it when there is no certainty to what they are pursuing? But let the matter rest. I'm aware of your political views, hence those famous and brilliant proposals about abandoning offspring, about abortion and about love, as well as suggesting that wives, children, wealth and land be held in common,

that women should perform active military service along with men, and that men be seen as merely sharing this institution of theirs with them[69]! A real literary masterpiece, full of artistry and morality! What light-headedness caused you to show such a lack of consideration for others by preaching things like that?

SOC. But what was disgraceful about those things, especially when they attracted such praise and renown? Surely, by that reasoning, everyone will consider universal friendship to be an admirable thing, and surely the current evils of the State seem to arise from the fact that people do not own everything in common? But what I'm really referring to here are things like perjury by witnesses, toadyism among the rich, and law-suits and other disputes about breach of contract.

THAM. But Socrates, none of these things is due to wealth not being held in common – there has to be viciousness and perversity for these things to happen. Why do I say this? Because we find that people who hold property in common are more likely to fall out with each other than those who keep their resources to themselves. But you've been led astray because you thought – after looking at the matter from every side and in all its forms – that it would be more expedient to have just one household and just one State. But that's not the case; indeed, if we pursued this line of argument then there wouldn't be a State at all, for by nature the city-state is a multitude of people unless, that is, your idea of harmony is the sound of one voice. And what, in the meantime, would your Producers actually receive from your Guardians[70]? What would the magistracy get out of it? What would their prospects be, and what would their remuneration be like? It also seems absurd, after putting women on the same level as wild animals[71], to insist that they should follow the same pursuits and perform the same functions as men. What have such roles got to do with wild animals, for in love, abortion and birth the laws of Nature would also be violated.

SOC. But I then went on to explain that the magistrates and governors of the State would be different from those who are subject to their rule, just as we see the warp arising from one kind of wool and the weft from another.

THAM.
Infelix o semper ovis pecus!
'Poor sheep, poor flock, forever out of luck!'[72]

What's the use of your high-flown language if it's not consistent?[73] I feel really sorry for you, Socrates, for surely this is incompatible with the unity and sharing that you propose? Solve that conundrum if you can, and find just one, out of all those sophisms, that can get you out of this quandary. But we'll let those things pass. You did actually seem to be explaining things with divine inspiration when you insisted that reason should prevail, and that passion and anger should be kept under control.

Reason is the way to assuage passion.
But that was a mistake, for it is not reason that summons us to duty by issuing an order or which discourages us from an act of dishonesty by prohibition; quite the contrary, for reason is the way to assuage passion, and it is entirely the matter that deceives and which is deceived, and unless intellect is present then, believe me, you are wasting your time trying to ascend on the wings of reason, for

> *Fertur equis auriga, neque audit currus habenas.*
> 'the charioteer is swept along by his horses and the chariot does not obey the reins,'[74]

even though there'll be some among your favourites in whom that deception
cannot be dispelled. To such people however I would strongly recommend not only mastery of their passions and anger but also of their reason – indeed I would recommend that the intellect alone should be supreme. Indeed, to bring the conversation back to you, that principle should have formed the substance of the Socratic state.

The life of Socrates.
SOC. And yet, as everyone knows, I lived a modest, honest life.
THAM. In a shady, lazy sort of way yes you did, and you were certainly ingenious too: nothing plain or frank, just a putrid sense of irony and a fastidious dissimulation. Your life was utterly useless, and you didn't even bring up your children properly[75].

The *dæmonion*[76] and self-adoption[77].
For by way of deception, that is to say by making use of the *dæmonion*, you, as it were, adopted yourself, so that it seemed to you to be a

fastidious judgement to declare that all the philosophers of your age were just country bumpkins compared with yourself.

SOC. But surely the decent thing to do was to challenge the dishonest and uncultured Sophists?

THAM. Which meant that for Socrates alone the trade and trafficking in trickery and shams would be free from taxes. But we'll let that pass too, though indeed the censure of the magistrate would, in such cases, have been more efficacious than the satire of someone who was a Sophist himself[78]. But tell me, what passionate frenzy was it that first got you interested in Anaxagoras[79]?

SOC. Surely moderation is worthy of praise?

THAM. Now you're wriggling, and I see you turning pale at the mention of his name. But I didn't think that you'd start talking about moderation, you of all people, who had such love of parties and who shamefully instructed people in the temptations of the flesh, such as the suspicions people had (which I'll omit here) about your interest in young boys, especially Alcibiades[80]. You know the rest:

> *Considera adolescentule, importuna esse omnia*
> *Quæ insunt, voluptatibus si priveris*
> *Puerorum, mulierum, ludorum, obsoniorum,*
> *Conviviorum, cachinnorum:*
> *Quale hoc ipsum erit vivere, his si privatus fueris?*
> 'Young man, just think what moderation actually involves, and what pleasures you'll deny yourself if you practise it: boys, women, drinking-games, food, banquets, laughter... Tell me, without these things, is life really worth living?'[81]

Indeed, they say you thought that young men should be ashamed if they didn't have male lovers.

SOC. But those are Aristophanes' words. Certainly no crime was ever committed.

THAM. Even so, your actions were not beyond criticism, were they?

SOC. But what if they were?

THAM. Well, they were certainly not beyond suspicion.

SOC. But what if they were?

THAM. Did they not at least set a bad example to others? But I see that you deny enjoying illicit sex. What is that 'love that is friendship' you talk about if not the love of ugly boys and good-looking old men?

SOC. But what about my famous tolerance? Xanthippe[82] bears witness to that.

THAM. I don't like people who are too tolerant: that was impious, inappropriate and the stuff of which bad examples are made.

SOC. But I used to walk around in my bare feet, and often stand motionless all day long!

THAM. But why all this showing-off in the first place? If a person couldn't do that then would anyone really think he was in a bad way, and if he didn't want to do it then would he immediately be seen as a fool?

SOC. But just a moment ago you were saying how sly and secretive I am. What could be less compatible with that sort of nature than despising human kindness or considering wealth to be a thing of no importance?

THAM. Nothing, certainly. Yet you've achieved nothing, and nor can anything to the contrary be said about Socrates.

SOC. But acknowledge my steadfastness at least, for how many chains was I was most tightly bound with after I was unjustly condemned? Go on, tell me, how many?

The death of Socrates.

THAM. But obviously you were hoping that you could be released from custody and that your chains would be removed, and took care to be seen with a serene expression, like someone who had nothing at all to fear from death. But when you saw that no hope remained for you, and that you were almost completely lost, and that your mind would also be condemned[83], how all that pretence and glowing resolve just evaporated! What prickings of grief did that give rise to? Although I must confess that with your death you assumed a mask as if out of a conviction of it being your duty[84], so that you seemed shattered and humbled not on your own behalf but on that of your children. Then, when it was time for you to depart, you displayed a certain smugness, as if you were about to suffer willingly what, in any case, you would certainly have had to endure whether you wanted to or not, to the extent indeed that you were happy to maintain your extreme stance of simulation and dissimulation so that, in your empty pride, you could continue to lay claim to that famous steadfastness of yours.

SOC. But I drank the hemlock, as you can even see from my legs, which are still puffed up and swollen.

THAM. But at first you drank it unwillingly. That was a sign of weakness. You're wasting your time arguing about this.

The disciples of Socrates.
SOC. But surely the integrity of my disciples is enough to protect my reputation from all these wagging tongues?

THAM. I'm certainly aware of Aristippus[85], who was dissolute and a drunk, and Plato, who also sought the favour of Dionysius[86] and was certainly even worse than Aristippus in that he wanted to be seen as a more saintly man. Haven't you heard how Plato urged Dion to murder his kinsman Dionysius? And if Plato was your enemy then why did you cosy up to him and accept his generosity? If he was indeed your friend then what example were you following when you decided to plot against him? And what can I say about that chap Xenophon[87]?

Antisthenes, student of the physical sciences[88].
SOC. Well, acknowledge Antisthenes at least.

THAM. Certainly I shall. For at least he recognised one true God when most people were claiming that there were many, was interested in women and disdained wealth. He it was also who encouraged the Athenians to become historians of your death. He also taught moderation to Crates[89], tolerance to Zeno, and peace of mind to Diogenes[90]. But what is that to you? For he was accustomed neither to listening to you speak nor to spending much time with you as you lived in Athens while he lived in the Piræus[91].

SOC. Well, you've certainly given me a good drubbing today Thamus! But how do you know all these things when you died centuries before they actually happened?

THAM. If I'm making all this up or telling lies then I'm happy to be corrected. But if these things *are* true then why are you so upset about them? How can you bear to think about what you've been responsible for? But I will not conceal this: I must certainly acknowledge Antisthenes, Crates and Diogenes, but hardly a day goes by without me hearing something you've have said or done that's harmful to us mortals.

SOC. Other people may find fault with me if they wish, but you used to have an obligation to be better-natured and more fair-minded than that. I think I can perhaps request your grace for displaying a certain consistency of judgement?

THAM. Even if it's appropriate to resist grace[92]? But consistency in what exactly, Socrates?

SOC. In the fact that, thanks to your influence, I never put pen to paper in my whole life!

An explanation of Thamus' opinion on writing.

THAM. Now *you're* finding fault with *me*! But I didn't say that people shouldn't write at all, but only that, through a sort of recovery action[93], the study of memory should be restored to the place that's currently occupied by writing[94]. Think about it: one person entrusts to writing those things that he has conceived in his senses[95]. That's one thing. Another doesn't do that and instead repeats it from memory – that's surely even better? But the person who does neither always strikes me as useless. Although I don't consider it 'to be worthy of a philosopher to appeal to authority and witnesses, whom you find to be either telling the truth by accident or, alternatively, to be telling lies and allowing their imaginations to run riot out of malice'[96]. We should be driven to pursuing certain courses of action by argument and the influence of reason, and certainly not by events, especially those that one cannot accept with a clear conscience. We should therefore accept something not on the basis of how it strikes us, but because it has been put together with strength and structure in reason and argument. But what am I doing, expecting strength or reasoning from Socrates, as if he was a proper philosopher!

Socrates takes his turn and ultimately prevails.

SOC. You're certainly an awkward character, Thamus. But now you must tell me in your turn whether it is right for the same person both to seek peace in wartime and to refuse to condemn the arts of war in peacetime?[97]

THAM. Yes, certainly it is.

SOC. And surely if we are able to conceive of things that are harmful to the forms of the State then we must also have conceived of things that are of advantage to them?

THAM. Yes of course.

SOC. And is it not the duty of the same person who identifies and repeals bad laws to also enact good and advantageous ones?

THAM. Perhaps.

SOC. And surely it is also appropriate that someone who has given an account of the shadow of death should seem to be able to have sat in the shadow of light so as to lead people to that shadow?

THAM. Yes, it would seem so.

SOC. So is it not therefore the task of that same Thamus, who discovered the substance of forgetfulness, to also reveal to us the potion for a good memory? When I tried to spend some time with you discussing this matter, starting with the very basics, your long-winded explanation of my teachings stopped me from doing so. So come along now, since you've recognised that I must now shuffle off this mortal coil by the judicial decision of my superiors,

Tu animum magnum
Contine in pectoribus: amicitia enim est melior.
'...keep your magnanimity in your breast, for friendship is better'[98]

and, if you are happy to have me as an interlocutor, then remind me about that form of memory that formed the subject of the discoveries made by Theutates.
THAM. My world is about people, destiny and love. And I have to explain all this to a Greek? But why not? You say 'friendship is better', but tell me what persuaded you and where you got the idea from that this is in any way relevant to any of the matters under discussion? If there's nothing in the way of a judgement, if there's no mechanism for passing judgement, then it follows that there's nothing that can be known or perceived, for all that remains is just rash opinionising:

Sacer est morbus, et visus mentitur.
'It is a deadly disease, and the appearance is deceptive.'[99]

And once we've got rid of opinionising and perception then all we have left is assertion. But we are going astray and clothing ourselves in deceit if we think that any judgements are handed down by Nature. But you're blushing! So what now? Are you sticking to your way of thinking?
SOC. And if I do?
THAM. Then there's nothing further to be said about the matter.
SOC. And if I don't?
THAM. It's not for sages to change their mind – right? Isn't that your opinion also?
SOC. The least you can do is show some respect for your own kind.
THAM. But it's wicked to yield and to show pity, for a wise man never allows himself to get upset. I thought that that's what you yourself

taught, O wisest of men, and that we should immerse ourselves in the river of your subtleties. But do as you wish. I shall do what I was never accustomed to do in life, seeing that I disputed about things that can only be sustained by doctrine and reason: I shall recall to mind, on this Earth of ours, that form of memory which, as you say, has been investigated for centuries, and with you as my interlocutor. If that's what you want of course. And yet:

Tua messis in herba:
'You are harvesting in the grass'.[100]

for you won't understand what is said to you until you have made your peace with Anaxagoras[101] who, I hear, has also passed on. So listen carefully!

Forgetfulness.
Forgetfulness is a defect occasioned by a weak and undisciplined mind, and is that primary material legacy that dissolves and attenuates the mind's principal powers.

From this statement it will be clear that forgetfulness does not originate in God or in Nature, for the role of Fortune is meaningless in this context, since an ignorance of causes gives a false impression of the effect of those causes[102]. I do however know that forgetfulness is located within us, and that, of our own volition, we enter into a sort of contract with it. Sophisticated people therefore hold forgetfulness in scorn, hence the saying:

Mos est oblivisci hominibus,
neque novisse, cuius nihili sit faciunda gratia.
'It's fashionable for people to forget (and even to pretend not to recognise) those whose favour has been acquired to no purpose.'[103]

When forgetfulness is present there will be no progression from the boundary[104], nor will there be any shadows, subjects, organisation or, ultimately, any resourcefulness of mind and spirit.

Nil igitur mirum est, animus si cætera nescit,
præterquam quibus est in rebus deditus ipse.

'It is no wonder that the mind loses sight of everything other than those things with which it is immediately preoccupied.'[105]

In such cases we are betrayed by our senses and by the functioning of the sensory apparatus. We also find ourselves plunged into a state of ignorance, and that's the very worst thing of all – indeed, it resembles a form of unjust slavery[106].

Memory.

Memory is the precise opposite of forgetfulness, as it is a power, an action, a shadow, and a beating of the wings of the mind[107] unencumbered by the servitude[108] of the physical body and the sensory faculties. Its primary virtue lies in the shadow of the good[109], and its secondary virtue in the actions that need to be undertaken to look back at what has been seen and observed.

Now every faculty, though it be impressed upon us by Nature, proceeds from God who is the author of all things, and whose footprints[110] we can however always see impressed in that faculty. Observing and experiencing those footprints enables the resources of our reason to come hurrying to our assistance. And that is the only correct form of reason, namely that which is created by Nature. If you finally succeed in rousing it from the dust[111] then you will have won everyone's esteem[112]. This arrangement will therefore be triple in character: it is natural[113]; it is also, and indeed first and foremost, innate; and it also coexists simultaneously with our innate thinking faculty.

Nature.

Indeed, man was contemplating and expressing this form of reason even before Theutates invented writing, and nor in those days did humanity have any need of letters and alphabets. But then people started to use letters of the alphabet to record those things that it wanted to record permanently, just as they had formerly engraved things in their minds. Unfortunately, being all too human, mankind – after that great and skilful sage Theutates had invented writing – came to prefer him to the natural way of doing things and so became his followers. It therefore became necessary to protect memory from the effects of his invention. Even so, a general decline in memory ensued, and humanity became less interested in working in accordance with the laws of Nature. Ultimately, mankind acted impiously towards her, which gave rise to an actually quite spurious allegation that humanity was developing a streak of weak-mindedness.

But thereafter either:

Ut varias usus meditando extunderet artes, pater ipse colendi
Haud facilem esse viam voluit.
'the Great Father Himself willed that the path of husbandry
should scarcely be an easy one, so that hard practice
accompanied by careful thought might hammer out the various
skills'[114]

or alternatively the gods did not share things out equally, so that our solution, namely the Art of Memory, although it everywhere took the place of those ineffective measures, did not, however, replace all of them.

Reason.
From this the second opportunity can be seen readily to follow, which is that of reason and the Art, which stimulates and invigorates Mother Nature who is otherwise latent. Indeed, that power is called forth from Nature's womb, and with her assistance that previous conception, which is also Nature herself, starts to glow with learning and reason, and of these things a sympathetic alliance is formed.

Simonides of Ceos.
It was once mistakenly believed that the Art of Memory, after remaining in the background for so many years thanks to the skill of the learned inventor of writing, first saw the light of day in your own country of Greece. Indeed, it's widely believed that it was that fellow from Ceos[115] who was the first to discover and promulgate it. But if you turn the pages of the annals of my Egyptian ancestors and you read the stories that are brought to life within them then you'll find that, long before that, it was gaining strength in the form of figures, marks, token, seals, signs and characters[116]. And, even if we set Egypt to one side, it's been established that the Celts also used it in their Druidic schools[117]. So much for Simonides and his Tyndarides![118]

Themistocles.
Other people, in an effort to appear more civilised, can persuade us with

a certain vein of humour that this Art of Memory is completely worthless, replying that they prefer to forget what they wish to forget rather than remember it[119], but they fail to take into consideration that there's a riposte to this, for although that probably is the point of view that's held by some poor wretches, speaking personally as someone who likes things to be relevant to the theme in hand I think you should be criticising the subject itself, not the man who invented it, and should be asking what is agreeable to Nature and what the best course of action is, not what this or that person would prefer to remember or forget.

Anyway, those are the origins of the Art of Memory – in other words, how it came about and how life was first breathed into it.

What memory is.
Surely only an impudent fellow would look for the blessing and influences of this shadow within the circuit of immortal God, and not by looking through the lattices of the windows of the temple either, but by gazing from its very heights, in an instant, with the light cast upon all things?

But if memory has its underlying causes; if it is conjoined with matter, with time, with the generative process and with its opposite, impotence; and if it is a useful thing in itself, then surely it should be allowed to flourish, and in other domains also? But does that mean that the advantages of memory help perfect the mind that is embedded in the planets[120] or the fixed stars, or the virtue of the world-mind[121]? Surely, if the planetary minds do not require any understanding of those things that come to pass in their midst, such as mankind passes judgement on, then they won't need the beating wings[122] of recollection either?

They do however recognise and arrange, one by one, whatever comes to pass. That may well be true, but it actually happens rather differently, for they are not deprived at any time of the opportunity to contemplate the lower world, since the rational memory[123] allows a representation of any physically remote object.

Again, if someone were to ask me whether the minds of the planets are aware that they've orbited the Earth during the previous day, month or year, then I would ask them to understand that, although nothing that is continuous and free from change can ever allow any variation, nonetheless certain features and traces of variation can be discerned in the day, month and year. No part of something constant can therefore ever belong to yesterday.

However, the human mind, whichever way one looks at it, is the father of the day, the month and the year, and just as someone walking along a road leaves footprints on various parts of the ground, so we divide the individual motions that the planets make within their minds into many parts, for in the celestial world the day is all one, and there is no transition from day to night.

So perhaps the minds of the stars and planets do have awareness, as you say. But they do not have awareness within a temporal framework, and we said above that time is something with which memory is conjoined. Yet you still persist in saying that the planetary minds are looking down on humans, and that it may perhaps follow from this that those minds are our rememberings.

But what kind of memory can this be? They look down on us, so by that same token it may ultimately be concluded that they ultimately participate in memory, but the opposite is in fact the case, for we do not go over in our mind what we are looking at in a process of recollection, but instead recognise it comprehensively.

From these facts we can simultaneously conclude that the minds of individuals cannot have the functions of a rational memory when they have risen to a memory-locus[124] that is known to them nor any faculty for acquiring such functions, unless perhaps:

Iterum ad Troiam magnus mittetur Achilles.
'again a great Achilles shall be sent to Troy'[125]

for either they do not see, or they do see but in a mirror.

So let's accept that a rational memory *is* present in other things, but since we've assumed that its function is conjoined with the body, and that rational memory itself is conjoined with time, then it certainly remains the case that the powers of this virtue are only present in animate beings and, indeed, only in those animate beings that have a sense of time. And if time is a number[126], and if only human beings were made by Nature to perform calculations with numbers and are suited to that task, then why waste any more time on dumb animals?

Nature and reason.

On no occasion therefore will the universal nature be absent, and on no occasion will its individual nature[127] be languishing, for only the related virtue of reason may prevail, as well as the addition of the art, which certainly either follows the virtue of reason and is overcome by it or, by chance, overcomes it, for that art does indeed serve the form of the substance in terms of representation, but not in the same way in number (if, indeed, the stomach rapidly digests all of the floating matter[128]). The art is indeed deficient in representation, but in number (by using distinctions) it is strong by virtue of the measure and duration of those objects for, once the object has passed away, its external form can be committed to a 'hard' picture or writing; bygone absent and present events can be restored; and words and concepts that are otherwise flowing forth can be transmitted and gathered together at any time and place one wishes.

This form of reason does not in any way rest on a branch[129] of the mind.
If you are positioned on the boundary of this virtue then how can it ensure rest and action at the centre? And even if it is at the centre then by what reasoning might it have crossed over from the boundary, as you cannot claim that it is properly leaning in any way on any branch of the mind? And, my dear friend, now Anaxagoras will assess your powers of acumen and judgement, and of those things that it is pleasing to recollect[130], if we may quote poetry at you, he may bring an acquaintance and an understanding to the fore.

Since we have three things in Nature – namely foresight, insight and hindsight – then who would dare to claim that, if you removed either or both of the first two, he would still have hindsight of something that, I think it's fair to say, would not actually exist and would be lacking in any sort of organisation? And, by the way, we'll be throwing you out of here if you think that what we're seeking to instil here is keenness of invention and skill in judgment, for you would err to no purpose.

The first influences.
For you are not seeking the prudence[131] of Nature and of reason but rather the shadow of its object and, indeed, a shadow that cannot be grasped by any reasoning at all unless its body be disencumbered, for that is the nature of shadows.

So when we finally decide to descend into the arena to begin combat, the first assertion we can make in an effort to understand this phenomenon is that willpower must be present, as well as Cupid, who is certainly the greatest and oldest of all the gods.

The next rule is that the mind must be free of anxiety[132] and in a state of readiness[133], and that you yourself must be undisturbed for otherwise you would be struggling rashly and in vain, just as if you were trying to use your signet-ring to place a seal on a rushing torrent.

To these requirements we need to add the advice that, just as someone who neither plants a tree nor looks after it properly after it has put out its first shoots ever gets any oil, figs, apples or whatever, so, in the same way, unless you first provide the necessities and then, certainly, cultivate what comes forth then you'll wait in vain for its 'oil' to be produced, and will work to no purpose and end up empty-handed. Which is why it is very truly said that:

Non fieri partum nisi concilio ante vocato principium.
'No birth can take place without a meeting having first been called.'[134]

Once we've decided what it is we wish to remember we must first, as it were, choose where to pitch our camp. We then, to continue our analogy, have to raise our troops. You may well ask, 'After our line of battle has been drawn up and we've motivated our soldiers, what more do we need? In this case foreknowledge comes first, and changes in discrimination second. But is that what memory is? Surely those things have already been banished?'

But if that's your response then you're dealing in superficialities. You're obviously making fun of me – most charmingly I should add, and I do like you above all the others.

Foreknowledge.
Foreknowledge of things must be sought in the sources of those things, and we have therefore banished the method of foreknowledge to the Island of Reason, while the foreknowledge of flight and pursuit have also perhaps been banished to the city, since for the time being we are permitted to remain among the shadows.

But the whole of this preliminary consideration lies within the subjects and shadows. Indeed, since forgetfulness and memory are polar opposites – the former corresponding to darkness and, as it were, death, and the latter, by analogy, corresponding to light – and since between darkness and light there is nothing except a progression by means of interposed shadows (if Nature allows), then we have reason to believe that the same is true in this instance, and that everything that is retrieved from forgetfulness and placed in the memory may be brought there by means of intermediary shadows, which act like female messengers[135], tempering the representations of the retrieved objects and then presenting them to the mind[136]. Indeed, it is fitting that everything that moves spontaneously rather than by necessity may anticipate representation of the object proposed, and this idea is in God, and for us is a shadow. And as Nature, through the innate and occupying idea, produces definite representations from indefinite material, so in the same way our mind, not only in the habit of recall but in every decision and action of any kind, acts only through shadows, which explains:

Quodcunque lubido
venerit, extemplo mens cogitat eius id ipsum
et simul ac volumus nobis occurrit imago.
'why, when the desire shall have come, our mind immediately thinks of that thing, and as soon as we experience the desire the image presents itself to us.'[137]

This is why shadows are useful, and why we find, innate in them:

causa videtur
cernendi, neque posse sine his res ulla videri.
'...the cause of seeing, and nor can anything be seen without them.'[138]

This should lead you to the conclusion that there must be subjects from which these shadows are extracted.

First therefore I need to talk about the nature and essence of a subject, and then about how it is selected, and the principle by which it is governed. Finally, and in a similar manner, I will need to talk about shadows.

Subjects.
A subject is a sort of pocket or receptacle into which the shadows are placed. This arrangement will enable you to recite from memory whatever you might have learned and conceived by thinking, but only those things that have been visible to you. So we are not concerned here

with logical extremes, nor with the actual *hyle*[139], nor with something made by Nature and related specifically to her, nor with things made by an art and related to an art. Instead we are wrestling, in various contexts, with things that have been made using the shadows of a construction that needs to be disencumbered, just as marks and seals need to be[140].

The whole question of subjects has a twofold aspect, for there is an absolute and primary subject which is clearly manifested either by nature or design, while the other is an adjuvant subject which is generally contained by the efficacy of the vision.

But when an adjuvant is the entire universe or the bowels of the Earth, or contains all sorts of different things, or is an entire political or economic system with all its constituent parts then absolute subjects are selected from the three categories[141] just mentioned as occasion demands. Other categories are neither useful nor perhaps even possible.

The adjuvant subject is that which has been adjoined to the absolute subject. It is the latter that actually contains the shadow. It is this process of adjunction that gives rise to a fertile memory and firm retention[142]. Although the adjuvant subject is fixed and immobile, it may be moved on a pretext provided by those shadows, as it is obviously assigned to the task of using and employing those shadows.

Let's take an example. In an intercolumnar space[143] let there be a sword. Now let Astraea[144], drawing attention to that innate and, by its very nature, clearly defined law of self-defence, stretch forth that sword. Now let those who want social change atone by the sword. In the same way, if at any time a shadow that has been previously imagined doesn't immediately spring to the mind of the person trying to recall it on the basis of its effects and contingencies, then recalling the sword's function will instantly point to that shadow, for in such a case the stones speak with their own voice and heed the commands and authority of the shadow of the guest[145].

However, situations may perhaps arise in which something in the material of these adjuvants seems to be so mathematical in character that it proves unsatisfactory. Why it may be unsatisfactory I shall explain elsewhere. For the time being I'm content to make the point that all subjects of this kind strike me as being mathematical, not because they're separated from the concretion of the material but because they also designate the number and sequence of the memory-loci and the guests[146]. Indeed, if they failed to do so then, in this instance, they would seem to have been adopted to no purpose. You should be able to decide for yourself whether this feature should be added to the existing utilities provided by the adjuvants.

Now we've discussed the nature and essence of subjects I'll provide some supplementary material on how they are selected and the principles they should follow.

On the principle that subjects should follow.

To begin with, let's deal with sensory objects. Whether the form is innate or has been assumed externally, each object should assume a form endowed with sensation[147] and suited to the eyes even if it may not always have been moved from the boundary by the sensory faculties, otherwise you will waste your time trying to recall things you cannot even represent or construct.

The object should then be moulded to suit the visual strength of the boundary, for just as a shadow is neither light nor darkness, so its seat is located neither in the latter nor in the former, as every piercing brightness hurts the eyes[148], for:

(nam quocunque loco fit lux atque umbra, tueri illorum est:)
'it is their task to see where light and shadow might be manifesting'[149]

and the same is true also for the senses and mental images. Subjects should not therefore be too bright lest they dazzle and hurt the eyes, but nor should they be too dark.

What's more, since they are to serve as containers for the shadows, let them be of a moderate and reasonable size, and make sure they maintain that size. If however anything should interfere with this process you can allow the subjects to be modified in accordance with the rules of Nature, for if they're too voluminous they can scarcely be considered images at all, whereas if they're too small they can look as if they're trying to keep the observer at arm's length. They should also be sufficiently prominent and distinct.

Spaces between subjects should also be moderate in size and must be kept parallel. In this task you'll need to use the cognitive apparatus to achieve satisfactory results. The central areas however need to be, as it were, effaced and erased[150].

Next, eliminate any dissimilarities of form as well as of essential character. Even so, you should use all your skill to ensure that the infinite variety of Nature is respected.

All subjects should be concave (or, at least, flat): they should never be convex. Let all the absolute subjects be characterised by their companion adjuvant subjects, which should serve as their guards.

Next, ensure that those objects that will be entrusted to the confidence of those guards are also guarded, and release those objects if the thinking process obtrudes. Do not allow them to stray into neighbouring territory, but always distribute them, as it were, among their decans[151]. The commanders and princes of the decans may, if you wish, be selected from among the images of the lunar mansions[152]. A permanent decemvirate[153] should take responsibility for the administration, and golden chains[154] should be provided for them in the individual stations. Finally, adjuvants that you think are suited to more than one purpose and movement should be made permanent. But make sure you keep all these things under careful observation, so that those that wish to can remain in position and stand fast. Great care and meticulousness must be brought to this task to ensure satisfactory results, and not with the eyes and with their external light of the mind (which should never be allowed to happen) but with their innate and integral light.

So that's how subjects should be dimensioned and delineated. Now let's move on to discussing shadows using a similar plan.

Shadows.

A shadow is defined as the representation of an object assigned to a subject and so selected as to ensure a firm perception[155] of that object, but it's not a representation to the same extent that we encounter in the First Mind[156], for that is Light and is always the same, whereas what we are seeking is a shadow of a kind that can be brought forth. Nor is it quite comparable to that which can be found in the heavens and those everlasting fires[157] or in the celestial circuits[158], nor to a thing in itself[159] or a thing in something that procreates[160], or something which can be produced by procreation. Finally, it is not comparable to a work of art or something that is moved within the boundary of the mind, but is, as it were, polished by the sensory faculties and by the file of the mind[161].

The object – the thing itself – is therefore entrusted to the subject. The result of that prior entrustment, as Mercury once explained to me, is understanding. The position of the antecedent[162] gives rise to a connection in the prudence of both Nature and wisdom; in the same way the virtue of the shadows is responsible for every firm and expanded retention of a memory-activity.

What we've just said may make acquiring this skill sound difficult and even pointless, or perhaps vain and laborious, but whereas those who adhere to the former opinion claim that memory is a wild and uncontrollable gift of nature, those who support the latter view see it as something knavish, and have also concluded that if you don't understand something when it's made patent then (need I say more?) it should remain abstruse.

Simple shadows.

Some shadows are simple, whereas others are modified.

Simple shadows are processed by the sensory apparatus, modified shadows by the conceptual apparatus.

Simple shadows are moved from and adopted from the boundary, whereas modified shadows are brought forth and represented within the sensory apparatus.

Consequently, when we are dealing with a memory-activity that involves an object that is visual, albeit to a modest extent, then whatever its exact nature that object will also be a shadow: hence, a man designates a man, Alledius stands for Alledius[163], and a wild animal for a wild animal. Everything that can be identified from its very nature as visual and can only be identified as such, albeit only to a modest extent, is therefore handed over to the cognitive faculties in the form of shadows of this kind.

I said 'from its very nature', since those objects that are perceived by the hearing and the cognitive faculties but which elude the vision and are *per se* intellectual will also assist in the process, with the approval of the eyes[164], but in the form of modified shadows. This is so that the construction may record these as invisible and, by their very nature, removed from the judgement of vision[165], which means that you won't be able to grasp them by reflecting upon them, just as you *can* grasp them by inspecting them. But even if this occurs in the case of very small objects (or, indeed, large ones) we are only concerned here with objects of moderate size.

Modified shadows.

If an object doesn't have its own shadow then necessity demands that you must obtain what you do not have from somewhere else. If no simple shadows are available then you should consider using imitative and representative simulacra[166], or things that are similar in some way.

This is what's known as a construction[167]: these *modified shadows* as they're known are not employed to provide amusement and a pleasurable stimulus as is usually the case with metaphors but to solve problems that have arisen and meet the urgent needs to which they have given rise, as the eyes of the intellect[168] are, as it were, drawn more readily to related abstractions. For what else can you do if necessity compels you to do something?

Modified shadows can be further subdivided into those that involve a modification of objects and those that involve verbal constructions[169].

Modification of objects.

Just as, in the case of those objects that fall within the scope of the vision, we see that the shadows are emanating from external forms so perhaps we should expect to find inflected and modified shadows emanating from internal forms. Certainly, if we are examining the true forms of objects then we will find that every construction will need to be evoked from those forms, but since in the case of absolute subjects we are not examining them on the basis of the underlying rationale then in the case of mathematical subjects we need to derive the construction from the basic arrangement.

Absolute shadows.

Absolute shadows are all those that do not involve any difference of number. They may be either simple or conjoined. I shall not dwell on this distinction here, provided that you remember throughout this discussion that we are investigating the simulacra of abstractions that elude the sensory apparatus. If objects fall within the scope of the visual apparatus then they have a simple formation.

We can fairly refer to this inflection[170] or modification of absolute shadows as a form of metaphor, not because it involves a word having to be substituted and used figuratively to add a certain lustre to an oration (which is essentially what your philosophy[171] consists of), but because it enables absolute shadows to, as it were, perform exchanges[172] of objects and serve as simulacra, since an object which eludes the sensory faculties is entrusted to the care of something different that *does* fall within the scope of those faculties[173]. So we don't select these shadows (which assume the role of changing these objects) in order to put them forward as strict replacements for the ineffective ones (which would be the sole cause of your selection) but so that, with the help of these shadows, which are latent in the cognitive apparatus, you can recall to mind and recite those objects which they have been selected to represent and which you would otherwise not be able to retain in the memory. That's why you won't find here any of the excessively daring metaphors you were warning us about[174], and indeed they can get in the way of our argument.

The efficient cause[175] of the created object undergoes certain changes, so that the 'father' of something is followed by his 'progeny'. So Theutates can stand for mathematics and writing, Vulcan for pyromancy[176], Nereus for hydromancy[177], Apollo for the sunrise and sunset, Chiron[178] for what's known as surgery, Minerva for wars and enterprise, Prometheus for foreknowledge[179], and, sadly, Epimetheus[180] for the pride than precedes repentance.

It shouldn't cause you any problems if these objects do not fall within the scope of the vision, for whether they are material or immaterial, connected or unconnected, due regard must still be paid to those objects that the ancients assigned to them,

Nam certe ex vivo, Centauri non fit imago:
Nulla fuit quoniam talis natura animantis.
Verum ubi equi atque hominis, casu convenit imago,
hærescit facile extemplo.
'for certainly no image of a Centaur is formed from a living
one, since no such kind of living creature has existed, but when
the image of a horse and a man come together by chance then it
immediately coalesces without difficulty.'[181]

So, for example, tools made of iron and other metals, and things like crowbars, will stand for building and construction, while what someone once said, did or wrote, or was able to do, can easily be repeated from that same act.

Now what about matter? And what about the end-result? But the efficient cause (and, indeed, every other cause besides) is recalled on the basis of *acts*. Who raised man from the dust and made him sublime?[182] Who fashioned the senses as the interpreters and messengers of things, and placed them in the head as if in a citadel? Who hollowed out the eyes and surrounded them with a form of rampart? Who sealed up in them the luminous fire? Who made the holes to create our nostrils? Who made the entrances to the ears as hard as horn? Who established the marrow with bone, the bones with sinews, and the whole with flesh? Who constructed that flesh with salt and acid, like a leaven? Who made the sinews from flesh and bone, the bone from earth and marrow, or the marrow from triangles[183]? Who constructed our ribs? Or made our heart in the shape of a pyramid?[184] Why is there this incredibly unanimous, harmonious and continuous alliance of all things[185]? Finally, is there anything terrestrial in which the shadow of intelligent nature does not appear?

Surely therefore you can see how even the infinite and the incomprehensible can be revealed by His effects? There is an infinite number of such examples from which you can usefully recollect, as if from traces and seals[186], God Himself, and eternity, and the world, and time, and procreation, and anything in general which might ever have brought anything into existence.

First of all the core value[187] of the shadow is conveyed to those adjuncts that you need to insert. To take an example, if you are investigating forms of government the construction will favour the general welfare[188] rather than tyrannical inclinations. A conception involving a few people (but more than one person) who are blessed with virtue will therefore give us Aristocracy, while a popular conspiracy in favour of the general welfare will give us a Polity or, when it involves some sort of confrontation with the patricians, Democracy. These are the distinctions that you yourself make[189].

Diseases, strength, virtues, wealth, beauty as well as the opposites of all those things are therefore expressed on the basis of their subjects, while the properties and accidentals of all those things that are of natural origin[190] are accordingly expressed by those same things, which serve as heralds.

Approval of the subject depends upon the adjuncts and the accidentals, e.g. springtime is derived from the swallow, the planting of beans, and similar things, while in the same way the toga is used to represent peace, and armour and spears stand for war[191]. We should also mention here that, irrespective of the nature of the subject, you can evoke common accidents[192] in sequence on the basis of the inclinations and sentiments of your will. We can even draw inspiration from subjects that are quite different to the objects they represent. These include, in the first instance, those things that differ by virtue of reasoning alone, e.g.

a badge of honour will inspire a search for victory, while the figure of a bandit will lead you to a search for treachery.

Then again you may have overlooked those examples in which, by the same reasoning, one object is set against many objects, e.g. a group of heirs might recall the memory of someone making a will; someone who has inflicted some injury or other might lead you to think of the victim; a wife might remind you of her husband; a father-in-law might call to mind his son-in-law; and a tenant his landlord.

If, for example, you recall to mind the memory of Pericles[193] you'll recognise Anaxagoras, while Hippolytus[194] can stand for an adulterer, and a slave for a freedman. Similarly, something that gives off heat may stand for something that is cold, a spendthrift for a miser, a sensible man for a fool, someone who's enjoying his wealth for someone who's been ruined financially, a blind man for a sighted one, and a drunkard for someone sober. All this is based on the effective use in the Art of Memory of material that makes you smile or which causes surprise.

But as the majority of people divine things quite differently, i.e. on the basis not of passion but of judgement, reflecting on the perpetual changes in things, and being aware that:

sperat infestis, metuit secundis
alteram sortem, bene præparatum
pectus,
'the heart that is well prepared for a happy or unhappy fate is one that is optimistic in adversity and anxious in times of good fortune'[195]

then why should the power of reminiscence[196] not also come to their aid in the same way? Similarly, Nature herself draws forth contraries from contraries[197], while an intimacy between opposites always involves a greater degree of attraction and more far-reaching consequences than does a relationship between things that are alike.

Furthermore, in the case of those objects that are distinguished from one another by means of comparison we can imagine infinity being inspired by a multitude, a wind by Ibycus[198], something of moderate size by something larger, and *vice versa*, for who doesn't understand how analogy works? Certainly there's nothing in Nature that cannot be illuminated at some time by the light of resemblance. Hence someone who is

os humerosque Deo similis,
'God-like in face and shoulders'[199]

can stand for God, a potter kneading his clay for God's divine authority, the head of a family for a prince, and an old lady standing between two adolescents for a lunar or solar eclipse. In the same way a tree made secure by its deep roots, which no force can shake, can stand for a type of virtue. And that ship where

Nudum remigio latus,
et malus celeri saucius africo,
antennæque gemant,
'the side has lost its oars, and the yardarms and the mast, damaged by the bitter south-westerly, are groaning'[200]

will suggest a badly affected and struggling republic, while whirlwinds and gales will stand for dangers and calamities. Thus

Fulvum fingatur in ignibus aurum,
'tawny gold is shaped in the flames'[201]

can stand for a similar sentiment, that loyalty is often to be proved in time of misfortune.

So numerous are the allegories that can be derived from various narratives that, generally speaking, you can achieve anything you wish by using your reasoning, especially if you're employing maxims and other types of saying.

As examples of differences in quality we can use Neoptolemus[202] to help us recall the idea of Achilles, while Socrates will serve the same purpose for Anaxagoras.

So I suppose we should be grateful to you for providing such an excellent example – thank you, Socrates!

Finally I'll review the advantages of the principle of distribution: wedding-flutes can stand for marriage; a single squadron for cavalry; and a roof, walls, ramparts and the individual parts of those things for a house or city. In this case, from the simulacrum and image of one word the construction of a whole sentence often comes to our aid. The same thing usually happens with a picture. So your Mercuries, your Æsculapiuses, Prometheuses and Chirons can stand for sages, and

Calatinuses[203] for distinguished citizens (even impoverished ones), while, all in all, *species* are taken to represent their *genera*[204].

So those are in general the things that seemed to me to be worth saying about the inflection of absolutes, unless by chance you expect me to go to the same trouble regarding how they should be arranged. In such a finely-detailed matter as that the diligence that I bring to my explanations should indeed enable me to flourish. If the harmony of Nature requires me to do so then so be it, but if it does not then it is clear that it is either a rare occurrence or, alternatively, that utility certainly prevails in this instance. Of course, every precept yields before necessity, so now you will need to learn how to recognise mathematical shadows which, in some situations, are the only solutions.

Mathematical shadows.

Since mathematical objects are abstractions and are separate from any concretion of matter[205] they are unable to project simple shadows, nor can they project those shadows that have been modified by the higher reason[206].

Of course, we must understand that we are dealing here with an adumbration of numbers. Since there is not the slightest suspicion that this arrangement – which, indeed, is one of great importance – could have arisen from any observation of nature, it is a subject that merits a brief explanation here.

First, let's deal with those elements that are able to properly stimulate the gaze of the mind[207].

*Humana ante omnes species est optima: nempe hæc
instrumenta capit quæcunque, et ad omnia nata est.*
'The human species is the best of all: it certainly understands these instruments whatever form they take, and it is born for all things.'[208]

It is generally agreed that these elements should be drawn from the shadows of the signs of the Zodiac and of the wandering planets, as also from the sequence of the letters of the alphabet. To avoid any confusion at any time due to excessive similitude you should take care not to use too many of these elements. Indeed, you should record them on the left-hand side, and should make sure that every arithmetical calculation is correct and that the counting-stone prevails over the counting-rod.[209]

In general, that's all that needs to be said about the adumbration of objects.

As long as we carefully notate the forms and shadows we can easily retrieve from our memory anything we wish to remember.

Verbal inflection.

But what we still need to discuss is the modification of *words*, in which regard, even if

Cui lecta potenter erit res,
nec facundia deseret hunc, nec lucidis ordo:
'he who has chosen a subject suited to his ability will be deficient neither in eloquence nor in clarity of organisation'[210]

    and

Verbaque provisam rem non invita sequantur.
'the words come without effort when the subject-matter is well-digested'[211]

we still need to pay close attention to this facet of our subject even if it seems to be a matter of opinion and dissimulation rather than of knowledge.

First we need to understand that words will also inevitably arise from most objects in the genera of both sensory objects and non-sensory objects due to the very nature of those genera. In this respect therefore, what we have already said about objects may also be considered to apply to words.

In situations where the approval of objects proves futile it is usually sufficient to use a notation (if you can find time to practice it) consisting of similar words, unchanged and unchangeable as to case[212], or translations. But since the joints follow the parts of the body of which they form an element[213] there is no need to take any further trouble over the words.

Since that's what your philosophy is all about that is something that is, of course, very much a part of your experience. But just in case you, as a ravenous Greek Sophist, should desire some further elucidation of this kind, it may help if I provide some.

First therefore, let the shape of the letters be placed in certain persons, then in their distinctive actions, and then in the same way in the adjuncts.

Now that the necessary preparations have been made in such a way that even Alledius[214] may promptly and expeditiously assign as many letters of such a kind, along with their effects and adjuncts, and do the same for the remaining ones, you should surely not be in any doubt that we can perform any matchings that might be required by an interchanging[215] of the letters and the effects/adjuncts?

Now arrange just the consonants, and also the five proper vowels[216], which should be arranged individually. You should look for the finals and liquids[218] in the person's gestures, but you should record everything by means of well-ordered 'masks'[219]. You will certainly be able to record everything you need to remember, just as if you were writing characters in wax.

The principle of the shadows.

So that is how the shadows are 'composed' as it were. Now let's deal with the principle of the shadows and the topic of adjuncts.

Since, with a bit of imagination, multiple shadows can be produced from any individual object,

Cum præsertim aliis eadem in regione locoque,
Longe dissimiles animus res cogitet omnes:
'when, especially for others in that same region and place, the mind may be reflecting upon things quite dissimilar'[220]

and a simple formation may be made more secure and the reflected shadow of the sense may prove effective, then because that same thing touches the boundary on both sides we seem to be presented with an opportunity to, as we expressed it above, 'levy some troops'[221]:

Scilicet arte madent simulacra et docta feruntur.
'for images are imbued with art and, suitably instructed, are carried about.'[222]

And since it is certain that what will be most firmly attached to people's minds will be that which has been conveyed and impressed by the sensory apparatus, but that the keenest sense is that of vision, you should first ensure that all the shadows, both simple and inflected, are only conveyed to the mind after receiving the approval of the eyes[223], and that they are described and defined in terms of light, colour, shape and size. Otherwise, of course

> *pars maxima fallit,*
> *propter opinatus animi quos addimus ipsi,*
> *pro visis ut sint, quæ non sint sensibu' visa.*
> 'the greatest part deceives because of the mental suppositions which we add to it, so that things which may not have been perceived by the senses are treated as if they have been.'[224]

If an object will permit it, allow it to retain its dimensional characteristics; if it will not, then modify it by using adjuncts.

Make sure also that the shadows are bright and sharp, and in every way of such a kind that they can quickly approach and rapidly penetrate the mind, since it is easy for:

> *uno commovet ictu,*
> *Qualibet una animum nobis subtilis imago.*
> 'any one subtle image to stimulate our mind with a single impression.'[225]

Make them distinctive therefore by imparting to them some novel or even amusing characteristic, and have them display some outstanding kind of beauty or even ugliness:

> *Creentque*
> *Tenuem animi natura[m] intus visumque lacessant.*
> 'and bring into being and excite the delicate substance of the mind within as well as the vision.'[226]

Make sure they are too not vague, for sometimes:

> *Species vanescit iacta in inane.*
> 'the representation vanishes, hurled into empty space.'[227]

If the cognitive faculties have increased then allow the subjects to escape[228].

In addition, make sure that the subjects are dissimilar to one another in form and variety. Even if the sense receives similar forms from the sensory faculties, or has itself created them, always re-examine the functions and work of the vision.

As for foreknowledge, we have already said quite enough about that topic.

Discrimination.

So what happens next? Of course, there will always be changes in discrimination, and it therefore remains for me to say something about this topic, employing similar reasoning to that which we used above.

First we need to define what discrimination is. The reasoning on the subject is certainly diverse, for sometimes discrimination is seen as a rule and a canon of how to live one's life, while at other times it's viewed as a yardstick of the truth.

In fact, this is the very point that has given rise to every quarrel that your Sages have been involved in, with some saying that judgements are a mental image and that there is accordingly a Truth that can be discovered (a view supported by Parmenides[229], Anaxagoras, Dionysodorus[230], and many others) while others contend that nothing can be known or perceived (whence has arisen your own cunning dissembling), while finally there are still others who feel that we should be reticent about making such an assertion, and would ask:

Quis novit autem an hoc vivere sit mori?
an vero mors sit quod vocamus vivere?
'Who has ever known whether this living may be dying, or whether dying is what we call living?'[231]

Evidently the reasoning of the elegant Pyrrho[232] has pleased many with its brevity. It is certainly very courteous towards other thinkers, and does not even exclude the donkey of Silenus[233] or Cyllenius[234]. But among those who actually hand down judgements there is less continuity of agreement. For such a person only sense and reason give satisfaction. Hence:

Ne te Deus ancipitem iuxta hanc viam cogat,
Iudicare inconsiderato visu, et resonante auditu:
Sed iudices ratione accuratam sententiam.
'Lest God force you, undecided, down this path of judging with heedless vision and with a clamour in your ears, always express

an opinion that has been carefully prepared by reason.'[235]

We ourselves however prefer the concept of discrimination to be defined in terms of the function and virtue of both vision and thought, for it is through the visual and cognitive apparatus that whatever is perceived as a result of the impulse of the faculties or which was fashioned by the work of the senses can finally be insinuated into the memory by a regular stimulus, for the mind[236] has its own sort of sphere and its distinct orbs, namely the senses, vision, thinking and memory. The memory is at the centre and, of course, we situate the sensory faculties on the boundary, but nothing can be moved to the centre except by means of all the intermediate orbs. That is why, when the faculties are stimulated, there is not an immediate folding-together[237] of our senses and our memory.

So that should be enough to make clear the value and contribution of our subject of enquiry, namely discrimination.

The task of the vision.

When the faculties have received a stimulus and that same sensation has been projected into the subjects and shadows, then the vision exerts its influence. Certainly the whole of the vision is expended in judging the arrangement, but since we set up the subjects like pockets or receptacles we shall first need to explain the rationale behind our organisation of the subjects, whatever form that organisation may take, for just as we grasp the objects themselves on the basis of simulacra, so in the same way we grasp the organisation of the subjects from those subjects.

First therefore, you should if possible establish just one prevailing idea in the subjects. This idea may soon need to be divided into common parts, which will themselves be divided into other less common parts, which are then divided into particulars[238]. Finally, the particulars are separated in a certain order into third-parts. Although this may perhaps seem to be at odds with the character of the memory-locus, in what way does it interfere with the task of naming?

So trust therefore in the idea of the idea, and observe closely the common parts of the common parts, the particulars of the particulars and the third-parts of the third-parts! You can add new tenths too, and (if it's any use) some 'veilings'[239] which may be constructed for the purposes of the adjuvants and for the support and convenience of the Golden Chain[240]. Indeed, there is nothing in this entire discourse from which you are more likely to reap greater rewards than this. If you assume the right 'gaze of the rational soul'[241], and take great pains to avoid an oblique or diametric one then you should find that light will be shed on everything.

Finally, you should make sure that the distance and interval of the field[242] from the eyes of the mind[243] is in proportion to the faculties.

Now it remains for us to discuss the role that thinking plays in the animation process.

But perhaps I'm mistaken, and you don't actually need any additional material on thinking, since someone who intrinsically grasps this method can do as much as he likes, whereas someone who does not will toil in vain and achieve nothing at all!

Good organisation can certainly achieve a great deal in any situation of this kind, but I would strongly deny that our skill can do just about anything in this task we have set ourselves, as you may recall from the controversy surrounding the assumption made regarding planetary motion[244].

First of all, don't spoil the work you do with the shadows by being lazy. Make sure the subjects in which the shadows are placed are clearly and distinctly identified. Use exaggeration to produce sharply-delineated events and striking circumstances, but do not judge in accordance with the rules of Nature, and do not judge rashly either, but rather by using your skill on the basis purely of the instruction you have received, for then the results will accurately reflect the stimulus and your strong feelings.

The Gatekeeper of Memory[245].
The intellect, which is itself a sense, will extend itself towards those things that have moved it and will seek to envelop and retain them[246], for:

Nam quia tenuia sunt, nisi se contendat acute,
cernere non potis est animus: proinde omnia quæ sunt,
præterea, pereunt.
'since images are delicate, you cannot discern them unless the mind makes an exceptional effort to do so. Hence all existing images pass away apart from those that the mind has struggled to discern.'[247]

This also occurs in the external eyes[248]. Finally negation asserts itself, and with it there occurs a dual transformation[249], namely of you into the object, and of the object into itself. This is that quickened power of the mind[250], and a carefully-achieved loosening of the mind from the body. Thus an (as yet unformed) thought-process[251], that of the shadows, forsakes matter and time and grasps the ideas and rationales, since it has a natural propensity for such an understanding.

Every skill is something to be admired, but this, which causes inanimate objects to appear as if they are living and breathing, is especially worthy of our admiration.

So, son of Sophroniscus, now you've heard what I have to say about memory. What happens next is up to you. It all depends on your intensive study, practice and hard work to ensure that nothing can escape your attention, so that everything sinks in, and so that you can acknowledge the hand of Anaxagoras in all this. This is a subject that requires especial dedication, and you must always abide by its rules. But since you're here on Earth, remember to give satisfaction to Anaxagoras, as I have just reminded you. Although I must admit that I find this whole change of outlook of yours quite suspicious, and get the impression that there may perhaps be some hidden motive behind it[252].

The End.

1   Latin *Arelii*. This use of the genitive is a most unusual way of indicating a person's origins. Normally one would expect *Areliensis*, but it is hard to see what else it could mean other than a person from the village of Errol (now in Perth and Kinross). Errol's location on the River Tay would help explain Dicsone's fascination with the ship of William Wallace. Henry Adamson (1581-1637), in his poem *The Muses Threnodie*, which is famous for its references to Masonry and Roscrucianism, makes flattering reference to 'Master Dickeson [sic]' as the finder and salvager of William Wallace's ship, scuttled in the Tay to stop the English fleet reaching the Scottish hero's fastness. Whether Dicsone's salvaging of the ship had a magical or other esoteric motive we do not know.
See Paul Ferguson, 'Where is the Ship of William Wallace?': https://www.academia.edu/37917652/WHERE_IS_THE_SHIP_OF_WILLIAM_WALLACE.

2   *Sub umbra illius, quam desideraveram sedi*, from the Song of Solomon 2.3: 'As the apple tree among the trees of the wood, so is my beloved among the sons. I sat down under his shadow with great delight, and his fruit was sweet to my taste.' This was a favourite quotation of Giordano Bruno (see, for example, the opening of his *Triginta Intentiones Umbrarum*, Intention I A).

2   Basson (1555 – 1613) appears to have been the first English publisher and printer in Leiden of any note. For reasons unknown to us he left his native England and lived first in Cologne and then, from around 1584, in Leiden where, from 1585 onwards, he had his own bookshop and imprint. Ten years later he was admitted to the University of Leiden, and from then on was closely involved with thesis-publishing, translation and related activities. He also seems to have been a member of the essentially Anabaptist *Familia Caritatis*, to which the famous printer Christopher Plantin also belonged. One of his efforts was *The Coniugations in Englishe and Netherdutche* of 1586, a translation of Gabriel Meurier's primer of the Dutch language and, apparently, the first book of its kind intended for English-speaking readers. Yates, in *The Rosicrucian Enlightenment* (Shambhala Books 1978, pp. 74-75), tells us that he was a protégé of the Earl of Leicester (the dedicatee of the *De Umbra*) and was interested in the occult. His son Godfrey, also a printer, published Robert Fludd's Rosicrucian booklets, the *Apologia* and the *Tractatus*. See J. A. van Dorsten, *Thomas Basson 1555-1613: English Printer at Leiden* (Leiden 1961) and the same author's 'Thomas Basson (1555-1613), English printer at Leiden, in Quærendo' 15(3):195-224 January 1985, as well as Keith L. Sprunger, *Trumpets from the Tower: English Puritan Printing in the Netherlands 1600-1640* (Brill 1994), p. 131 et seq.

4   The same year that James I published his *Dæmonologie*, a philosophical dissertation on necromancy and related matters which is believed to have been used by Shakespeare as one of the sources for his *Macbeth*.

5   Latin *horizon*. Though this is a Brunonian term, Dicsone seems to be using it to signify a part of his model of the human mind based on his reading in natural philosophy. See footnote 237.

6   Giordano Bruno: *De Innumerabilibus et Immenso*, Book VII, Ch. 1, lines 37-38.

7   Lucretius, *De Rerum Natura*, Book I, lines 331 and 336. Dicsone seems to have 'discovered' Lucretius in the

interval between the *De Umbra* and the *Thamus*, possibly through coming into possession of Michel de Montaigne's copy of the famous Lambin edition (see footnote 148).

8   In his *Phædrus*, 274b–278d.

9   Horace, *Art of Poetry*, lines 114-116. Davus is a name commonly held by slaves in Roman comedy.

10 A type of narrative in which an author communicates with his or her audience by speaking as a different person or as an object.

11 Lucretius, *De Rerum Natura*, Book IV, lines 614-615.

12 Or, in Hazlitt's translation, 'Olus, what is't to thee/What with themselves does he or she?' These lines are from the opening of the 10th Epigram of Martial's Seventh Book, which is about a slanderer and gossip called Olus. Dicsone misquotes this passage (*faciat* instead of *faciant*), as does Michel de Montaigne in his 'Essay on Vanity' from his *Third Book of Essays*, which was published in March 1580 and from which, given the error and the date, Dicsone may well have drawn the quotation. It is worth noting here that Lucretius, from whom Dicsone quotes extensively in the *Thamus*, was also one of Montaigne's favourite authors. See Michael Screech, *Montaigne's annotated copy of Lucretius: a transcription and study of the manuscript, notes and pen-marks,* Librairie Droz, 1998.

13 Lucretius, *De Rerum Natura*, Book VI, line 16, in a passage where Lucretius renders homage to Epicurus by describing how the great philosopher saw that humanity was unhappy despite all its blessings because he himself (the 'vessel') was corrupt ('leaky and full of holes') rather than because of external circumstances.

14 Possibly a reference to the passage in Plato's *Symposium* (212c et seq.)

where a drunken Alcibiades, the lover of Socrates, gate-crashes the party. Alternatively, Dicsone's may have been trying to flatter Dudley's classical scholarship by referring to the *Frogs* of Aristophanes, in which the god of the wine-harvest, Dionysus, makes ludicrous appearances at the doors of Hercules and Pluto.

15 Giordano Bruno: *De Innumerabilibus et Immenso*, Book VII, Ch. 1, lines 6-7.

16 Presumably of the mind, a favourite metaphor of Dicsone's.

17 Latin *naturæ vestigia*, see Lucretius, *De Rerum Natura*, Book III, line 310 for this term. See also footnote 109.

18 The text has *iudicium*, judgement, but we suspect this is a typographical error for *indicium*, a sign or token, and we have translated it accordingly.

19 Giordano Bruno, *De Monade Numero et Figura*, Introduction, last two lines. These lines (and, indeed, the whole Introduction to *De Monade Numero et Figura*) were a favourite text of the Romantic poet Samuel Taylor Coleridge, who was a lifelong admirer of Bruno. See Hilary Gatti, *Essays on Giordano Bruno*, Princeton, 2010, Chapter 10, 'Romanticism: Bruno and Coleridge'. This whole latter section is, of course, a riposte to the 'G.P. of Cambridge' who had written the *Antidicsonus* (see the section *Decoding Dicsone*).

20 This is closely based on a similar passage in Plato's *Phædrus* 274C-275B, in which Socrates recounts the interview between Thamus, King of Egypt, and Theuth (here: Theutates), who has just invented the art of writing.

21 i.e. Hermes.

22 For Theutates see, for example, William Reeves, *The Apologies of Justin Martyr, Tertullian, and Minutius Felix* (1716): 'And in his 3d Book de Divinat[ione], he [Cicero] mentions

five Mercuries, and makes Mercury Theutates the fifth, who slew Argos, and for that flew into Egypt, and there instructed the Ægyptians in Laws and Letters, from which Theutates the first Month of their Year, that is September, was called Theuth. This was the Mercury the Gauls sacrifice to, and which Lucan in his First Book refers to: *Ex quibus immitis placatur sanguine diro/Theutates, horrensque feris altaribus Hesus,* i.e. 'And they for whom the ruthless Teutates is appeased with bloodshed horrible, and Hesus awful with his cruel altars' (Lucan, *Pharsalia*, Book I, lines 444-5). Note the reference to the Gauls, which helps underline the Celtic character of Theutates.

23 Latin *adumbratio*, from *adumbro*, 'to cast a shadow over something' and, by extension, 'to represent an object artistically with due mingling of light and shadow'. See Cicero, *De Natura Deorum*, Book I, Ch. 27: 'You argue that [the gods according to Epicurus] have figures without consistency or solidity, and which are neither modelled nor projecting but are only pure, light and luminous... so in Epicurus's deity there are no things as such, but merely the similitude of things. Try therefore to convince me of what one cannot even conceive: go on, draw the outlines and shapes of those *foreshadowed deities*' [*adumbrati dei*].

24 Latin *vas*, a vase, vessel or dish. This is reminiscent of the *sinus* (pocket) or *receptaculum* (receptacle) whereby the subject acts as a container for the shadow (see Ch. VI).

25 See Aristotle, *On the Heavens*, Book 3, Section 8: 'Earth, again, they call a cube because it is stable and at rest. But it rests only in its own place, not anywhere; from any other it moves if nothing hinders, and fire and the other bodies do the same. The obvious

inference, therefore, is that fire and each several element is in a foreign place a sphere or a pyramid, but in its own a cube...Again, combustion of a body produces fire, and fire is a sphere or a pyramid. The body, then, is turned into spheres or pyramids.'

26 See the *Corpus Hermeticum*, Book VII (VIII), 1: 'Whither stumble ye, sots, who have sopped up the wine of ignorance unmixed, and can so far not carry it that ye already even spew it forth?' (G. R. S. Mead's translation).

27 It is hard to know what is meant here, unless it is a reference to the importance that the Ancient Egyptians and Greeks attached to the washing of the hands before religious ceremonies associated with the Mysteries, or perhaps it refers to the passage in Book II (III), 8 of the *Corpus Hermeticum*: 'Regard the animals down here, a man, for instance, swimming! The water moves, yet the resistance of his hands and feet give him stability, so that he is not borne along with it, nor sunk thereby.' (G. R. S. Mead's translation).

28 See the *Corpus Hermeticum*, Book VII (VIII), 2-3: 'But first thou must tear off from thee the cloak which thou dost wear, the web of ignorance, the ground of bad, corruption's chain, the carapace of darkness, the living death, sensation's corpse, the tomb thou carriest with thee, the robber in thy house, who through the things he loveth, hateth thee, and through the things he hateth, bears thee malice. Such is the hateful cloak thou wearest, that throttles thee [and holds thee] down to it, in order that thou may'st not gaze above, and, having seen the Beauty of the Truth, and Good that dwells therein, detest the bad of it; having found out the plot that it hath schemed against thee, by making void of sense those seeming things which men think senses' (G. R. S. Mead's

29 Latin *sinistra*, 'the left (hand)', here apparently used as a synonym for Hell. The left was the side of ill-omen for the Greeks, just as it was the side of good tidings for the Romans. It is interesting that another Latin word for *left*, *scævus*, is derived from the Greek word σκαιός, 'skaios', which seems to be derived from the Proto-Indo-European word *skeh$_2$-i-uo-, via the Proto-Italic *skaiwo, meaning *shadow*. In the northern hemisphere, when one faces eastwards the sun is always on the right-hand side and one's shadow is therefore always on the left-hand side, which may explain this relationship.

30 See the *Corpus Hermeticum* XVI, *The Perfect Sermon* or the *Asclepius*, VII.1: 'Asclepius: Are not the senses of all men, Thrice-greatest one, the same? Trismegistus: Nay, [my] Asclepius, all have not won true reason; but wildly rushing in pursuit of [reason's] counterfeit, they never see the thing itself, and are deceived. And this breeds evil in their minds, and [thus] transforms the best of animals into the nature of a beast and manners of the brutes' (G.R.S. Mead's translation).

31 Latin *virgine cæsa*. See Virgil, *Aeneid*, Book II, lines 116-117: 'O Greeks, you appeased the winds with blood and a *virgin slain* when you first came to the Trojan shores'. This is a reference to the story of Iphigenia, in which Artemis, the goddess of hunting, wild animals and chastity, punishes Agamemnon after he kills a stag in a sacred grove and boasts that he is a better hunter than Artemis herself by becalming the winds at Aulis and so keeping the Greek fleet, which was about to leave for the Trojan War, in port. The seer Calchas tells Agamemnon that the only way to appease the goddess is to sacrifice his daughter Iphigenia. Artemis then snatches her from the altar and substitutes a deer. In one version of the legend she then becomes the immortal companion of Artemis. It may also be a reference to the Virgin Queen Elizabeth: see, for example, the pre-Armada propaganda ode quoted in Tucker Brooke, 'Some Pre-Armada Propagandist Poetry in England (1585-1586)', *Proceedings of the American Philosophical Society*, Vol. 85, No. 1 (Nov. 17, 1941), pp. 71-83, which contains the line *Gaudentne cæsa virgine Cælites*, 'Do the Immortals really rejoice in a virgin slain?'

32 Latin *materiæ vindices*. In the *Art of Memory* (Routledge 1999), p. 269, Frances Yates translates this phrase as 'punishments of matter', but *vindex* means someone who takes revenge or who defends something.

33 Contrast with the use of 'soul' (*anima*) in the *De Umbra*.

34 The atmosphere of this passage is strongly reminiscent of Book IV of the *Consolation of Philosophy* by Boethius, another Latin author with whom Dicsone seems to have been familiar: '...whence it comes to pass that the bad cease to be what they are, while only the outward aspect is still left to show they have been men. Wherefore, by their perversion to badness, they have lost their true human nature. Further, since righteousness alone can raise men above the level of humanity, it must needs be that unrighteousness degrades below man's level those whom it has cast out of man's estate. It results, then, that thou canst not consider him human whom thou seest transformed by vice. The violent despoiler of other men's goods, enflamed with covetousness, surely resembles a wolf. A bold and restless spirit, ever wrangling in law-courts, is like some yelping cur. The secret

schemer, taking pleasure in fraud and stealth, is own brother to the fox. The passionate man, frenzied with rage, we might believe to be animated with the soul of a lion. The coward and runaway, afraid where no fear is, may be likened to the timid deer. He who is sunk in ignorance and stupidity lives like a dull ass. He who is light and inconstant, never holding long to one thing, is for all the world like a bird. He who wallows in foul and unclean lusts is sunk in the pleasures of a filthy hog. So it comes to pass that he who by forsaking righteousness ceases to be a man cannot pass into a Godlike condition, but actually turns into a brute beast' (Book IV, Section III, in H. R. James' translation).

35   Along with Minos and Rhadamanthus, one of the three judges of the dead in the Underworld.

36   Possibly a reference to the story found in the Greek satirical writer Lucian's *The Tyrant*, in which Hermes (sometimes identified with Theutates) manages to 'lose' one of the dead mortals he is supposed to be presenting before the three judges of the Underworld.

37   Naucratis (or Naukratis) was a city of Ancient Egypt on the Canopic branch of the Nile. It was the first and, for a long time, the only permanent Greek colony in Egypt, and was a meeting-point for Greek and Egyptian culture. See Plato, *Phædrus*, 274, where Socrates says, 'Well, I heard that in the neighbourhood of Naucratis, in Egypt, there lived one of the ancient gods of that country; the same to whom that holy bird is consecrate which they call, as you know, Ibis, and whose own name was Theuth.' See also the start of the second prosopopœia in the *De Umbra*.

38   This is a rehearsal of the argument about the discovery and value of writing in Plato's *Phædrus*, 274-275.

39   Virgil, *Aeneid*, Book I, line 140, from a passage where Neptune calms down a storm that the vengeful Juno has ordered Aeolus, the god of the winds, to unleash against *Aeneas* and his fleet and reminds Aeolus that he is simply a sort of 'jailer of the winds' who should only release them from custody on his instructions. It is a common retort to pedants working futilely within a narrow compass.

40   Latin *in animo...scriberent*. Cf. Seneca the Elder, *Controversiæ*, Book I, pr. 18, referring to the remarkable memory of his friend Marcus Porcius Latro (died 4 BC), a celebrated Roman rhetorician considered to be one of the founders of scholastic rhetoric: *aiebat se in animo scribere*, i.e. 'He used to say that he wrote his meditations in his soul.' Earlier in that same book Seneca boasts about his own astonishing memory, claiming to have been able in his youth to memorise 2000 names at random and repeat them in the correct sequence, as well as 200 lines of poetry which he would then repeat to his school-chums in reverse order. See Patricia Fairweather, *Seneca the Elder* (Cambridge University Press 2007), chapter on *Memoria*, p. 228ff.

41   An allusion to Bruno's contention that the Art of Memory was designed to teach ethics as well as train the mind.

42   Frances Yates (*Art of Memory*, p. 269ff.) follows John Durkan ('Alexander Dickson and S.T.C. 6823', *The Bibliothek*, 3 (1962)) in stating that the Socrates portrayed here is intended as a satirical portrait of Petrus Ramus.

43   See Plato's *Apology* 21. 'You are doubtless familiar with the name of Chærephon... Upon the occasion of his having visited [the temple dedicated to Apollo in] Delphi once he ventured upon inquiring of the oracle, and do not express displeasure at what I say my friends, for he asked if there was

any one wiser than me? Upon this the Pythian priestess announced, that there was none wiser.' (Charles Stuart Stanford's translation). To be fair to Socrates he subsequently devoted a great deal of energy to trying to prove the oracle wrong.

44 The eponymous hero of a lost work by the philosopher Phædo of Elis. We know some of its contents from a passage in Cicero's *Tusculan Disputations* 4.80. Cicero tells us that Zopyrus claimed to be a master of face-reading, and made some unflattering comments about Socrates in a public assembly after examining him. Socrates admitted to the vices, which he claimed were perfectly natural, and said he had mastered them by the use of his reason.

45 This and the later quotations in this dialogue seem to be based on the 1538 Latin translation by Andreas Divus of Aristophanes' *Clouds* (lines 926ff.), in which the Greek playwright lampooned the fashionable intellectual movements of contemporary Athens. The trial and execution of Socrates may have been an indirect result of the play's unflattering portrait of him.

46 One of Cicero's favourite expressions (see, for example, its use in his *Epistulæ ad Atticum* 8.16). It is taken from Homer's *Iliad* 6.442. Cicero used it to mean 'a fear of public opinion'.

47 One of the founders of the Cynic school of philosophy and a noted ascetic. Once described by Plato as 'a Socrates gone mad'.

48 A lieutenant and friend of Hector during the Trojan War who was blessed with second sight.

49 More correctly, *Falsus honor juvat, et mendax infamia terret,/Quem? nisi mendosum et mendacem?* Horace, *Epistles*, Book I, XVI, lines 39-40, *Ad Quintum.*

50 This is a translation of line 319 from Book IX of Homer's *Iliad.* Thomas

Aquinas quotes it in his unfinished commentary on Aristotle (though the translation may not be by him) and so does Denis Lambin in his 1567 translation of Aristotle's *Politics*, which may be where Dicsone got it from. Lambin, Professor of Latin (from early 1561) and then of Classical Greek (from later in 1561) at the Collège de France in Paris, is an interesting figure in the present context as he was both a close friend of Ramus (Lambin is alleged to have died of shock on hearing of the death of his friend in the anti-Protestant Massacre of St. Bartholomew) and also the target of allegations of heresy and paganising tendencies by the Italian Catholics. In the Introduction to his famous annotated edition of the Roman poet Lucretius (1563) Lambin set out his stall: 'Should we really ignore a poet who not only delights our minds but who also unravels the most obscure problems of natural philosophy in the most beautiful poetry?'

51 The father of Socrates and, according to some (e.g. Timon of Philius, as quoted in Diogenes Laertius, *Lives of the Eminent Philosophers*, Book II, Ch. XIX), a mason by profession, as indeed Socrates may have been in early life.

52 A quotation from a work by Cicero, *Hortensius*, which was largely lost in the 6th century. Fragments are known to us through the work of writers such as the late Roman lexicographer Nonius Marcellus, who compiled a 20-volume compendium of Latin literature. In the *Hortensius*, Cicero, Hortensius, Quintus Lutatius Catulus and Lucius Licinius Lucullus discuss the best use of one's leisure. Hortensius argues that oratory is the greatest art, but Cicero appeals strongly for the study of philosophy. St. Augustine attributed his own

interest in philosophy to reading this work.

53 *Calculum reducam*. A *calculus* was a counting-stone. Another quotation from Cicero courtesy of Nonius Marcellus.

54 Latin *complexio*, a rhetorical figure by which one constantly refers to something that has recently been said.

55 Another reference to Plato's *Phædrus* (261), where Socrates refers to the 'arts of speaking' compiled by Nestor, Odysseus and Palamedes in their leisure-time at Troy.

56 *Genesis* I.4.

57 Latin *radii [Dei]*. This phrase has a distinctly Hermetic ring to it. Dicsone may have been reading the recently-published *Traité de la vérité de la religion chrétienne contre les athées, épicuriens, payens, juifs, mahométans et autres infidèles* (Antwerp, 1581) by Philippe de Mornay (1549-1623). In this much-translated publishing sensation De Mornay, a Protestant open to esoteric ideas, quotes extensively from the *Divine Pimander* of Hermes to demonstrate the essential truth of Christianity, e.g. in Chapter II he writes: 'But, says Hermes, the rays of God are actions, the rays of the world are the rays of Nature, and the rays of man are the arts and sciences'. See Florian Ebeling, *The Secret History of Hermes Trismegistus: Hermeticism from Ancient to Modern Times*, Cornell University Press, 2007, pp. 84ff.

58 See Marsilio Ficino, *De raptu Pauli ad tertium cælum et animi immortalitate*, Ch. XXVIII, *Corpora sunt umbræ Dei, animæ vero Dei imagines immortales*, 'Bodies are the shadows of God; indeed they are the immortal images of the soul of God.'

59 Latin *anima mundi*, dealt with extensively in Plato's *Timæus*.

60 Another paraphrase from the Divus translation of Aristophanes' *Clouds*.

61 Presumably a sarcastic reference to Plato's analogy in the *Timæus* of the Receptacle (the material or spatial substratum of the universe) as an ointment that serves as a neutral base for various fragrances (50e5-8).

62 Timæus of Locri is a character in two of Plato's dialogues, *Timæus* and *Critias*, where he appears as a philosopher of the Pythagorean school. He may not have been a historical figure but simply a creation of Plato's.

63 Latin *in fictæ simulationis specie*. See Cicero, *De Natura Deorum*, Book I: *In specie autem fictæ simulationis, sicut reliquæ virtutes, ita pietas inesse non potest*, 'But piety, like the other virtues, cannot involve itself in a kind of dissimulation'.

64 Lucretius, *De Rerum Natura*, Book IV, lines 508-509.

65 Latin *in naturam...intrandum erat, eaque quid postularet, penitus videndum*. See Cicero, *De Finibus Bonorum et Malorum*, Book V, Ch. 16: *Intrandum igitur est in Rerum Naturam et penitus quid ea postulet pervidendum; aliter enim nosmet ipsos nosse non possumus*, 'We must therefore penetrate into the nature of things, and come to understand its requirements thoroughly, otherwise we cannot know ourselves'.

66 Lucretius, *De Rerum Natura*, Book IV, lines 518-522. A passage that no doubt especially appealed to Dicsone as a Mason.

67 It is worth comparing this passage with the corresponding lines in the *De Umbra*, 'a soul that doesn't understand any of the things that exist falls blindly into the physical passions.'

68 See Cicero, *De Finibus Bonorum et Malorum*, Book II.ii.5 for this phrase and a discussion of the related issues.

69 See Plato's *Republic*, respectively Book IV 423e and Book V 457c-d; Book III 415e-416e; and Book V

457b-c.

70 Plato divides his Just Society into three classes: Producers (all professions other than warrior or guardian), Auxiliaries (warriors), and Guardians (or philosopher-kings, chosen from among the auxiliaries). In a Just Society the Producers have no share in ruling but simply obey the Guardians.

71 i.e. as chattels held in common by men.

72 Virgil, *Eclogues*, Book III, line 3.

73 A direct quotation from Cicero, *De Finibus Bonorum et Malorum*, II.89.

74 Virgil, *Eclogues*, Book I, line 514.

75 Socrates and Xanthippe had three sons: Lamprocles, Sophroniscus and Menexenus. Aristotle had a low opinion of all of them, calling them 'silly and dull' (*Rhetoric* 1390b30–32).

76 Socrates claimed to have an 'inner voice' (the *dæmonion*) which warned him against certain courses of action but never told him what to do. Plutarch assumed that this was a 'familiar spirit', and even wrote a book about it entitled *De Genio Socratis* ('On the genie of Socrates'), as did Apuleius (*De Deo Socratis*, 'On the God of Socrates'). The Neoplatonists and some of the Church Fathers also seem to have seen it as a personal demon, though whether they considered it to be good or evil they did not always make clear. Xenophon, in his *Memorabilia*, describes it in detail: 'It was in the mouths of men that Socrates declared that the Deity, or Dæmonion made things known to him, or gave him signs by which to know them... He used to say that the Dæmonion signified (things) to him: and that he often advised those who were with him to do some things, and not to do others, as the Dæmonion forewarned him... For he thought that the gods had care of men in a way unlike that which most men imagine: for they suppose that the Gods know indeed some things, and do not know others. But Socrates believed the Gods to know all things: whatsoever things are said, or done, or purposed in secret: and that they are everywhere present: and that they make known human things to men.' And Plato gives a number of instances where the inner voice came to the aid of Socrates, e.g. in the *Phædrus*, 242: 'When I was about to cross the river, the Dæmonion, the accustomed sign, came, which restrains me when I am about to do anything; and I seemed to hear a certain voice, which did not suffer me to proceed until I should have expiated myself, as having in some way offended against God.' See Henry Edward Manning, *The Dæmon of Socrates, A Paper read before the Royal Institution*, Jan.26, 1872.

77 This was Cicero's abusive term for changing one's name to improve one's social status. See *Brutus*, 68, where Cicero tells us about C. Stalenus, 'who had adopted himself and so changed himself from a Stalenus into an Ælius'.

78 A paraphrase of a line from Cicero, *De Republica*, Book IV, Ch. 10, referring to the criticism, on the stage, of politicians: *Patiamur, inquit, etsi eiusmodi cives a censore melius est quam a poeta notari*, 'We may tolerate that, though indeed the censure of the magistrate would, in these cases, have been more efficacious than the satire of the poet.'

79 Anaxagoras of Clazomenæ (born *c.*500 – 480 BCE) was the first of the Presocratic philosophers to live in Athens. He propounded a physical theory of "everything-in-everything," and claimed that *nous* (intellect or mind) was the motive cause of the cosmos. See Plato, *Phædo* 46 and *Apology* 14.

80 Alcibiades, son of Cleinias (c. 450 – 404 BC), from the *deme* of Scambonidæ, was a prominent Athenian statesman, orator, and general. Xenophon attempted to clear Socrates' name at trial by relaying information that Alcibiades was always corrupt and that Socrates merely failed in attempting to teach him morality.

81 Another quotation from Divus' translation of Aristophanes' *Clouds*, lines 1071ff.

82 The wife of Socrates, a notorious nagger and shrew.

83 Latin *capite damnatus*. For this technical term, see Cicero, *Tusculan Disputations*, Book I, *De Contemnenda Morte*, XXII, 50. A Roman citizen was said to be *capite damnatus* when he was deprived of his rights of liberty, of citizenship, and of family. By the Roman law if any one was to be punished with death (*morte multatus*), he had first to be *capite damnatus*.

84 Latin *officii iudicio*, another phrase from Cicero. See *Tusculan Disputations*, Book III, Ch. 27.

85 Aristippus of Cyrene (c. 435 – c. 356 BCE) founded the Cyrenaic school of philosophy. A pupil of Socrates, he adopted a very different outlook, teaching an ethical hedonism.

86 Dionysius the Younger (c. 397 BCE – 343 BCE), also known as Dionysius II, ruled Syracuse from 367 BCE to 357 BCE and from 346 BCE to 344 BCE. When his father died in 367 BCE Dionysius, still in his twenties, inherited supreme power and ruled under the guidance of his uncle Dion, who became increasingly concerned about his nephew's dissoluteness and so summoned his old teacher Plato to Syracuse. Dion and Plato tried to restructure the government and establish Dionysius as the archetypal 'philosopher-king', but without

success. See Plato, *Seventh Letter*.

87 Xenophon of Athens (c. 430 – 354 BCE) was a philosopher, historian and student of Socrates. He was also probably the greatest military commander of his time. Diogenes Laertius reports how Xenophon met Socrates: 'They say that Socrates met him in a narrow lane, and put his stick across it and prevented him from passing by, asking him where all kinds of necessary things were sold. And when he had answered him, he asked him again where men were made good and virtuous. And as he did not know, he said, 'Follow me, then, and learn.' And from this time forth, Xenophon became a follower of Socrates.'

88 Antisthenes (c. 445 – c. 365 BCE) was an ardent disciple of Socrates, developing the ethical side of his teaching and recommending an ascetic life conducted in accordance with virtue. Later writers saw him as the founder of the Cynic philosophy. He was present when Socrates was executed and never forgave his master's persecutors. His work on Natural Philosophy (the *Physicus*) contained a theory of the nature of the gods, arguing that although humanity believed in many gods, there was only one God. He also argued that God is like nothing we know on Earth and therefore cannot be portrayed.

89 Crates of Thebes (c. 365 – c. 285 BCE) was a Cynic philosopher who gave away his personal fortune to live on the streets of Athens.

90 The links between these philosophers and Socrates may have been fabricated by the later Stoics to establish a line of succession from Socrates to Zeno, the founder of the Stoic school.

91 Quite true, but according to Diogenes Laertius in his *Lives of the Eminent Philosophers* Antisthenes walked from the Piræus to Athens every day to converse with Socrates, a distance of

some five miles.

92 Presumably a sly reference by the very Catholic Dicsone to the Reformers' belief that it was impossible for man to resist grace.

93 Latin *repetundarum iudicium*, a legal term denoting, in its narrowest sense, a recovery through legal action of extorted money.

94 *Reponendum* carries the idea of something being revived or restored, as the Art of Memory was a partial revival of previous habits of humanity in pre-literate times, rather than something entirely new.

95 Latin *sensus*. Compare with Dicsone's use of the much rarer *sensa*, nominative plural of *sensum*, in this passage in the *De Umbra*.

96 A quotation from Cicero, *De Divinatione*, Book II, Ch. 11.

97 Another quotation from Petrus Ramus. See his *Præfatio Tertia, Rami de Cæsaris Militia* (1559), where, referring to Cæsar, he remarks that 'it is fitting for a great prince both to seek peace in wartime and to refuse to condemn the arts of war in peacetime'.

98 This is a Latin version of lines from Homer, *Iliad*, Book IX, lines 257ff. They seem to be a paraphrase drawn from the marginal Latin translation in Henri Estienne's famous 1566 edition of the *Iliad*. In this passage Odysseus reminds Achilles how his father Peleus must have taught him to be kind to his friends and to control his fearsome temper.

99 This seems to be a splicing of phrases from Ramus and Bruno; see *P. Rami Scholæ in liberales artes*, Book I, Ch. 2, *De Logica Mathematicorum*, Basel 1569 for a similar phrase, *Sacer est morbus, et aspectus fallitur*, which means more or less the same thing, and Giordano Bruno, *De Immenso et Innumeralibus*, Book 3, Ch. 1 for *visus mentitur*.

100 A Latin expression for someone who

is acting rashly. From Ovid, *Heroides*, XVI, line 263: 'But you are in too much of a hurry, for your harvest is only just starting to sprout.'

101 Socrates was initially strongly attracted to and then repelled by the view of Anaxagoras that the cosmos is controlled by *nous*, i.e. mind or intelligence (see Plato, *Phædo*, 97b8ff.).

102 A paraphrase of Petrus Ramus, *Dialecticæ libri duo*, Beauvais, 1556, Book I, p. 36, *Et quidem ignoratio caussarum, temerariam caussarum efficientiam confinxit*, 'And, indeed, an ignorance of causes gives a false impression of the random effect of causes', by which I assume he means that we believe in good or bad fortune because we do not always understand the chain of causes which precedes events.

103 Plautus, *Captives*, Act V, Scene 3, line 8.

104 As we explain in the section entitled *Dicsone Decoded*, Dicsone's microcosmic model of the intellect seems to hypothesise memory as being located at the centre of the mental 'universe', with the sensory and cognitive apparatuses, which contribute material to the memory, located at the boundary that surrounds it.

105 Lucretius, *De Rerum Natura*, Book IV, lines 812-813.

106 Cf. Cicero, *De Republica*, Book III, 25: 'For I consider it to be a form of unjust slavery when someone who is capable of being his own master is enslaved to another, but not when that person is unable to govern himself.'

107 Latin *remigium alarum animi*, literally 'a rowing with the wings [of the mind]', but *remigium* was also used by Virgil and others to mean *flying*. This expression occurs on page 7 of the 1567 Latin translation of a work by the Middle Platonist philosopher

Alcinous called Ἐπιτομὴ τῶν Πλάτωνος δογμάτων *(An Epitome of Plato's Doctrine)*. The translation, entitled *Alcinoi ... Elementa atque initia, quibus quis imbutus, ad Platonis decretorum penetralia facilè introire, ac pervenire possit*, was by Denis Lambin, whom we have already met (see footnote 50) and with whose work Dicsone seems to have been familiar. Marsilio Ficino also translated this work by Alcinous into Latin as *Alcinoi philosophi Platonici de doctrina Platonis liber*. An English translation by George Burges of the Greek original will be found in volume 6 of the *Works of Plato* in Bohn's Classical Library: Chapter IV deals with perception and memory.

108 As opposed to *help* in the *De Umbra*.

109 See Giordano Bruno, *Triginta Intentiones Umbrarum (The Thirty Intentions)*, Intention I A: *Qui autem fieri potest ut ipsum cuius esse non est proprie verum, & cuius essentia non est proprie veritas; efficaciam & actum habeat veritatis? Sufficiens ergo est illi atque multum: ut sub umbra boni, verique sedeat. Non inquam sub umbra veri bonique naturalis atque rationalis (hinc enim falsum diceretur atque malum) sed Methaphysici, Idealis, & supersubstantialis*, 'But how is it possible that what is not strictly true and whose essence is not strictly the truth still has the effectiveness and action of truth? In that case it is enough...to sit in the shadow of the good and the true, i.e. in the shadow not of the natural and the rational (for this should be defined from this perspective as false and evil) but of the metaphysical, the ideal and the super-substantial.'

110 Latin *vestigia Dei*. The 'father of Christian theology' Tertullian (c. 155 CE – c. 220 CE) and, later, St. Augustine had sought for signs of the Trinity in mankind and in Nature. Tertullian, in his *Against Praxeas*, had given one such example as 'sun, ray and apex', while Augustine's *De Trinitate* had cited 'object seen, attention of mind, and external vision' among others. Augustine followed Plato and Plotinus (see, for example, the *Enneads* III.8) in assigning the term *vestigium* (as a Latin equivalent to Plato's *ichnos*) to such evidence of God. Giles of Viterbo (*fl.* 1500) further developed this idea along lines that may have influenced Giordano Bruno and, therefore, Dicsone. In his *Sententiœ ad mentem Platonis* Giles describes the *vestigium* as the 'shadow of an idea', the mid-point between darkness and light. See Hilary Gatti (ed.), *Giordano Bruno: Philosopher of the Renaissance*, Ashgate 2002, p. 111 ff. The *vestigium* is, of course, on the twelve categories of the 'Idea of Nature' to be found in Book II of Bruno's *De imaginum, signorum et idearum compositione*. See footnote 140.

111 Literally, 'if you rouse it up with a rod and with dust', another phrase from Cicero – see the *Tusculan Disputations*, Book V, chapter xxiii, where Cicero describes his rediscovery, during his quæstorship, of the tomb of Archimedes, whose memory he sought to 'pull up from the dust'.

112 Latin *omne punctum tulisse*, literally 'to have carried off every point', because votes in ancient Rome were often cast by pricking wax tablets with a stylus.

113 See Cicero (attrib.), *Ad Herennium*, Book III, xvi, 28: *Sunt igitur duœ memoriœ: una naturalis, altera artificiosa. Naturalis est ea quœ nostris animis insita est et simul cum cogitatione nata; artificiosa est ea quam confirmat inductio quœdam et ratio prœceptionis*, 'There are, then,

The Hermetic Art of Memory

two kinds of memory: one natural, and the other the product of art. The natural memory is that memory which is embedded in our souls, born simultaneously with thought. The artificial memory is that memory which is strengthened by a kind of training and system of discipline' – Caplan's translation for Loeb, slightly adapted.

114 Virgil, *Georgics*, Book I, lines 133 and 121-122.

115 Simonides of Ceos (c. 556 – 468 BCE) was a Greek lyric poet born at Ioulis. According to legend, during the excavation of a collapsed dining-hall from which Simonides had luckily escaped the poet was asked to identify the body of each guest, which he accomplished by correlating them with their places at the dining-table. He later used this experience to develop the mnemonic system of the 'memory theatre' or 'memory palace'.

116 *Figura, nota, indicium, sigillum, signum, character* – this is, of course, Brunonian terminology. See footnote 140.

117 See, for example, Cæsar, *De Bello Gallico*, Book VI, 14: 'Report says that in the schools of the Druids they learn by heart a great number of verses, and therefore some persons remain twenty years under training. And they do not think it proper to commit these utterances to writing, although in almost all other matters, and in their public and private accounts, they make use of Greek letters. I believe that they have adopted the practice for two reasons – that they do not wish the rule to become common property, nor those who learn the rule to rely on writing and so neglect the cultivation of the memory; and, in fact, it does usually happen that the assistance of writing tends to relax the diligence of the student and the action of the memory'

(translation for Loeb by H. J. Edwards).

118 i.e. the sons of King Tyndareus, Castor and Pollux, who, according to legend, saved Simonides from certain death in the collapsing dining-hall (see footnote 115) by asking him to step outside.

119 See Cicero, *De Oratore*, Book II, lxxiv, 299: '...we are told that the famous Athenian Themistocles was endowed with wisdom and genius on a scale quite surpassing belief, and it is said that a certain learned and highly accomplished person went to him and offered to impart to him the science of mnemonics, which was then being introduced for the first time; and that when Themistocles asked what precise result that science was capable of achieving, the professor asserted that it would enable him to remember everything; and Themistocles replied that he would be doing him a greater kindness if he taught him to forget what he wanted to forget rather than teaching him to remember' (E. W. Sutton's translation for Loeb 1967, slightly adapted).

120 The known planets in Dicsone's day were Mercury, Mars, Venus, Jupiter and Saturn.

121 Latin *communis animus*. Dicsone probably encountered this term in the 1571 Latin paraphrase of the fourteen books mistakenly attributed to Aristotle on the secret wisdom of Ancient Egypt, *Libri quattuordecim qui Aristotelis esse dicuntur, De secretiore parte divinæ sapientiæ secundum ægyptios*, by Jacques Charpentier (Jacobus Carpentarius, 1524-1574), a professor at the Collège Royal and an arch-enemy of Petrus Ramus. The work is now known to be a mediæval Arabic redaction of parts of Plotinus's *Enneads*. After a copy was discovered in Damascus in the early sixteenth century it was

translated into Latin and published in 1519. Given the date of publication of Charpentier's paraphrase of it and the rarity of the term we think we can conclude that Dicsone was familiar with it.

122 See footnote 107.

123 Latin *ratiocinans memoria*. Another term from Jacques Charpentier's edition (Book IX this time) of the pseudo-Aristotelian *Libri quattuordecim qui Aristotelis: esse dicuntur, de secretiore parto divinæ sapientiæ secundum Ægyptios* (see footnote 121). It was a book much drawn on in later times by, among others, Emanuel Swedenborg. Cf. Swedenborg's *Hieroglyphic Key to natural and spiritual mysteries, by way of representations and correspondences* translated from the Latin by J. J. G. Wilkinson, 1847, p. 26: 'It follows then, that there is a correspondence and harmony between all things, namely, of natural with spiritual, and vice versa; and that in universal nature we have nothing but types, images and likenesses of particular things in the spiritual sphere, which is the region of exemplars or antitypes. Were it not so, it would be permanently impossible for a spiritual intelligence of any description to comprehend the objects of a lower sphere, which yet spirits do comprehend spontaneously and instinctively, *ex se* and *in se*. The Egyptians appear to have cultivated this branch of learning, and to have signified these correspondences by a vast number of different hieroglyphics, not merely expressive of natural, but also at the same time of spiritual things. Respecting this science of the Egyptians we have an entire treatise by Aristotle.'

124 See Cicero (attrib.), *Ad Herennium*, III, 17: *Constat igitur artificiosa memoria ex locis et imaginibus. Locos appellamus eos qui breviter, perfecte, insignite aut natura aut manu sunt absoluti, ut eos facile naturali memoria conprehendere et amplecti queamus: ut ædes, intercolumnium, angulum, fornicem, et alia quæ his similia sunt*, 'The artificial memory is therefore established on the basis of memory-loci and images. By memory-loci I mean those things that are naturally or artificially complete in themselves concisely, perfectly and distinctively, so that we can easily understand and grasp them with the natural memory, e.g. a building, an intercolumnar space, a recess, an arch, or something similar.'

125 Virgil, *Eclogues*, IV, line 36. Virgil's *Fourth Eclogue* is one of the most famous of all Latin poems. Probably written around 42 BCE, it describes the birth of a boy who will eventually become divine and rule the whole world. In the Christian era it began to be seen as a prediction of the birth of Jesus Christ. This was one of the roots of the mediæval idea that Virgil was a prophet and even a magician. Constantine the Great, St. Augustine, Dante and Alexander Pope all believed in this interpretation. See *Vergil* [sic] *in the Middle Ages* by Domenico Comparetti, translated by E.F.M. Benecke. Lines 34-36 of the poem, from which this line is taken, describe the two conditions for the return of the Golden Age: war, and a second Argo, the ship in which the Argonauts sailed in search of the Golden Fleece. This quotation can therefore be interpreted as 'when the Golden Age returns'. It will also be found in Giordano Bruno's *Expulsion of the Triumphant Beast*, 1st Dialogue, 1st Part.

126 See Aristotle, *Physics*, Book IV, 219b 1-2. For a detailed treatment of this subject see Ursula Coope, *Time for Aristotle*, Oxford University Press, 2005, ISBN 0199247900.

127 Cicero discussed this distinction between universal nature (*universa natura*, the general laws of nature) and individual nature (*propria natura*, the things that make each person different from another) in his *De Officiis*, Book I, Ch. 31, though we know that he had a lost work by the Stoic philosopher Panætius, *On Duties*, at his elbow while writing it.

128 A phrase from Giordano Bruno, *Ars memoriæ*, Part I, Ch. VI: *Considerato igitur, qua intentione possimus expressisse, artem in quibusdam excellere naturam, eandemque in aliis ab illa superari. Id enim esse minime potest, quam ubi naturam in actibus remotioribus quasdam rationis majores, quam in mage propinquis, ostendere conspexerimus. Ipsa perpetuare fertur in eadem specie formam substantialem, quam non valet secundum numerum eandem perpetuasse, in quibus artis facultas non extenditur. Forma vero extrinseca atque figura inventoris clavis magnæ per artem duro committitur lapidi, vel adamanti. Item conditiones, actus et nomen memoriæ et cogitativæ objectis perpetuanda committuntur; quæ tamen natura retinere non potuisset, quandoquidem fluctuantis materiæ stomachus mature omnia digerit,* which I take to mean: 'Consider therefore what our intention was when we were able to bring forth an art to surpass Nature in some respects and be surpassed by her in others. For this can be nothing more than when we have observed Nature displaying certain greater instances of reason in more remote acts than in nearer ones. That is done in order to perpetuate in the same representation the substantial form, which is not strong enough to have perpetuated that representation according to number, for the ability of the art does not extend that far. The extrinsic form and figure of the discoverer of the great key is committed by means of the art to a hard stone or adamant. In the same way the conditions, acts and the name of the memory and the object which have been imagined and which need to be perpetuated are committed to objects. Yet Nature had not been able to retain these, since the stomach rapidly digests all of the floating material.'

129 Latin *ramus*, a play on the name of Petrus Ramus.

130 Latin *repetentia*, another word from Lucretius, Book III, line 863 (according to Denis Lambin, whose edition Dicsone would certainly have used, although his reading has been disputed). In a note, Lambin interprets it as equivalent to *recordatio* (a recalling to mind) or *retinentia* (a 'sticking' in the mind): 'If, after we have died, time should gather together the material of which we are currently made and restore it to its present locations, and the light of life was restored to us, would it really be of any interest to us that this had been done, now that the chain of our recollection had been broken?'

131 Latin *prudentia*. See Cicero, *De Inventione*, Book II, Ch. liii: *Prudentia est rerum bonarum et malarum neutrarumque scientia. partes eius: memoria, intelligentia, providentia. Memoria est, per quam animus repetit illa, quæ fuerunt; intelligentia, per quam ea perspicit, quæ sunt; providentia, per quam futurum aliquid videtur ante quam factum est,* 'Prudence is the knowledge of good and bad things and of things that are neither good nor bad. Its parts are memory, intelligence and foreknowledge. Memory is that through which the mind repeats those things which have been, intelligence that through which it perceives those things that are, and foreknowledge that

through which something is seen before it has occurred.' See also Spencer Pearce, 'Dante and the Art of Memory', *The Italianist* 16, 1996, p. 22: 'The renewal of interest in the art of local memory was instigated...by Albert the Great and his pupil Thomas Aquinas… It is highly significant... that the context in which St. Augustine and St. Thomas offer their mnemonic device is not a treatise of rhetoric but of ethics: for both writers memory is a fundamental aspect of the virtue of prudence.'

132 Latin *vacuum animum*, another term from Cicero, indicating a mind so occupied with a task that it is free of anxiety, see his *Letters to Atticus,* XII, 38.3.

133 Cicero again, *animus acer et præsens*, 'a keen and ready mind', one of the requirements for a good orator. See his *De Oratore*, Book II, 20.84.

134 A very strange paraphrase (or misquotation?) of Lucretius, *De Rerum Natura*, Book IV, line 934, which usually reads *Non fieri partum, nisi concilio ante coacto*, i.e. 'birth cannot occur unless intercourse has taken place beforehand'.

135 Latin *nuncias*, specifically female messengers or, perhaps, eagles (*nuncia fulva Iovis*, 'Jupiter's tawny messengers').

136 Latin *animus*, in contrast to *anima,* the soul considered as the vivifying substance of every human being, which Dicsone used in this passage in the *De Umbra.*

137 Lucretius, *De Rerum Natura*, Book II, from lines 780-784.

138 Lucretius, *De Rerum Natura*, Book IV, lines 238-239.

139 Greek ὕλη, defined by Aristotle as 'matter' but in the sense of 'the substratum which is receptive of coming-to-be and passing-away: but the substratum of the remaining kinds of change is also, in a certain sense, 'matter', because all these substrata are receptive of 'contrarieties' of some kind' (*On Generation and Corruption*, Book I, Ch. 4, in Harold Joachim's translation).

140 Latin *notæ* and *sigilla* respectively. These and some related Brunonian terms are ably explained by Johann Gottlieb Buhle in Volume II Part II pp. 762ff. of his *Geschichte der neuern Philosophie seit der Epoche der Wiederherstellung der Wissenschaften* (Göttingen 1801):

'In Book II of his *De imaginum, signorum et idearum compositione,* Bruno depicts Nature as a sort of living mirror in which we perceive the images of natural things, the shadows and the Divinity. This mirror contains the idea (the form) which is its causal principle, just as the image of the object in the mind of the artist is the cause that determines the work that he or she produces. But Nature contains the idea as the substance itself, for matter is nothing other than this substance, which draws forth from itself an incalculable number of forms subject to an infinite number of variations, i.e. it is nothing other than the idea (the form). But the idea of Nature can be shared in twelve different categories which make it knowable by the spirit: 1. the idea (*idea*), which is the metaphysical principle, the absolute form, the cause of which is supernatural; 2. the trace (*vestigium*), the form of the physical world; 3. the shadow (*umbra*), the form of the universe in the intelligence; 4. the mark (*nota*), everything that indicates something medially or immediately through a proximate or remote cause; 5. the character (*character*), which indicates something by a series of lines and points, e.g. the alphabet; 6. the sign (*signum*), which encompasses everything by which something is designated; 7. the seal (*sigillum*), which designates an object according to one of its more remarkable parts or qualities; 8. the token (*indicium*), which does not express the thing in itself but serves only to announce it and draw our attention to it; 9. the figure (*figura*), which indicates not the interior, like the idea, trace and shadow do, but the exterior, and contains a space through which the figure is distinguished from the character; 10. the resemblance (*simile*), a form perceived by the senses and conserved in the imagination and corresponding to an object; 11. the analogy (*proportio*), which expresses a relationship between several things; and finally 12. the image (*imago*), which denotes a more or less perfect identity with its object, and consequently plays upon an expressive force that is greater than simple resemblance. However, all the forms of nature which are knowable by the intelligence, however they might be expressed, must be related to the visual sense, i.e. they must be images.' (Our own free translation).

It should be mentioned in passing that Buhle had interesting views on the origins of Freemasonry, arguing that speculative Freemasonry arose in England between 1629 and 1635 through the work of Robert Fludd, who had earlier been introduced to Rosicrucianism by Michael Maier. For more on the Brunonian terms, see Manuel Mertens, *Magic and Memory in Giordano Bruno: The Art of a Heroic Spirit*, Brill 2018, p. 107ff.

141 We take this to mean the three categories of universals, subjects that contain many other subjects, and entire systems.

142 Latin *firma retentio*. Contrast this with the phrase *firma perceptio*, 'firm perception', used in the corresponding passage in the *De Umbra*. Dicsone may have been reading a work on natural philosophy by the Flemish Franciscan scholar Franciscus Titelmans (1502-1537), the *Compendium Philosophiæ Naturalis, Seu De Consideratione rerum Naturalium, earumq[ue] ad suum Creatore reductione, Libri XII* of 1558, which contains a section on memory (in Book X) in which the term *firma retentio* is used. Titelmans is known to have influenced the thought of Petrus Ramus. This relatively rare term is also found in the works of mediæval medical writers such as Arnaldus de Villa Nova in the negative sense of a memory that it is impossible to get rid of and which is a cause of 'love sickness', a topic that Arnaldus dealt with in his treatise *De Amore Heroico*, which was republished several times during the 16th century and which may have been familiar to Dicsone.

143 See footnote 124.

144 According to legend, Astræa, the virgin goddess of justice, innocence and purity, was the last of the immortals to live among mankind during the Golden Age, and will one day return to Earth to restore it to its former glory. We find a possible reference to her in Virgil's *Fourth Eclogue*, line 6 (see footnote 125): *Iam redit et virgo, redeunt Saturnia Regna*, ('Now the virgin returns, and the Saturnian powers return with her'). In Dicsone's time Astræa was identified with Elizabeth I, the virgin queen presiding over a Golden Age. See Frances Yates, *Astræa: The Imperial Theme in the Sixteenth Century* (1975).

145 Latin *hospes*, which would seem to be Dicsone's own term, synonymous with *subject*. *Hospes* can mean both a *guest* and a *host*, but *guest* would seem to be more appropriate here. Perhaps Dicsone borrowed the notion from the

story of Simonides (see footnote 115).

146 See footnote 145.

147 Latin *sensilis*, a word Dicsone undoubtedly picked up from his reading of Book II of *De Rerum Natura* by Lucretius (see Book II, lines 888, 893, 895, 902). It has a very different meaning to the *sensibilis* (perceptible) which Dicsone used in the corresponding passage in the *De Umbra*.

148 Paraphrased from Lucretius, *De Rerum Natura*, Book IV, lines 330-332, but Dicsone's paraphrase, *ut splendor omnis acer adurit oculos* is so uncannily close to Montaigne's handwritten annotation of Lambin's text (see footnote 12), which reads *omnis splendor acer adurit oculos*, that one wonders whether Dicsone actually owned Montaigne's copy of Lambin's edition or, at least, had sight of it. Montaigne died in 1592, and the *Thamus* was published in 1597, so it is a possibility. A digital version of Montaigne's annotated copy is available on-line at http://cudl.lib.cam.ac.uk/view/PR-MONTAIGNE-00001-00004-00004/1. See also Michael Screech, *Montaigne's annotated copy of Lucretius: a transcription and study of the manuscript, notes and pen-marks*, Librairie Droz, 1998.

149 Lucretius, *De Rerum Natura*, Book IV, line 381.

150 We take this to mean that the spaces between subjects should not be allowed to intrude on the mind's eye.

151 Latin *tribus*, 'third-parts'.

152 Here Dicsone gives the reader the option to use the lunar mansions, but does not insist upon it as he seems to do in the *De Umbra*.

153 The *decemviri* ('ten men') were Roman magistrates with absolute authority, originally appointed in 451 BCE to protect the interests of the lower classes from the predations of the patricians. After a promising start, including the enactment of the Laws of the Twelve Tables, the *decemviri* fell into bad ways and the consular system was reintroduced.

154 Presumably a reference to the decemvirs' chains of office, but also to one of the most famous of all esoteric images, the Golden Chain of Homer. The tradition is too long and complex to trace in detail here. Suffice it to say that in the opening of the 15th book of his *Iliad* Homer portrays Zeus awakening after being seduced by Hera to find the Trojans in retreat. He scolds Hera with the words, 'Do you not remember how once upon a time I had you hanged? I fastened two anvils on to your feet, and bound your hands in a chain of gold which none might break, and you hung in mid-air among the clouds.' Plato and Kircher, among others, took this literally to be a reference to the Sun, but a more esoteric interpretation can be traced via the commentaries by Favonius Eulogius and Macrobius (both 5th century CE) on the 'Dream of Scipio' to be found in the 6th Book of Cicero's *De Republica*, in which the disembodied soul of the Roman general Scipio Æmilianus has a vision of the nine celestial spheres of the universe. In Book I Ch. 44 of his commentary Macrobius argues that the Golden Chain is an uninterrupted connection of causes that bind themselves together by mutual bonds and run from God to the vilest dregs of matter. Petrus Ramus, however, saw it as a chain of dialectic, e.g. in his *Aristotelicæ animadversiones*, Paris, 1543, pp. 2 recto-3 verso, and his 1549 edition of Euclid, page 1: *Hic enim prima mediis, media postremis, omniaque inter se, velut aurea quadam Homeri catena sic vincta, colligataque sunt* ('For here the first are thus bound and connected to the middles, and the

middles to the finals, and everything to each other, just like that Golden Chain of Homer'). According to Plotinus it is possible to ascend to the world of ideal forms by moving up the Golden Chain, and the image became an essential component of the strictly contemplative systems of Pseudo-Dionysus, Aquinas, Cusa and Ficino and eventually of Giordano Bruno's hermetic memory system. See Joshua Ramey, *The Hermetic Deleuze: Philosophy and Spiritual Ordeal,* Duke University Press 2012, Chapter II; Leo Catana, *The Concept of Contraction in Giordano Bruno's Philosophy,* Routledge 2005; Robert Lamberton, *Homer the Theologian: Neoplatonist Allegorical Reading and the Growth of the Epic Tradition,* Univ. of California Press 1989; and Pierre Lévêque: *Aurea catena Homeri: une étude sur l'allégorie grecque,* Paris: Les Belles Lettres 1959. But the Golden Chain almost certainly pre-dates even Homer, e.g. Proclus, in Book II of his commentary on Plato's *Timæus,* tells us that Orpheus made use of this image.

155 See footnote 142.

156 Or Primal Mind, Latin *mens prima.* A term from Giordano Bruno (found in his *Summa terminorum physicorum. Intellectus. Seu Idea*), who may have obtained it from Dante's *Convivio,* Book II, 3.8-12: 'And tranquil and peaceful is the place of that supreme Deity which alone completely sees itself. This is the place of the blessed spirits, according to the Holy Church, which cannot tell lies; and Aristotle also seems to hold this view, to anyone who follows what he is saying, in the first book of *On Heaven and Earth.* This heaven is the overarching edifice of the universe, in which all the universe is enclosed, and outside of which nothing exists; and it is not in any place but was formed alone in the

First Mind *(ma formato fu solo ne la prima Mente),* which the Greeks call *Protonoe.* This is the magnificence of which the Psalmist spoke, when he says to God: 'Elevated above the heavens is your magnificence'.' Dicsone may also have been reading Marcantonio Flaminio's paraphrase of Book XII Aristotle's *Metaphysics,* published in 1536, in which the term occurs.

157 See Cicero's *Dream of Scipio* (see footnote 154): 'For men were created subject to this law, to keep to that globe, which you see in the centre of this region and which is called the Earth; and to them a soul was given formed from those everlasting fires, which you mortals call constellations and stars, that, round and spherical in form, alive with divine intelligences, complete their orbits and circles with marvellous swiftness' (Pearman's translation).

158 Latin *periodus cæli.* See Giordano Bruno, *De Umbris Idearum,* Conceptus VI.F: *Rerum formæ sunt in ideis, sunt quodammodo in se ipsis; sunt in coelo; sunt in periodo cæli,* 'The forms of things are in ideas; they are, in a certain way, in themselves; they are in the heavens; they are in a circuit of the heavens.'

159 See footnote 158.

160 Presumably he means 'in an animate being.'

161 Latin *lima mentis.* Cf. the mediæval hymn to St. Catherine: *'Tandem ista margarita/Lima mentis expolita/Et fracturis carnis trita/Paradisum adiit',* 'At last that pearl/Polished by the file of the mind/And burnished by the breaking of the flesh/Has entered Paradise.'

162 A term from syllogistic logic: the position (i.e. positing or assertion) of an antecedent leads naturally to the position (positing) of the consequent, e.g. If a man has feeling then he is an

animal/But a man has feeling/ Therefore he is an animal.

163 It is difficult to know who is being referred to here. Titus Alledius Severus is mentioned in Book XII of the *Annals* of Tacitus as marrying his niece (which was perfectly legal at that time and place). There was also a famous glutton called Alledius who is mentioned in Juvenal's *Fifth Satire*: 'Before Virro is put a huge goose's liver; a capon as big as a goose, and a boar, piping hot, worthy of yellow-haired Meleager's steel. Then will come truffles, if it be spring-time and the longed-for thunder have enlarged our dinners. "Keep your corn to yourself, O Libya!" says Alledius; "unyoke your oxen, if only you send us truffles!" ' (G. G. Ramsay's translation). Cicero's *Letters to Atticus*, Book XII, Letter IV, also mentions someone of this name, but Dicsone makes him sound like a leader in the Servile Wars, though no one of that name seems to have been involved in them. Perhaps it is a satirical reference by Dicsone to a famous glutton of his time with radical sympathies who was known by that nickname or, perhaps, to Petrus Ramus.

164 Cf. Cicero, *De Oratore*, Book II, 87: *Vidit enim hoc prudenter sive Simonides sive alius quis invenit ea maxime animis affigi nostris, quæ essent a sensu tradita atque impressa; acerrimum autem ex omnibus nostris sensibus esse sensum videndi; quare facillime animo teneri posse ea, quæ perciperentur auribus aut cogitatione, si etiam oculorum commendatione animis traderentur*, 'For Simonides or whoever it was who discovered it was wise enough to see that those things are most likely to stick in our minds are those which are communicated to or impressed by the senses. But the keenest of all our senses is that of seeing, which means that those things which can most readily be retained in our minds are those that are perceived with the ears or cognition if they are also conveyed to our minds with the approval of the eyes.'

165 Latin *aspectus iudicium*. Cf. Carl von Morgenstern, *Commentatio de Arte Veterum Mnemonica*, Dorpat (Tartu) 1835: *Imago autem, quæ collocatur in loco quodam, etiam perfectior esse potest, ita ut ea non solum admoneamur rei, sed ut eius vi etiam repræsentetur et in aspectus iudicium vocetur res ipsa, cuius memoria opus est*, 'But an image which is positioned in a certain memory-locus can be even more perfect, so that we are not just reminded of the thing itself but also in such way that the thing itself which needs to be recalled to mind is represented in all its vigour and is called before the judgement of vision.'

166 Latin *imitata et efficta simulacra*, a phrase lifted from Chapter III of Cicero's uncompleted translation of Plato's *Timæus*, known as the *De Universitate*.

167 Latin *conformatio*. This seems to be a term of Dicsone's devising.

168 Latin *mentis oculi*, a term used by Cicero in his discussion of metaphor in *De Oratore*, Book III, 163: 'for the eyes of the intellect are drawn more readily to things we have seen than to things we have heard of'.

169 Latin *conformatio verborum*. See Cicero, *De Oratore*, Book III, Ch. 52.

170 Latin *inflexio*. Dicsone seems to use this term synonymously with *modificatio*.

171 i.e. the Sophistic philosophy.

172 Latin *commercia*. Compare with *mutuationes*, 'borrowings', in the related passage of the *De Umbra*.

173 Cf. Cicero, *De Oratore*, Book III, 156: 'Metaphors are therefore a kind of borrowing, since you take from something else that which you have

not of your own. Those that display a slightly greater audacity are the ones that...add a certain lustre to an oration.'

174 Cf. Cicero, *De Oratore*, Book III, 165: 'A metaphor ought not to be too daring, but should be of such a nature that it may appear to have been substituted for another expression rather than have leapt into its place, to have entered by entreaty, and not by violence.'

175 Latin *efficiens*, one of Cicero's favourite words (see, for example, the *Topica* 14, *De Divinatione*, I, 55, etc.). According to Aristotle the efficient (or moving) cause of a process of change consists of things apart from the thing being changed or moved which interact so as to be an agency of the change or movement. So, to take one of Aristotle's own examples, the efficient cause of a boy is his father.

176 Fortune-telling using fire. Like hydromancy (see footnote 177) it was one of the seven *artes magicæ* or *artes prohibitæ* (practices forbidden by canon law, and mirroring the seven 'respectable' arts of the trivium and quadrivium). Others included necromancy (divination by contacting the dead), geomancy (divination using markings on the ground, tossed stones or earth, or specially-constructed domino-like figures), aeromancy (divination from weather phenomena, comets etc.), chiromancy (palmistry) and scapulimancy (divination from animal bones, especially shoulder-blades).

177 Fortune-telling using water, more specifically by dropping pebbles into a pool.

178 A Centaur, born in Thessaly.

179 It has been claimed that his name means 'foresight', just as his brother's name Epimetheus seems to denote 'hindsight'.

180 The foolish brother of Prometheus: his lack of foresight led to regret, which he was able to experience thanks to his gift of hindsight.

181 Lucretius, *De Rerum Natura*, Book IV, lines 743-746.

182 The whole of this passage is a mélange of Book II, ch. 46-47, of Cicero's *De Natura Deorum*, Plato's *Timæus* and Book V (VI) 6 of *The Divine Pimander*, and Jean Fernel's *Physiologia* (see footnote 185).

183 See Plato, *Timæus*, 73c: 'Concerning the bones and flesh and all such substances the case stands thus. The foundation of all these is the marrow: for the bonds of life whereby the soul is bound to the body were fastened in it throughout and planted therein the roots of human nature. But the marrow itself comes from other sources. Such of the primal triangles as were unwarped and smooth and thus able to produce fire and water and air and earth of the purest quality, these God selected and set apart.'

184 See *The Divine Pimander*, Book V (VI), 6: 'If thou would'st see Him too through things that suffer death, both on the earth and in the deep, think of a man's being fashioned in the womb, my son, and strictly scrutinize the art of Him who fashions him, and learn who fashioneth this fair and godly image of the Man... Who [then] is He who traceth out the circles of the eyes; who He who boreth out the nostrils and the ears; who He who openeth [the portal of] the mouth; who He who doth stretch out and tie the nerves; who He who channels out the veins; who He who hardeneth the bones; who He who covereth the flesh with skin; who He who separates the fingers and the joints; who He who widens out a treading for the feet; who He who diggeth out the ducts; who He who spreadeth out the spleen; who He who shapeth heart like to a pyramid; who He who setteth ribs together; who He

who wideneth the liver out; who He who maketh lungs like to a sponge; who He who maketh belly stretch so much; who He who doth make prominent the parts most honourable, so that they may be seen, while hiding out of sight those of least honour?' (G. R. S. Mead's translation).

185 Latin *consentiens, conspirans et continuata cognatio*, a phrase taken from the *Physiologia* of Jean Fernel (1497 – 1558), a highly successful physician and an important pioneer of the subject of physiology, the name of which he seems to have invented. Fernel's text contains a section on the physiological aspects of memory. This reference is further evidence that Dicsone was reading widely in the natural sciences at this time. Fernel's Latin text has been published by the American Philosophical Society with an excellent English translation by John M. Forrester as *The Physiologia of Jean Fernel (1567)*, American Philosophical Society (2003). See Book V, section 8 and especially pp. 339ff. of that text for Fernel's discussion of the memory function.

186 See footnote 140.

187 Latin *id quod subest*, literally 'that which lies underneath.' I take this to mean that you should choose a general underlying expression of the shadow concerned rather than something extreme or partial.

188 Latin *communis utilitas*, a concept much discussed by Cicero, especially in his *De Officiis*, e.g. Book III, section 52: 'What say you? comes Antipater's argument on the other side; 'it is your duty to consider the interests of your fellow-men and to serve society; you were brought into the world under these conditions and have these inborn principles which you are in duty bound to obey and follow, that your interest shall be the interest of the community and conversely that the interest of the community shall be your interest as well; will you, in view of all these facts, conceal from your fellow-men what relief in plenteous supplies is close at hand for them?' (Walter Miller's translation for Loeb). Aquinas also examined it extensively in his commentary on Aristotle, *In Libros Politicorum Aristotelis Expositio.*

189 See Book VIII of Plato's *Republic* for the discussion between Socrates and Plato's brother Glaucon about the various forms of government.

190 Latin *natura constant*. See Lucretius, Book II, line 378.

191 A phrase from Cicero, *De Oratore*, Book III, 42.

192 'Property is an accident that is proper; or, it belongs to its subject; hence its name, property. It differs from accident that is common, in this: property belongs to the species of the object; i. e., agrees with an object on account of its specific nature or form, the *common accident* agrees with an object or individual in virtue of its matter, or quasi matter; e.g., 'Man limps, because Peter is lame; Peter laughs, because man is a laughing being.' Lameness is an accident that is common to individuals of many species of animals that walk; laughter, strictly so-called, is peculiar or proper only to man' (Rev. W. H. Hill S.J., *Elements of Philosophy*, 1873).

193 The great Greek statesman, patron of the arts and promoter of democratic principles was a great admirer of Anaxagoras, and may have spoken up for him at his trial for impiety.

194 In Greek mythology Hippolytus was a son of Theseus and was killed after rejecting the amorous advances of his step-mother.

195 Horace, *Odes*, Book II, 10, lines 13-15.

196 Latin *repetentia*, another word from Lucretius. See *De Rerum Natura*,

Book III, line 851. Though corrected by some later editors to *retinentia*, Denis Lambin, in his famous edition of Lucretius which Dicsone seems to have owned, gives *retinentia* and, in a long footnote, glosses it as equivalent to the Greek ἀνάμνησις, 'reminiscence' as used in Aristotle, *De memoria*, 451a21.

197 Latin *contraria ex contrariis*, a phrase from (and a topic discussed in) the section on the contrariety of motion in *Super Aristotelis libro V, de physica auscultatione lucidissima commentaria, cum nova interpretatione* by the English scholastic philosopher Walter Burley (c.1275-1344/5). An edition of this work had been published in Venice in 1589, around the time that the *Thamus* was being written, and we strongly suspect that Dicsone may well have owned a copy. See p. 694 et seq. of the Venice edition.

198 Presumably a reference to the Greek erotic poet of that name (6th century BCE), who once compared falling in love to a down-rush of the Thracian north-wind armed with lightning (Fragment 286).

199 Virgil, *Aeneid*, Book I, line 589. A description of Aeneas as he meets Dido for the first time in Carthage.

200 Horace, *Odes*, Book I, 14, lines 4-6.

201 A paraphrase of Ovid's *Tristia*, Book I, V, lines 25-26. Ovid has: '*Scilicet ut fulvum spectatur in ignibus aurum, tempore sic duro est inspicienda fides*', i.e. 'It is clear that just as tawny gold is *tested* in the flames so loyalty must be proved in times of stress'. I wonder if this (presumably deliberate) misquotation is an alchemical reference by Dicsone?

202 The son of Achilles by Deidamia.

203 Presumably a reference to Aulus Atilius Calatinus, a distinguished Roman general in the first Punic war, who was twice consul (BCE 258 and 254) and once a dictator (and the first to wage war outside of Italy). Cicero mentions him admiringly in, among other places, his *De Finibus Bonorum et Malorum*, Book II, 116: 'You will not find anyone extolled for his skill and cunning in procuring pleasures. This is not the purport of laudatory epitaphs, like that one near the city gate:
HERE LYETH ONE WHOM ALL MANKIND AGREE
ROME'S FIRST AND GREATEST CITIZEN TO BE.
Do we suppose that all mankind agreed that Calatinus was Rome's greatest citizen because of his surpassing eminence in the acquisition of pleasures?'

204 In the Aristotelian sense, whereby the genus is a larger group of which the species is merely one proper subset, see Aristotle, *Categories*, V, 2b.

205 Latin *materiæ concretio*. Another phrase Dicsone may have picked up from his reading of Jean Fernel's *Physiologia*. See footnote 185.

206 Latin *superior ratio*, a term that has its *locus classicus* in St. Augustine's *De Trinitate* XII 3:3, where he argues that the human reason is superior insofar as it contemplates spiritual things, and inferior insofar as it contemplates the mundane: they are not separate powers, but are distinguished only in terms of function. This debate was taken further by the Scholastics, and especially by Thomas Aquinas (*Summa Theologica* Ia, q. 79).

207 Latin *acies animi*. *Acies* is the *pupil* of the eye but is here meant metaphorically. The term is found in Cicero, but was used most extensively by St. Augustine in his analysis of visual perception in his *De Trinitate* XI. See Vernon Joseph Bourke, *Augustine's Love of Wisdom: An Introspective Philosophy*, Purdue University Press, 1992, Ch. 4, *Memory*

and its Wonders.

208 Giordano Bruno, *De imaginum, signorum et idearum compositione,* Book I, Ch. XI, lines 16-17.

209 A rather obscure passage. I think he means that the number of elements should be kept as small as possible and that the calculations should be rigorously checked.

210 Horace, *De Arte Poetica*, lines 40-41.

211 Horace, *De Arte Poetica*, line 311.

212 This remark only applies, of course, to inflected languages like Latin, where the endings of nouns change to reflect their role in the sentence.

213 See Cicero, *De Oratore*, Book II, Ch. 88: 'verbal memory, which is less necessary for our business, is distinguished by a greater variety of figures: for there are many words which, like the joints of the human body, connect the members of a discourse, and are entirely abstracted from all sensible ideas; yet we must affix some determinate qualities to those words, which we must always make use of' (Guthrie's translation of 1808).

214 See footnote 163.

215 Latin *vicis*, taking the place of the term *mutuatio*, 'borrowing', used in the *De Umbra.*

216 i.e. the vowels *a, e, i, o, u.*

217 i.e. letters that end a word.

218 In English the letters *l, m, n, r, s.*

219 Taken from Cicero, *De Oratore,* Book II, 359: *Rerum memoria propria est oratoris; eam singulis personis bene positis notare possumus, ut sententias imaginibus, ordinem locis comprehendamus*, 'A memory for the concrete is the unique possession of the orator; we are able to imprint this memory on our minds when the individual 'masks' have been well ordered, so that we assimilate ideas by means of images and their sequence by means of places.'

220 Lucretius, *De Rerum Natura*, Book IV,

lines 787-788.

221 Latin *delectus habendi*, a military term used by Cæsar. This echoes the military metaphors used in the section *The first influences.*

222 Another Dicsonian paraphrase, this time of Lucretius, *De Rerum Natura*, Book IV, line 793. What Lucretius actually said was *Scilicet arte madent simulacra, et docta* vagantur,/ *Nocturno facere ut possint in tempore ludos'*, in other words 'Are images so imbued with art and so suitably instructed that they can wander about putting on performances in the night-time?'

223 See footnote 164.

224 Lucretius, *De Rerum Natura*, Book IV, lines 466-468.

225 Lucretius, *De Rerum Natura*, Book IV, lines 750-751.

226 Lucretius, *De Rerum Natura*, Book IV, line 734-735. What Lucretius actually wrote was *cientque./Tenuem animi naturam intus sensumque lacessunt,* i.e. 'And disturb and excite the delicate substance of the mind within as well as the *sense.'*

227 Giordano Bruno, *De imaginum, signorum et idearum compositione,* Book I, Ch. XI, line 12.

228 We take this to mean that the rational faculties should not be allowed to interfere with what is essentially an irrational (or, more correctly, non-rational) process.

229 Parmenides of Elea (*fl.* late sixth or early fifth century BCE) founded the Eleatic school of philosophy, which rejected the epistemological validity of sense experience and used logical standards of clarity and necessity as the criteria of truth. They were hostile to the early physicalist philosophers, who explained everything in terms of primary matter, and to Heraclitus, with his theory of perpetual change. Only fragments of one work by Parmenides (*On Nature*) have survived. Dicsone

was familiar with it and subsequently quotes from a Latin translation of it (see footnote 235). Dicsone would also seem to have known the work of Diogenes Laertius entitled *Lives of the Eminent Philosophers*.

230 Dionysodorus (c. 430 BCE – late 5th century or early 4th century BCE) was an ancient Greek Sophist and teacher of the martial arts, generalship, and rhetoric. He is unflatteringly portrayed by both Plato (in his *Euthydemus*) and Xenophon (in the *Memorabilia* 3.1) as the worst kind of Sophist, using logical fallacies to defeat arguments and taking people's hard-earned money from them in return for shoddy teaching.

231 A Latin translation of a fragment from a lost play by Euripides called *Phryxus*, quoted in the section on Pyrrho in Diogenes Laertius, *Lives of the Eminent Philosophers*, Book IX, Ch. XI, No. VIII.

232 See footnote 231.

233 The companion and tutor of the Greek god of wine Dionysus. He was often so drunk that he had to be carried around by a donkey. He was however thought to possess secret knowledge and the gift of prophecy when he was in his cups.

234 A surname of Hermes (Mercury), which he derived from Mount Cyllene in Arcadia, where he had a temple, or from the circumstance of Maia having given birth to him on that mountain. See Virgil, *Aeneid*, Book VIII, lines 139ff. He makes an appearance in Book II, Ch. 16, of Giordano Bruno's *De imaginum, signorum et idearum compositione*, where 'The first ass of Cyllenius' makes an appearance as one of his memory-images. In Book II, Ch. 6, of that work he also has a section entitled *Asinus Cyllenicus* ('The Cyllenian Ass'), where he describes the ass as spare transportation should Hermes require it, for *Nullum sane*

esset Mercurii numen, nisi equitabile pecus aliquod subesset, 'Mercury's divine nature would not be intact unless he could mount some horse-like animal'. This would seem to be Bruno's own invention.

235 A Latin version by an unknown translator of lines from Part 7 of *On Nature* by the Greek pre-Socratic philosopher Parmenides.

236 Latin *animus*, as opposed to *cerebrum*, 'brain', in the *De Umbra*.

237 Latin *complicatio*. This section of the text, with its description of the brain as a microcosm, with the memory located in the solar position in the centre and the sensory faculties in orbit around it, seems to be Dicsone's clearest explanation of what he means by the 'boundary' (*horizon*). This was of course written during the time of the Copernican revolution, in which Bruno was an important figure.

238 Latin *partes communes* and *partes propriæ*, so for example the 'common parts' of an eyelid are skin, adipose tissue etc., because these are common to most parts of the human body, whereas the 'particular parts' are the eyelashes, which are unique to the eyelid. Dicsone's system therefore seems to allow parts or aspects of objects to be studied and memorised and not just parts of them.

239 Latin *velificationes*, literally 'sailings', or 'settings sail', but it is hard to see how this meaning could be relevant in this context. It is perhaps being used here in a very specialised sense to mean the 'veiling' used to signify deity in Roman art, whereby the god or goddess in question holds a cloak over their head so that it billows in the form of an arch, which 'recalls the vault of the firmament' (Karl Galinsky, *Augustan Culture: An Interpretive Introduction*, Princeton University Press, 1996, pp. 158 and 321). Its

esoteric meaning in this context is not entirely clear.

240 See footnote 154.

241 Latin *aspectus animi*, a phrase that Dicsone probably got from St. Augustine (see the latter's *De Immortalitate Animæ*, 6.10).

242 Latin *campus*. This seems to be the only use of this Brunonian term in the two texts. See, for example, the 3rd Dialogue of Bruno's *De la causa, principio, et uno*.

243 Latin *oculi animi*, another phrase which Cicero seems to have introduced into Latin. See, for example, *De Natura Deorum*, Book I, Ch. 8. For a discussion of phrases of this kind in Cicero and Lucretius, see P. H. Schrijvers, 'Seeing the Invisible', in *Oxford Readings in Lucretius*, OUP 2007.

244 Copernicus's ground-breaking *De Revolutionibus Orbium Cælestium* ('On the Revolutions of the Heavenly Spheres') proposing a heliocentric model of the universe was published in 1543, just before the astronomer's death.

245 Latin *memoriæ ianitor*. This may well be a term of Dicsone's own invention, but see the 84th saying of the *Liber Sententiarum* of Bernard of Clairvaux (1090 – 1153): *Ianitor memoriæ, recordatio professionis: voluntatis ianitor, memoria patriæ cælestis: portitor intentionis, consideratio gehennalis*, 'Gatekeeper of the memory, recollection of one's vows; gatekeeper of the will, memory of the celestial kingdom; ferryman of the intention, contemplation of Hell.' For modern physiologists the *hippocampus* seems to be associated with the process of recollection and is accordingly sometimes known as the 'gatekeeper of memory'. As William Newell Hull put it: 'Recollection is the doorkeeper of Memory... The swinging door from Memory into

Consciousness has by it always the faithful servant – Recollection. A fact is wanted. Recollection stirs himself, searches the vault of Memory for the fact, finds it, brings it out into the light of Consciousness. Consciousness recognizes the fact and disposes of it as desired; it may go to the factory of thought for elaboration or it may go out to the world in the same form in which it came in, as a percept through the senses; but in any case, Memory cannot lose it and, like a pebble on the beach, a fact may be polished or made more easily recognizable by use in transition back and forth. We call this repetition.' (Hull, *New Light on Psychology*, Flanagan, 1905, p. 42.)

246 See Cicero, *Academica X, 30: Mens enim ipsa, quae sensuum fons est atque etiam ipse sensus est, naturalem vim habet, quam intendit ad ea, quibus movetur. Itaque alia visa sic adripit, ut eis statim utatur, alia quasi recondit, e quibus memoria oritur,* 'For the mind itself, which is the source of the senses, and which itself is sense, has a natural power, which it directs towards those things by which it is moved. Therefore it seizes on other things which are seen in such a manner as to use them at once; others it stores up; and from these memory arises.' (Yonge's translation).

247 Lucretius, *De Rerum Natura*, Book IV, lines 801-803.

248 i.e. the physical eyes, in contrast to the eyes of the mind.

249 Latin *gemina transformatio*. Dicsone may have borrowed this term from Dialogue IV of the *Necyomantia* [*sic*] of Étienne Forcadel (Stephanus Forcatulus, 1519-1578), a famous lawyer, Neo-Latin poet and esoteric writer. Forcadel published a series of bizarre books exploring the intersection of law, satire and the occult. See Wim Decock, Law on Love's Stage: Étienne Forcadel's

(1519-1578) *Cupido Jurisperitus* in Inszenierung des Rechts / Law on Stage, München: Martin Meidenbauer, 17-36: 'In his Oracle of a Jurist or Dialogues on Occult Jurisprudence (*Necyomantia iurisperiti sive de occulta jurisprudentia dialogi*) of 1544, for example, Forcadel had staged a fictitious encounter between classical Roman jurists, famous representatives of the Medieval *ius commune*, and lawyers of his own time. They discussed perennial legal issues against a magical background highly reminiscent of the fantastic setting of the witty dialogues written in Greek by the satirist Lucian of Samosata (*c*.125-180).'

250 Latin *vivata animi potestas*, a phrase from Lucretius, *De Rerum Natura*, Book III, line 680. It is the power that is infused into us at the moment of our birth and which animates the body.

251 Latin *informata cogitatio*, a phrase used by Cicero (see *Letters to Atticus, Book I, Letter I*) to denote a thought-process that has begun but which has not yet been completed, i.e. 'a partly-baked idea'.

252 Presumably a reference to Socrates' disillusionment with the philosophy of Anaxagoras.'Having one day,' says [Socrates], 'read a book of Anaxagoras, who said the divine mind was the cause of all things, and drew them up in their proper ranks and classes, I was ravished with joy. I perceived there was nothing more certain than this principle that mind was the cause of all things.' Socrates purchased the books of Anaxagoras, and began to read them with avidity, but he had not proceeded far till he found his hopes disappointed. The author, he said, 'makes no further use of this mind, but assigns as the cause of the order and beauty that prevailed in the world, the air, water, whirlwind, and other agencies of nature' (Rev. John Hunt, *An Essay on Pantheism*, London, 1866, p. 68).

Alexandri Dicsoni Arelii Thamus,
Sive De Memoræ Virtute,
Consideratio Prima.

Sub umbra illius quam desideraveram sedi.

LUGDUNI BATAVORUM.
Ex officina Thomæ Basson.
CI⊐. I⊐. XCVII.

PRÆFATIO AD LECTOREM.

UIDNAM esse putem (inquis) in umbra, lucis, cum in eius, illa quidem horizonte consistat? certe cum duo sint momenta in causa, natura et ratio, in altero quidem audentibus esse licet: omnes enim et singularem et insitam esse memoriæ virtutem, sine recusatione fatentur: in altero vero quæstio est. Nam et sitne rationis hic ulla virtus et artis accessio, eaque data, quid ipsi primum secuti simus et consequuti, requiri fortasse possit. Atque hic quidem primum omnis protervia valeat: nam et veri videndi cupidis modo scribimus, et aliorum animantum genios non moramur. Atque ut leves aliquos esse necesse est, et minime proinde nobis graves, ex suis ingeniis et misero eodemque beato sensu, statuant de nobis:

Nam satis est dives, cui sensus pauperiei nullus adest:

a medico petere bonitates eas et momenta malint: meam auctoris memoriam requirant: putrem esse putent viam hanc, aut nullam, aut certe gravem: (nempe obscurari a nobis quod per se ipsa natura tenere potuisset) denique me vanum, et macri fortasse pectoris hominem. Omnia impune: neque enim levium avicularum rostris et impetu commoveri solemus. Imo vero eiusmodi animantes esse necesse est.

namque est in rebus inane:
Quod si non esset nulla ratione moveri
res possent,

nec solidi quidquam esset: sicut quoque ni leve sit in rebus, nihil etiam erit quod proprie grave definire queas: et nisi de tenebris fateri velis, nulla etiam neque lucis neque umbrarum regio futura est: ea nimirum sunt fœdera naturæ. Verum alterum occurrit genus eorum, qui nimis hæc abscondite a nobis, et obscure instituta queruntur. Atqui si æqui iudices esse volent, nihil est quod expedire tam facile possimus: nam et verba inflectere, et vocabula constituere necess[e] fuit: quod in aliis etiam artibus contingit: et cum Thami regis antiquissimi et gravissimi, persona a nobis assumpta sit, et idonea maxime visa, qui de memoria et literarum inventione, ea ipsa dissereret, quæ allata ab eo adversus Theutatem, memorasset Plato: quis nescit orationem brevem, pressam et fere etiam obscuram esse decuisse? quæ scilicet personam atque tempus referre et exprimere posset. Quippe in omni sermone

Intererit multum Davusne loquatur, herusne,
maturusne senex, an adhuc florente iuventa
fervidus.

Etenim si quidquam difficile est, prosopopeia est: ubi et videndum ut personis consonet oratio, et interim verendum, ne tua de conformatione solliciti, persona neglecta sit. Quo loco quia necessaria contingit aliquando ab altera, declinatio, cærte ea quæ introducta est iure superat, eique imprimis cautum esse velis. Tum nulla res tam facilis, quin primum ea difficilis occurrat: et

Cernere nemo
se supra potis est; at voces excipere extra.

Ac sanis quidem et generosis procis, hæc ipsa respondeo. Qui autem capti animis feruntur, sic accipiunto.

Ole quid ad te,
De cute quid faciat ille, vel ille sua?

mea cutis est, arbitratus meus, et nihil ad Olum. Quid si autem

Vitium vas efficit ipsum,

Fluxum quidem illud atque pertusum? Et certe facit: neque enim defectus hic in luce, sed in lumine cernetur. Quanquam ipsa etiam lux nec omnibus lucet, nec uno modo: cæca animi vis est, aut imbecillis, aut nulla contentio. Nunc quibus in Socratem (exorientur enim et illi) iniquus esse videor, servierint illi quidem patiente me, meque etiam meis sensibus permittant. Quod si autem fieri non potest ut impetrem ab illis, non me sed Thamum loqui hoc loco meminisse velint. Cæterum ista quæcunque commentatio, si gravissima principum populorumque negotia reputet, resistat sane: valdeque caveto, ne si magnatum ianuas pulset nuda præsertim, ebria esse videri possit. Et populo quidem,

Cui scire est quod fama virum vulgataque fides
suggerit,

expedita ac vendibilis non erit: nec certe debet: iuvat enim Platonice loqui, naturam rerum invenire difficile, et ubi inveneris, indicare in vulgus nefas. At quibus et amor, et alœ, et certa voluntas, opportuna (nisi fallor) erit, et grata ac probata. cœrte sana est, et ex naturœ radiis ac vestigiis expressa. Quanquam hoc loco, me nihil potius definire malis, quam efferentem alioqui, aut contra etiam vituperantem, vanitatis aut stultitiœ suspectum iri. quippe omnis eiusmodi ratio esse tumidi videtur: altera quidem simplicis et aperti, altera vero esurientis et certe vani. Tu igitur videris, eademque opera de tuo candore iudicium esse putes. mihi quidem

Si cum natura sapio et sub numine,
id vere plus quam satis est.

ALEXANDRI DICSONI ARELII THAMUS,
SIVE DE MEMORIÆ VIRTUTE
CONSIDERATIO PRIMA.

[Nil simile Deo, neque eius ulla adumbratio.] HAM. Sunt ista vera Mercuri: neque enim quidquam simile aut par esse possit, omnibus impari et uni ac soli. una est omnino unius idea, unique nota, corporis illa quidem expers, at ævi, mundi, temporis, ortusque ideas omnes corporibus immersans. Et poterit vas cuiusquam, quod sola mente complectimur, imaginatione prehendere? At hæc est earum rerum quæ sub ortum cadunt: et ipsa fortasse generatio quædam, ut ne radios quidem tantæ lucis perferre possit. Ergo ignorantiæ pravitas terram inundat et alluit, materiæ sarsinam baiulantem; eaque est absoluta malitia: nempe ignis pyramidem in speciem cubi mutans, ad orbes cognatos appellere non sinit.

[Ridicula multitudo Deorum.]
At non hic finis. o quam ridiculum! una generatio, tempus unum, et mundus et ævum: ipsum autem unum quotum esse contenderint? Sed viderint: nisi potius evomere malint.
MER. At immersas habent in aquas manus. Nam quid ego de amictu dicam? aut quando erit ut perrumpere velint, aut etiam forte possint?
THAM. amictum?
MER. an non dixisti? aut quotum est, quod non sit in imagine sepulchri?

[Ignorantiæ pravitas.]
THAM. ignorantiæ texturam dicis, et in ambitu tenebroso, furem inquilinum: sat est. Cæterum quando et otium est, et deambulandi potestas data, visne ut reliquo sermoni operam dantes, ad orci fauces et spacia contendamus? nam et hoc, tua etiam tradentis umbras, officia fortasse requirant: nisi tu quid aliud malis.
MER. at me senatus, et concio iam frequens vocat: est enim ne forte nescias, in certi generis feras, rogatio ferenda: qua in re decernenda solus fortasse desideror.
THAM. quid hic ad feras? an non in terris, una cum corpore penitus extinguntur?

MER. cærte homines ita existimant: et solas tamen feras sinistra admittit. THAM. at quotidianum est homines huc commigrantes videre: at feras non videmus.

[Feræ.]
MER. nescis o Thame, nescis: feræ sunt, humanam illæ quidem speciem ementientes.
THAM. rem incredibilem narras: sed Mercurio credendum: quamvis hoc tamen ad efferatos hominum mores transferri possit. perge.

[Homo.]
MER. nequitiæ quidem regio terra est, et doli mali rea, ac virgine cæsa, natura mentitur. hominis enim veri, forma mens est: quæ ubi materiam suscepit, in lucis umbra et horizonte sedens, ad ipsam inclinat: et ad ea quæ sub intelligentiam cadunt, et quæ revera sunt convertitur.

[Materiæ vindices.]
Non patitur hic a sensibus affectis, neque a corporis vinculis tenetur, sed materiæ vindicum securus, et superbis illis dominis sopitis, quasi ex obscuro quodam et nocturno die, ad id quod est ascendere conatur, huius animi pacem, nulla res delibrat, nullus hic cupedinis ardor, aut rigor metus. Qui vero suos animos corpore constrinxerint et abiecerint, feræ sunt immanes; quibus de metamorphosi fortasse metuendum.
THAM. tenere mihi videor: sed quos vocas materiæ vindices?
MER. discrepantias inquam. Sed properantem me moraris curiose nimis interrogando.
THAM. atqui. Sed abiit: et quis est iste? cærte Theutates est: agnosco radium, numeros, calculos, tesseras, ipsa etiam elementa: totus denique, is est. Hoc illud fuit o Theutates, nempe Deus etiam orcum subisti?
THEUT. utique Deus, o Thame, Theutates est, neque hoc dubitant Ægiptii tui: at ego umbra eius.
THAM. sed quid interim Æacus? elusisti in simili, nonne?
THEUT. sic est.
THAM. prorsus assentior, et is es vere.
THEUT. ergo rides o bone? at si circa Naucratem esses, de numine nostro, absurde dubitare, desineres.
THAM. cærte et nunc etiam absurde, dubitare desiero. Sed erras: homo es: nec hoc, sed fera, ut nuper Mercurium disserentem audivi[.]
THEUT. calumniaris o Thame: ergo literarum usus, ergo mathematicæ,

et tanta momenta, feræ esse tibi vestigia videntur?

[Literarum usus.]
THAM. de mathematicis viderit Mercurius: et hic forte aliquid subesse possit. Cæterum de literis, nihil affers.
THEUT. at hæc o Thame disciplina, sapientiores Ægyptios tuos, memoriaque promptiores effecit: memoriæ enim et sapientiæ, ea a nobis adiumenta profecta sunt.

[Memoriæ pestis.]
THAM. at amor tibi pectus obscuravit: et contra tu quidem ostentas quam ipsa possint. ea siquidem attentione sublata, oblivionis et non curantiæ, certissimas causas afferent. quippe externis scripturæ formulis confisi, internas ipsas, a se ipsis recordatione repetere et excolere desinent. Non igitur memoriæ sed oblivionis affinitate contenderis, tuaque hæc omnis solertia,

illa se iactet in aula.

[Sapientiæ fucus.]
Accedit alterum, in altera propositi tui parte, non parvum incommodum: neque enim ea re, sapientiæ veritas Ægyptiis meis, sed fucus et opinio successit. Nam cum multa sine præceptore perceperint, multa quoque scire videbuntur: cum tamen vulgo ac passim ignari sint, atque in hominum congressu et consuetudine graves, molesti, et importuni: quippe qui, sapientiæ opinione, non ipsa sapientia, tuo nimirum beneficio sint imbuti. Atque hæc quidem quondam, in civitate superioris loci, quam vulgus Ægyptias Thebas appellat, me tibi hæc ipsa venditanti, respondisse memini: cum tu te iure perculsum, ipso pudore significares.

[Tabula naturæ.]
At fuit illud tempus, cum omnia omnes in animo scriberent. Hic autem quia vivit, iniurias ulcisci potest, novitque quæ apud quosque dicenda ac tacenda sint. Tua vero soboles, ab indoctis contumeliose et iniuriose tractata, paternum semper auxilium, inanimis illa quidem et ignava desiderat. neque enim acceptas iniurias ulcisci, neque ipsa sibi opem afferre potest. Falso ergo etiam sapientiæ secula prætexis: cum contra reputando, posteros omnes, laudatissimi studii patrimonio exhæredaris. Quid tergiversaris mi homo? iste Dei radius et efficientia, an potius

immanis feræ (quod initio proposui) vestigium videtur?

[Socrates Thamum adit.]
SOCR. Audivi o Thame a maioribus meis, et ipsi verum norant, circa
Ægypti Naucratem, antiquorum Deorum quendam fuisse, et ipsi nomen
Theutati, cui et sacra sit avis, quam ibin scilicet vocant: tum vero te,
universæ Ægipti regem, multa quidem in utramque partem cum eo
disseruisse: cum autem ad quæstionem de literis ventum esset, nulla
ratione probasse: quod homines literis confisi minus memoriæ studerent.
THAM. Quorsum ista?
SOCR. nempe ob eandem causam nihil ipse scripsi:
THAM. fortasse, et quis tu?
SOCR. Socrates ille, sapientissimus Apolline teste iudicatus.

[Sophista et pernicies hominum.]
THAM. ergo tu es sophista ille, pernicies hominum, et certe græcus?
SOCR. At Zopirus erravit, inquam.
THAM. imo vero talem descripsit, qualem te postea civitas tua, fraude
comperta, ex vestigiis certis esse iudicavit.
SOCR. Sed probavit Apollo.
THAM. nihil affers, et postea videro. verum

Qualia docuisti rudes?
heu insania tua, civitatisque
quæ tu nutriit,
corrumpentem adolescentulos!

SOCR. At hæc sunt Aristophanis, cuius est hoc loco, certis de causis,
suspecta fides.
THAM. nihil igitur illi credatur: ipsi tecum agamus. Nunquid igitur in
terris, o Socrates, insidiator aliquando pro fido, et fidus pro insidiatore
habetur?

[Socratica in differendo ratio.]
SOCR. At meæ sunt si nescis interrogantis vices: eas ego semper quasi
meo quodam iure vendicavi. Verum quia metuo Troianos, et præsertim
hunc polidamanta Diogenem, et ne tergiversari videar, respondebo
tamen. sic est.
THAM. An non medicus ille, ex levibus morbis magnos efficit, et populi

tamen comprobatione iactatur: alter autem vix habet, qui se fidei suæ credere velint?

SOCR. Et illud.

THAM. An non in his, et aliis quoque rebus, qui emerita virtute aliquid consequuntur, mendacio fere debere solent?

SOCR. fortasse.

THAM. An non ut ait ille,

Falsus honos iuvat, et mendax infamia terret?

Et ille,

Fortis et ignavus parili afficiuntur honore?

An non etiam in iudicibus suus quoque contingit error? cum nihil tam sincerum, et incoruptum esse debeat, quam lata sententia?

SOCR. cærte: nam et me licet innocentem, Athenienses morte mulctarunt.

THAM. an non bonus ille vir, sceleratus et nefarius putatur? ut inde vexetur, damnetur, explodatur, et egeat? contra autem improbus ille laudetur, colatur, omnes fortasse ad eum honores, laudes, et imperia ferantur?

SOCR. fortasse.

THAM. an non illi, cum sit rerum omnium ignarus, populi clamor et approbatio contingit?

SOCR. assentior: quanquam et illud video, quem hoc petat.

THAM. bene est, at hæc et talia humano generi sunt pernitiosa, nonne?

SOCR. sunt.

THAM. at unde orta?

SOCR. a mendacio fortasse.

THAM. mendacium ergo pernitiosissimum?

SOCR. pernitiosissimum.

[Socrates mendacii pater.]

THAM. At tu o Sophronisci fili mendacii pater es, et ipse mendax.

SOCR. unde illud?

THAM. quid? tu si æra singula probasti, summum quæ ex his confecta est, non soles probare? visne ergo, si te dati alicuius pœnitet, ut calculum reducam?

SOCR. captum me ut video putas, et id quod nollem fateri coactum: non sic. sed unde est inquam ista complexio?

THAM. quæ tua fuit dissimulantia?

SOCR. non agnosco.

THAM. dic igitur, sapiens fuisti, an non?

SOCR. si non?

THAM. cur igitur laudatus ab Apolline? quove etiam tanta de sapientiæ laude contentio? ut ne hic quidem etiam te contineas: etenim cum Nestore, ut audio, et Palamede plerumque nugaris.

SOCR. si sapiens?

THAM. si nihil scire est? si nulla perceptio? comprehensio? regula? aut nota veritatis? sapientia vero si se ipsa ignorabit, quæ neque de se dubitare debet, quo modo obtinebit nomen sapientiæ? mira est omnino ea sapientiæ ratio, nihil scire, aut certi habere, idque ostentantem de sapientiæ tamen palma contendere: sic enim et pueros omnes, et idiotas etiam sapientes esse dixeris.

SOCR. nempe Apollinis designatio pollet.

[Oraculi expositio.]

THAM. tamen in ista vanitate perstas? fuit ergo dissimulantia, et vaferrimus scilicet fuisti: sed ne dissimula: nullum hic invenies, aut fugæ effugium, aut divorticulum fucis. Non ipse hoc dissimulat Apollo: at is optimus interpres oraculi sui: constat enim te nulla doctrina, nullis artibus fuisse imbutum.

[Socrates in mathematicis itemque in physicis rudis.]

Quod si negas, responde mihi, quot sunt numerorum affectiones? circuli tetragonismus, aut cubi diaplasiasmus, qua fieri ratione possit, ostendito. distingue si potes, corporum cœlestium motus, cælique viam. Quid vis amplius, et quid habes de Deo? quis universa distinxit? Deus notus, an ignotus, in patre, mente, et amore? quæ Dei essentia? virtus? radii? quæ vestigia? quæ etiam umbræ?

SOCR. at tu si Deus esse posses, qualem te esse velles?

THAM. Iugulasti me Socrates. sed ad citeriora discendere placeat. dic si potes, de ævo, de mundo, de tempore, de generatione. quæ est tandem anima animæ mundi? quæ rerum origo? quæ perseverantia? quæ mundi fabrica? quæ forma? quis ordo? motus? vita? mors? quæ tandem restauratio? dic quæ bonis expectatio melior, cum potestate tantum sint, habeantque essentiam imperfectam? solvi etiam, et migrare oporteat? ut eadem esse omnium regio videri possit. ecquonam imperfecta? multa? mista? singularia? ipsa etiam instrumenta naturæ? Quid? lunæ quæ lineamenta sint, potesne dicere? cur eius nascentis alias hebetiora, alias acutiora, cornua videntur? dic etiam de mari, si cæruleum ipsum, cur eius unda pulsa purpurascit?

[Socratis Dii.]
At hic vocem contines, indicem imperitiæ tuæ, et testem ignorantiæ. unde illud agnosce amici:

> *Putabas Deum nullum præterquam hos,*
> *Et chaos, et nebulas, et linguam, tria hæc.*

hinc tuus ille Plato, quem hic etiam unguenta olentem, et delibutum vix ferre queas, tibi quidem alioqui devinctissimus, de naturæ rebus sermonem instituens, non te, ut alias fere semper, sed Timæum Locrum disserentem inducit.
SOCR. atqui in cælum scandere nequibam: proindeque illa ut vana semper contempsi, ac philosophiam eiusmodi rebus intentam, et hoc ipso in cælum ascendere meditantem, revocavi, et in domos civitatesque deduxi.

[In naturam intrandum ut ne in moribus erres.]
THAM. o dementiam incrediblem, in fictæ simulationis specie latentem! Et naturæ fœderum extremam ignorantiam! Quid igitur tibi et Deo? non erit

> *hoc violare fidem primam, et convellere tota*
> *fundamenta, quibus nixatur vita salusque?*

in naturam, o bone, intrandum erat, eaque quid postularet, penitus videndum:

> *nam libella aliqua si ex parte claudicat hilum,*
> *omnia mendose fieri atque obstipa necesse est,*
> *prodita, iudiciis fallacibus, omnia primis.*

animus enim nihil intelligens eorum quæ sunt, dementit, et errans liquitur in morbos.

SOCR. at non ita est: quin potius, quæ de moribus a me profecta sunt, et instituta cognosce. Quamvis enim superiora illa iure contempserim: in reipublicæ tamen administrandæ formis, et privatorum vita recte instituenda, sedulo laboravi.

THAM. etiam cum dubitares, quod esset extremum et ultimum bonorum? atqui illud perspicuum est, constitui necesse esse initium, quod omnes cum quid agere incipiant, sequantur.

[Quæ Socrati in moribus et republica visa.]

qui autem suscipere aliquam rem, aut agere audeant, cum certi nihil erit quod sequantur? verum esto. agnosco: et inde fuit præclara illa et speciosa rogatio, de exponendis partubus, abortu, amore: tum etiam de uxorum, liberorum, facultatum, et fundi communione: nam et mulieres etiam, una cum viris, belli munera suscipere, eiusdemque atque viros institutionis participes esse visum. o literas! o artes! o mores! quæ te vertigo capitis impulit, ut ista tam inconsiderate præciperes?

SOCR. Verum quid ista probra, probra præsertim laudis et gloriæ plæna? an non erit ista ratione, admirabilis omnibus inter omnes amicitia? malaque quæ nunc sunt in reipublicæ administrandæ formis, ex eo cærte nasci videantur, quod non sint omnium cuncta communia. dico autem falsorum testimoniorum iudicia, divitum assentationes, tum etiam lites et controversias, de rerum contractarum fide.

THAM. at nihil horum o Socrates, quod non sit bonorum communicatio, sed eiusmodi omnia ex pravitate et perversitate contingere necesse est. Quid? quod eos qui bona communicant, magis inter se dissidere videmus, quam qui seorsim facultates habent? tibi vero fraudis originem dedit, quod omni ex parte, atque omnibus modis, unam esse domum et unam civitatem expedire existimasti. at contra reputando, isto modo longius progressa, ne civitas quidem erit. multitudo est enim civitas natura: nisi concentum etiam, unius vocis sonum esse velis. Quid intcrim opifices a custodibus? quid præmii qui magistratum gerent? qua spe? quo precio? Absurdum autem esse videatur, facta cum beluis comparatione, eadem studia, eademque munera atque viros, obire mulieres. quid hic ad beluas? nam in amore, abortu et partubus, naturæ etiam iura violata.

SOCR. præterea magistratus et Reipublicæ præfectos, ab iis qui imperio subiecti sunt, differre oportere disserui: sicut etiam ex alia lana stamen, et ex alia subtemen fieri videmus.

THAM. *infelix o semper ovis pecus!*

quid enim attinet gloriose loqui, nisi et constanter etiam loquare? Atque equidem me miseret tui. Nonne hoc, positæ a te unitati et communioni repugnat? dic igitur si quid potes, et e tot sophismatis, unum aliquod quod te hinc expediat adhibeto. Sed ista transeant. Insuper divine ipse tibi disserere visus es, cum rationis imperium, cupiditatis et iræ obtemperantiam inculcares.

[Ratio libidinis lena.]
At falso: neque enim ratio est quæ vocet ad officium iubendo, aut vetando a fraude deterreat. Imo vero contra, ratio libidinis lena est; eaque omnino est quæ decipit quæque decipitur: et nisi mens adsit, frustra mihi crede rationis alis ascendere contendas.

Fertur equis auriga, neque audit currus habenas.

Quamvis erunt e nepotibus tuis, quibus fucus ille non possit avelli. quibus tamen non modo cupiditatis et iræ, sed rationis etiam obtemperantiam, solius vero mentis imperium valde suaderem. Ac talis quidem, ut ad te revertar, Socraticæ politeiæ materia fuerit.

[Socratis vita.]
SOCR. at vita mihi verecunda et proba fuit.
THAM. nimirum in umbra et ocio, et certe capitalis: nihil simplex, nihil apertum, putris ironia, et morosa dissimulantia: ignava omnino vita, et nulla liberum cura.

[Demon et adoptatio sui.]
Nam et simulatione Demonis, te ipsum adoptasti: itaque es ipse tibi elegans visus, ut omnes tui temporis philosophos, præ te, esse agrestes existimares.
SOCR. nempe improbos et populares sophistas arguere decebat.
THAM. Et Socrati soli, fallaciarum et fuci commercia et cauponantum vectigalia vacare. esto: (etsi eiusmodi a censore melius est, quam ab ipso etiam sophista notari) sed quis te furor in Anaxagoram commovit?
SOCR. an non est tamen laudanda temperantia?
THAM. tergiversaris, et in eius ut video nomine palles: at ego te de temperantia dicturum non putabam: qui et convivia captaris, et libidinis etiam irritamenta flagitiose docueris: ut suspitiones hoc loco omittam de puerorum, præsertim Alcibiadis: nosti cætera. unde illud,

Considera adolescentule, importuna esse omnia
quæ insunt, voluptatibus si priveris
puerorum, mulierum, ludorum, obsoniorum,
conviviorum, cachinnorum:
Quale hoc ipsum erit vivere, his si privatus fueris?

Imo vero opprobrio te iudice fuisse dicitur, si amatores adolescentibus non essent.

SOCR. at hæc sunt Aristophanis, et crimen abfuisse certum est.

THAM. at non carent reprehensione.

SOCR. si reprehensione?

THAM. at non suspitione.

SOCR. si illa?

THAM. at non saltem exemplo malo. Sed enim negatis, amorem stupri esse. quis est ergo amor iste amicitiæ, neque pueros deformes, neque formosos senes amantis?

SOCR. sed patientiæ nostræ testis est Zantippe.

THAM. non amo nimium patientes fuitque ea res profana, et minus consentanea, atque exempli mali.

SOCR. at nudis pedibus incedere solebam, et toto sæpe die immobilis stare consuevi.

THAM. quorsum hæc primum ostentatio? tum, si quis hoc idem facere non possit, continuo malus; aut si non velit, continuo stultus erit?

SOCR. at ubi me occultum et astutum paulo ante finxisti, quid est, quod minus cadere in eiusmodi naturam possit, quam aut hominum aspernari benevolentiam, aut opes nullius esse ducere?

THAM. certe nihil: sed nihil effeceris: nec repugnantia, de Socrate dici queant.

SOCR. at constantiam saltem agnosce. quanta enim illa vincula, quibus quidem constantissime me iniuste damnatum astringi ferebam, quanta sunt?

[Socratis mors.]

THAM. Nimirum emitti posse ex custodia, et levari vinculis sperabas: et interrito vultu videri visum, ut qui mortem nihil omnino formidares. Verum ubi spem nullam reliquam esse videres, quasi totus esses periturus, atque animus etiam capite damnatus esset, quam illa tibi simulatio excidit, et luculenta constantia! quæ vero punctiunculæ? quanquam hic quidem fateor, tuo more, quasi officii iudicio persona assumpta est, ut non tua, sed liberum causa afflictus et humilis esse viderere. Cæterum cum emigrandi tempus adesset, confidentiam quandam præ te ferebas: quasi volens id esses passurus, quod alioqui nolenti, volenti, omnino fuerat ferendum. usque adeo tuum illud placuit, simulantis et dissimulantis tenere ad extremum: ut constantiam istam tuam in sola vanitate possis agnoscere.

SOCR. at venenum hausi: quod et ex inflatis et tumidis adhuc cruribus, videri potest.

THAM. primum invitus: aut erat imbecillitas: et frustra pugnas.

[Socratis discipuli.]

SOCR. verum discipulorum meorum integritas, mei nominis famam, a malevolorum iniuriis vindicabit.

THAM. agnosco Aristippum, dissolutum illum et ebrium: et Platonem, Dyonisii quoque gratiam captantem, tanto illo certe peiorem, quanto sanctior scilicet voluit videri. An non audisti, ut Dionem ad Dyonisii coniuncti sui cædem invitarit? si inimicus, cur adis, et eius opibus uteris? si vero amicus, quo exemplo insidias paras? Nam quid ego de Xenophonte dicam?

[Antisthenes in phisico.]

SOCR. at Antisthenem saltem agnosce.

THAM. certe: nam et unum verum Deum agnovit, cum multos populares esse diceret, et fœminas amavit, et opes sprevit: idemque, quod tibi gratissimum est, Athenienses in tuæ necis authores incitavit. Ille etiam Crateti, continentiæ, Zenoni, tolerantiæ, et tranquillitatis author Diogeni fuit. Quid hoc ad te? nam neque te audire, neque tecum etiam commorari solebat: Tu Athenis, ille in piræo.

SOCR. utique me hodie perculisti o Thame: cæterum quo modo ista omnia sic esse nosti, qui multis ante seculis e vita discesseris?

THAM. si fingo, si mentior cupio refelli: Sin autem ista vera sunt, quid ergo præterea sollicite labores? aut qui potes denique intueri quæ gesseris? verum nec hoc celabo: Antisthenem igitur hunc ipsum, Cratetem et Diogenem agnosce. Quamvis præterea quotidianum est, aliquid audire de te, quod in mortalium perniciem dixeris aut feceris.

SOCR. at ut alii calumnientur, tu tamen facilior et æquior esse debebas: tuamque fortasse gratiam, pro meo quodam et certo iudicio, repetere possem.

THAM. etiam, si gratiæ resistere convenit? Sed unde est hoc o Socrates?

SOCR. nempe tua authoritate adductus, nihil in terris scripsi.

[Sententiæ Thami de literis expositio.]
THAM. calumnia est: neque enim absolute non scribendum, sed quasi in repetundarum iudicio, memoriæ studium in literarum locum, reponendum esse contenderam. Ille igitur suos sensus literis commendat? aliquid est. non commendat autem, sed memoria repetit? hoc etiam maius. at vero qui neutrum, ille mihi inutilis semper visus. Quamvis hoc ego philosophi non arbitror, authoritate et testibus uti: quos aut casu veros, aut malitia falsos fictosque esse comperias. Argumentis et rationum momentis oportet ad persequenda impelli, non certe eventis, iisque præsertim quibus integra fronte non credere liceat. Non igitur ita hoc nobis visum, sed argumenti et rationis vi ac designatione confectum, amplecti oportuit. Quamquam quid ago, qui a Socrate rationis vim dignitatemque, ut a philosopho requiro?

[Socrates occupat vices suas et denique impetrat.]
SOCR. certe difficilis es o Thame. Verum dic vicissim iam nunc tu. An non eiusdem est, et bello pacem quærere, et hic illius artes non contemnere?
THAM. certe.
SOCR. an non si ea quæ sunt reipublicæ administrandæ formis perniciosa, animo teneamus, et ea quoque quæ salutaria, congruit tenere?
THAM. sic est.
SOCR. Et eiusdem qui leges malas deprehenderit et abrogarit, bonas et salutares condere?
THAM. fortasse.
SOCR. an non etiam eius, qui mortis umbram demonstrarit, in lucis etiam umbra sedisse, ad eamque ducere posse videatur?
THAM. videtur.
SOCR. an non igitur eiusdem Thami est, qui oblivionis materiam deprehenderit, memoriæ quoque pharmacum exhibere? atque hoc quidem, me tecum ab initio agere conantem, tua nostri instituti expositio non tulit. Ergo age, et quoniam ex superum rescripto transire datum est,

Tu animum magnum
contine in pectoribus: amicitia enim est melior:

et me si placet internuncio, Theutatis arte exactæ memoriæ, memoriam excita.

THAM. circulus est mi homo, et fatum, et amor. verum ego ut homini græco? Et cur non enim? atque esto ut inquis amicitia melior, cæterum unde tibi obsecro succurrit, de hoc omni proposito dici omnino posse? si nihil est iudicii, si nihil est quod iudicat, nihil etiam sciri aut percipi posse consequitur. Nam reliqua illa opinandi temeritas,

Sacer est morbus et visus mentitur.

ergo opinatione, ergo perceptione sublata, assertio omnis retinenda videri possit. Scilicet erramus alioqui, ac nos in fraudem induimus, si ulla a natura data esse iudicia putemus. Sed erubescis: et quid nunc vero? in sententia manes?

SOCR. si maneo?

THAM. nihil igitur de re proposita dici potest.

SOCR. si non maneo?

THAM. at non est sapientis mutare sententiam. quid? anne et hoc etiam tuum?

SOCR. at genus saltem respice tuorum.

THAM. sed flecti et misereri nefarium est: quippe nulla in sapientem cadit perturbatio. Sic enim urges o sapientissime, et laqueorum tuorum flumine mersamur. Verum fiat sane quod vis, faciamque quod ne in vita quidem facere solebam, ut iis de rebus quæ doctrina et ratione contineantur, disputarem: memoriæque memoriam, tot ut inquis seculis exactæ, te etiam internuncio, (siquidem hoc ita vis) in terris excitemus. At erit interim

tua messis in herba:

nec prius quæ ponentur intelliges, quam cum Anaxagora, quem transisse etiam audio, in gratiam redieris. Sic igitur accipe.

[Oblivio.]

Oblivio nequitia est impotentis animi, atque demissi: eademque materiæ soboles prima, potentias animi principes dissolventis et attenuantis. Ex quo apparet, neque divinitus eam, neque a natura contingere (nam fortunæ nomen inane est, cuiusque efficientiam ignoratio causarum effinxit) sed in nobis sitam, et nostra sponte contractam. Nunc enim a cognoscente res ipsa contemnitur: et

Mos est oblivisci hominibus,
neque novisse, cuius nihili sit faciunda gratia.

unde nulla sequitur ab horizonte progressio, nulla umbra, subiectum nullum, nullus ordo, aut animi denique spiritusque solertia.

Nil igitur mirum est, animus si cætera nescit,
præterquam quibus est in rebus deditus ipse.

Tum, sensus fiducia et muneris instrumenti functione decipimur. Et quod omnium pessimum, in ignoratione versamur. ut servitutis iniustæ genus quoddam esse videatur.

[Memoria.]
Huic contraria memoria, potentia quidem illa, et actus et umbra, remigium est alarum animi, corporis servitio, et sensuum instrumentis expeditum. Huius virtus prima est in umbra boni: Altera vero in agendis, et visa et perspecta respicere. Nunc omnis quidem, natura ipsa inculcante, facultas a principe Deo est, cuius tamen in ea ipsa, impressa vestigia cernimus: ex quorum observatione et experientia, rationis etiam solertia succurrit: eaque est sola recta ratio, quæ a natura profecta est: quam si radio denique, et pulvere sollicitaris, omne quidem punctum tulisse videri possis. Triplex igitur hic erit opportunitas, naturalis quidem et insita prima, eaque simul cum cogitatione nata.

[Natura.]
Quam cum ante inventas literas homines tuerentur, expresserunt sane, neque erat, ut literas et elementa requirerent. atque ut nunc homines literis consignant quæ volunt manere, sic illi in animis res insculptas habebant. Postea vero quam Theutatis acumine perfectum esset, ut illum quam naturam homines esse mallent; quem sequerentur, et a quo memoriæ præsidium petendum esset, secuta declinatio est, defuitque naturæ industria humana: unde nata tandem in matrem impietas, et falsa de impotenti vena querimonia. Deinceps autem, Sive

Ut varias usus meditando extunderet artes, pater ipse colendi
Haud facilem esse viam voluit,

Sive est inæqualis proportio superum, et nostra solutio, ubique imbecillis neque omnibus eadem memoria successit.

[Ratio.]
Inde altera illa rationis et artis opportunitas sequuta videri possit: quæ latentem alioqui naturam evocet atque confirmet: ex illius etiam utero et ipsa evocata. Namque, illius ope, præceptio, et illa, ratione ac doctrina nitescit; ea est rerum earum cognata conspiratio.

[Simonides Chius.]
Atque hæc quidem, cum multis annis doctoris illius solertia latuisset, in Græcia primum vestra falso emersisse putatur: et Chius quidem ille, primus eam invenisse et protulisse creditur. At si meorum replicentur annales, et excitentur historiæ, multo ante in figuris, notis, indiciis, sigillis, signis, et characteribus viguisse reperias. Idemque, si separetur etiam Ægiptus, apud Celtas in Druidum institutis, usuvenisse compertum est. valeat igitur cum suis Tyndaridis ille.
[Themistocles.]
Nunc alii ut elegantuli scilicet esse videantur, et artem hic nullam esse, facetiola quadam persuadere possint, malle se quidem oblivisci, quam meminisse respondent: neque tamen attendunt, reciprocam plagam esse: estque ea sane digna misero afflictoque sententia. Atque ut quisque quod opus est malit, tu tamen, opinor, de reipsa, non de homine quæris: et quid naturæ consentaneum, et per se bonum, non vero quid quisque aut oblivisci, aut meminisse malit. Ac istæ quidem memoriæ causæ fuerint, is occasus, et ea respiratio.

[De memoriæ subiecto.]
Et non sit impudens, qui in immortalis Dei circo, et ipsa, non per cancellos, sed ex vortice templi, et puncto tempore, omnia contuente luce, umbræ huius bonitatem et momenta quærat? Etenim si suas causas habet, si cum materia, tempore, generatione, et imbecillitate coniuncta, si utilis et ipsa, valeat, et in aliis esto. Ergo animus ille qui in sideribus errantibus aut inerrantibus inest, aut communis etiam animi virtus, ea opportunitate perficitur? certe si rerum earum quæ in medio geruntur, ut homines quidem existimant, cognitione non egent orbium animi, nec recordationis etiam remigiis egebunt. At enim cognoscunt, quæque geruntur a singulis dispensant. verum fortasse: sed alio modo: neque enim unquam inferioris orbis contemplatione privantur: est autem

absentium et præteritarum rerum omnis recordatio. Porro, si quis hoc quoque percontetur, an orbium animi, die vel mense vel anno superiore, se terram circuisse agnoscant: sic accipito. Nihil continuum et commutationis expers declinationem admittit: in die autem mense et anno, declinationis quædam extrema et vestigia cernuntur. Nihil igitur in eo quod constans est, hesternum esse possit. Verum animus humanus, in hoc omni sermone, diei pater est, et mensis et anni. Atque quemadmodum qui in itinere est, pedis eiusdem vestigia, variis terræ partibus imprimit; sic orbium motus in suis animis uni, a nobis quidem in multas partes distinguuntur. Etenim in cælesti mundo dies unus est, nullæ noctis vices. Quare stellarum et orbium animi, cognoscunt illi quidem fortasse: at non in tempore: et memoriam cum tempore esse coniunctam, positum est a nobis. Verum perstas adhuc, et orbium inquis animi in homines intuentur: ex quo etiam et memores esse fortasse possint. At quale est hoc? intuentur: ergo etiam, eodemque loco, memoriæ denique participes esse constet. imo vero contra est neque enim quæ intuemur, recordatione recolimus, sed absolute cognoscimus. Ex quibus et illud simul intelligi potest, nec singulorum animos ubi ad locum sibi cognatum ascenderint, ratiocinantis memoriæ functiones habere posse, nec ullam etiam ad eam rem potestatem: nisi forte

Iterum ad Troiam magnus mittetur Achilles.

aut enim non vident, aut certe in speculo vident. In aliis igitur esto. Quando autem eius munus cum corpore, ipsamque cum tempore coniunctam esse posuerimus, relinquitur quidem certe, in solis animantibus, atque iis quidem animantibus, quæ temporis sensum habent, virtutis huius habilitates inesse. Atqui si tempus numerus est, et solus homo natura factus et aptus ad numeros subducendos, quid moror amplius in brutis?

[Natura et ratio.]
Nusquam igitur universa natura aberit, nusquam cuiusque propria languebit: superet modo cognata rationis virtus et artis accessio: quæ aut eam certe sequitur, et superatur ab ea, aut forte superat. Illa enim substantiæ formam in specie quidem servat: at numero non item. siquidem fluctuantis materiæ stomachus mature omnia digerit. At vero ars, in specie quidem deficit, in numero autem differentibus, earumque rerum mensura et duratione pollet. Nam et pereunte re, extrinseca eius

forma, adamanti, picturæ et scripturæ committi possit, et absentia atque præterita præsentia reddi, et profluentes alioqui conceptus, et fluentia verba, ad quælibet loca et tempora transmitti et contrahi certe possunt.

[Nulli animi ramo ratio hæc innixa.]
Nunc si virtutis huius in horizonte sedes, ecquonam modo requiem et actum in centro præstare possit? sive etiam in hoc, ecquanam ratione ex horizonte transmitteret? ut nulli animi ramo proprie innixam agnoscere possis. Cæterum o bone, de acumine et iudicio tuo viderit Anaxagoras: rerumque earum quarum repetentia placet, si canimus tibi, notitiam et intelligentiam ante præstet. Nam cum tria sint in rerum natura, prospexisse, perspexisse, et hæc ipsa respicere, quis est qui sublato aut altero aut utroque, id quod non est, credo, quodque indigestum est, respicere se audeat dicere? hic igitur si inventionis acumen, aut iudicandi solertiam inculcari a nobis existimas, dimittimus te: et certe nequidquam erras.

[Prima momenta.]
Neque enim naturæ rationisque prudentiam, sed eius rei umbram quæris: et eam quidem umbram, quæ nisi expedito suo corpore (ea est enim natura umbrarum) nulla ratione apprehendi possit. primum itaque (ut denique in arenam descendere placeat) ipsum intelligere sit positum a nobis: voluntas et Amor adsit, maximus ille quidem et antiquissimus omnium deorum. proxima ratio est, vacuum esse animum, præsentem, et nullos motus. frustra enim alioqui et temere, quasi torrentem annulo consignare contenderis. his accedit uti qui neque vitem serit, neque quæ sata est diligenter colit, oleum, ficus et poma non habet: ita hoc loco, nisi quæ opus provideas primum, et certe colas, frustra hic oleum sperabis, et vacuus operam ludes. Ex quo verissime dictum est,

Non fieri partum nisi concilio ante vocato principium.

Posito ergo eo quod repetendum, primo quasi castra quæruntur, et delectus habentur: tum vero acie instructa, militibusque confirmatis et animatis, quid præterea quispiam requirat? Prima hic igitur providentia pollet: criterii vices alteræ. Sed hoc est memorem esse? an non ea, inquis iam ante relegata? At blande ludis, et amo imprimis te.

[Providentia.]

Omnis enim rerum providentia, e suis illa quidem fontibus quærenda: eiusque rei methodus in rationis insulam a nobis relegata est: et potuit fugiendi et persequendi quoque providentia, in civitatem etiam relegari: cum nobis interim in umbris esse liceat. Verum hæc omnis consideratio prima, in subiectis et umbris est. Etenim cum oblivio et memoria extrema sint, et illa tenebris et quasi morti, hæc vero luci ex proportione respondeat: certe ut a tenebris ad lucem, nulla est nisi per interiectas umbras, patiente natura progressio, idem etiam hoc loco credere par est: Omne igitur quod ab oblivione in memoriam fertur, per medias umbras quasi nuncias, quæ rerum species temperent et animo propinent, feratur oportet. Imo omne non necessitate sed sponte movens, propositæ rei speciem anticipet oportet: eaque est idea in Deo, et umbra nobis. Atque ut natura per insitam et inquilinam ideam, ex indefinita materia, definitas illa quidem species producit: ita animus noster non solum in instituto repetentiæ, sed in omni omnino consilio et actione, non nisi per umbras agit: et,

> *Quodcunque lubido*
> *venerit, extemplo mens cogitat eius id ipsum*
> *et simul ac volumus nobis occurrit imago.*

sunt igitur opus umbræ: omnisque in iis sita

> *causa videtur*
> *cernendi, neque posse sine his res ulla videri.*

unde, et subiecta etiam e quibus ipsæ exprimantur agnosce. Primum igitur de subiecti natura et essentia, tum vero etiam de delectu et lege, postremo de umbris simili modo dicendum erit. [De subiectis.]

Est autem subiectum sinus et receptaculum umbrarum. hinc potes quæ didiceris, quæque ipse cogitando conceperis, et sola tamen quæ visa tibi, memoriter pronunciare. Non sumus ergo in enunciati extremis, non in ipsa hyle, neque in re natura facta et ad ipsam, aut arte facta et ad artem relata: verum in hac et illa, facta cum expediendæ conformationis umbris, quasi notis et sigillis contentione versamur. Nunc omnis de subiecto duplex est quæstio: nam et absolutum quoddam est et principale, natura quidem illud aut manu denique promptum: et aliud adiuvans, ac visionis efficientia plerumque contentum. Cum sit autem ipsum universum, et ima tellus, et continens hæc aut illa, et politeia, et œconomica dimensio, et partes eius: e proximis quidem tribus generibus, absoluta subiecta pro occasione assumuntur: reliqua illa nec sunt opus, nec usuvenire etiam fortasse queant. porro adiuvans est quod absoluto et continenti adiunctum est. inde est ubertas, et inde firma retentio. atque cum illud immotum sit et fixum, hoc tamen pro umbrarum occasione movetur: quippe quod earum servitiis sit addictum. Esto autem in intercolumnio gladius. hic igitur innatam et ex ipsa natura expressam, sui defendendi legem, Astræa commendans, gladium porrigat: et novis rebus studentes gladio luant. Idemque si quando non protinus repetenti umbra omnis occurrat, ab effectis et contingentibus, officii quidem ille memor, sine omni cunctatione designet. lapides hic habent vocem suam, et hospitis umbræ, nutus et imperium observant. Sed exorientur fortasse, quibus horum aliud in materia tantum, aliud mathematicum esse videatur non placet: cur non placeat, alias ostendemus: id nunc admonuisse contenti, omnia quidem huius generis subiecta, mathematica nobis videri: non quod a materiæ concretione separata sint, verum quia locorum et hospitum numerum etiam et ordinem designent: et nisi designent, frustra hic fere assumi videantur. videris ergo, an et hoc etiam ad rerum earum utilitates adiiciendum putes. Atque sic quidem fuerit subiecti natura, adiuncta sequuntur in delectu et lege.

[De lege subiectorum.]
Sunto igitur primum e genere rerum earum quæ sub sensum cadunt: inhærentem inquam, vel extrinsecus assumptam formam, sed utramque tamen sensilem atque oculis opportunam habento: quamvis forte interim, non semper ab instrumentis et horizonte moveantur. nam frustra alioqui repetas, quæ ne effingere quidem et collocare potueris. Tum ex horizontis in aspectu proportione conformantor. Ut enim neque est umbra lux, neque etiam tenebræ ita nec in his, nec illa, sedes eius. Atque ut splendor omnis acer adurit oculos:

(nam quocunque loco fit lux atque umbra, tueri illorum est:)

idem etiam in sensu et visis usuvenire solet. Hic igitur nec nimis illustria, ne præfulgenti splendore offendant, nec vehementer etiam obscura sunto. Cæterum cum sint umbrarum receptacula, mediocri et modica magnitudine providentor ac definiuntor. Si quid autem prohibessit, ex naturæ præscribentis arbitratu modificantor. Nam si præter modum ampla, vix umbræ statum impetrassint: angusta vero fortasse etiam repellere videri possint. Porro explicata et distincta ipsa, intervalla vero mediocria et parallela sunto: idque ut opportune succedat, cogitationis apparatum adhibento. Mediæ autem areæ quasi abolitæ deletæque sunto. Tum dissimili forma, dissimili etiam natura similitudinis insolentiam amovento: naturæ autem in varietate solertiam exprimunto. Concava omnia aut certe plana, at nusquam convexa sunto. porro absoluta omnia, sociis illis et adiuvantibus, quasi custodiis, insignita sunto. Quæ autem illorum fidei credentur, hæc ipsa custodiunto. si cogitatio creverit, dimittunto. In viciniam ne digrediuntor. At in suas quasi tribus distribuuntor. Tribuum autem præfecti et principes, ex lunæ mansionum imaginibus si placet, assumuntor. Decemviratum perpetuum exercento. Suas in singulis stationibus catenas aureas providento. Adiuvantia denique quæ ad plures usus et motus, apta esse videas, æterna sunto. Hæc autem omnia ut maneant, et hærere possint, qui volent observanto. Qui operæ suæ precium requirent, non quidem oculis et externa (quæ neque semper usuvenire queat) sed insita illa, ac integra et sua animi luce diligenter et accurate censento. Sic igitur subiecta dimensa atque descripta sunto.

[De umbris.]
Nunc autem ad umbras simili ratione transire placeat. Est igitur umbra, efficta rei species credita subiecto, ad firmam illa quidem perceptionem assumpta. Et species quidem, non quatenus in mente prima: hæc etenim lux est, atque eadem semper: nos quærimus umbram, eamque quæ gigni possit: non quatenus in cælo et sempiternis ignibus illis, aut periodis cæli: non quatenus in se, eove quod procreat, aut ipso etiam eventu: neque denique quatenus artis opus est, aut in animi etiam horizonte movetur[.] Sed qua sensus apparatu et cogitationis lima polita est. Huius fidei res ipsa creditur: hæc ipsa, subiecti. Atque quemadmodum ex antecedente fide (ut Mercurium aliquando disserentem audivi) consequitur intelligentia: et in naturæ rationisque prudentia, ex antecedentis positione complexio: sic ex umbrarum etiam virtute, negotii omnis sequitur firma et explicata retentio. Nunc quibus hæc ardua et desperata videtur, aut vana et operosa fortasse solertia, illud modo norint, ut ne quid amplius dicam, quod explicatum non capias, vel involutum esse tenendum.

[Umbræ simplices.]
Sunt autem umbrarum aliæ simplices, aliæ modificatæ. simplices quidem, rerum earum quæ sub aspectum cadunt, et modificatæ conceptuum. Illæ ab horizonte moventur et accipiuntur: hæ vero in sensu gignuntur et effinguntur. Itaque cum de re sub aspectum cadente, sit modica modo, negotium erit, qualis illa, talis erit et umbra. Hic homo hominem, Alledius Alledium, et beluam belua designat. Omnesque adeo res, quæ sua natura sub aspectum cadere possint, sint modicæ modo, sub huius generis umbris cogitationi traduntur. Sua natura dico, quia et ea quoque quæ percipiuntur auribus et cogitatione, quæque ab aspectu abhorrent, et sub intelligentiam per se cadunt, aspectus etiam commendatione, sed modificata succurrunt: ut cæca hæc, et ab aspectus iudicio, sua natura remota, ita notet conformatio, ut quæ cogitando complecti nequieris, quasi intuendo tenere possis. Quod si autem occurritur in parvulis quidem rebus, aut certe magnis: de modicis modo dictum est a nobis.

[Modificatæ.]
Atenim si res suam umbram et propriam non habeat, necessitas cogit, quod non habeas, aliunde assumere. Ergo cum simplices non occurrent umbræ, bene agi existima, si imitata et efficta simulacra, aut quoquo modo similia afferentur. Hæc est illa conformatio, hæ umbræ modificatæ: non quidem voluptatis et delectationis causa inductæ (quod in translationibus usuvenire solet) sed angustiis et necessitate premente: ut ad ea quoque quæ abstracta, quæque coniuncta sunt, quasi facilius mentis oculi ferantur. Quid enim aliud restet, si necessitate cogaris? Porro modificatio alia rerum est, alia vero in verborum conformatione cernitur.

[Rerum.]
Atque quemadmodum in iis rebus quæ sub aspectum cadunt, a formis externis, umbras emanare videmus: sic peti ab internis, inflexæ et modificatæ fortasse debeant. Et certe si rerum formas veras cerneremus, omnis esset inde evocanda conformatio: nunc cum non cernas, in absolutis quidem, a rationum fontibus, in mathematicis vero, a nudo institutione, petenda.

[Absoluta.]
Absoluta autem sint, quæ nullam numeri differentiam afferunt. simplicia

sint, coniuncta sint, nihil moror: dum illud in hoc omni sermone memineris, rerum quidem abstractarum, et a sensuum instrumentis abhorrentium, simulacra quæri. siquidem rerum earum quæ sub aspectum cadunt, efformatio simplex est. Atque hæc quidem rerum absolutarum sive inflexio, sive modificatio, tropus sane vocetur: non quidem immutandi et transferendi verbi, quod orationi splendoris aliquid arcessat (quæ vestra philosophia est) sed quo rerum quasi commercia fiant, et simulacra suppetere possint: cum id quod a sensuum instrumentis abhorret, alterius sub hæc ipsa cadentis, officio creditur. Quæ tamen non ideo a nobis assumuntur, ut pro impotentibus illis, hæc quidem quæ rerum earum vices subeunt, proferantur (quæ vestræ assumptionis causa sola est) sed ut horum in cogitationis apparatu latentium adiumentis, illa ipsa pro quibus assumpta sint, quæque alioqui complecti nequeas, et retinere et pronunciare possis. Ob eamque causam, quod a vobis de verecunda translatione præcipitur, nusquam aderit, et obesse imprimis fortasse possit. Nunc igitur efficiens rei factæ vices subit. hinc patrem sequitur sua proles: hinc Mathematicas et elementa, Theutates: pyromantiam, Vulcanus: Hydromantiam[,] Nereus: ortum et occasum, Appollo [sic]: eamque quæ chirurgia dicitur, Chiron: molitiones et bella, Minerva: providentiam, Prometheus: et triste, Epimetheus, pænitentiæ supercilium præstare possit. Nec illud interim te conturbet, si neque hæc etiam sub aspectum cadunt. sive enim corpora sint, sive corporum expertia, et sive cohæreant, sive non: ad ea tamen corpora respiciendum est, quæ ipsis a veteribus tributa.

Nam certe ex vivo, Centauri non fit imago:
Nulla fuit quoniam talis natura animantis.
Verum ubi equi atque hominis, casu convenit imago,
hærescit facile extemplo.

hinc etiam ferramenta, ministri et vectes, molitionem et fabricam designant. Atque adeo, quæ quisque dixerit, fecerit, aut etiam scripserit, aut certe possit, ex ipso illo expedite repetere licet. Nam quid ego de materia dicam? quid vero de fine? Sed ab eventis, efficiens et omnis præterea causa repetitur. Quis hominem humo excitatum, celsum fecit? quis vero sensus quasi interpretes et nuncios rerum, in capite tanquam in arce collocavit? quis oculos tornavit, et quasi vallo munivit. quis vero iis ipsis ignem luminosum inclusit? quis nares perfodit? aut auribus duros et quasi corneolos introitus subiecit? quis osse medullam, ossa ipsa nervis, et omnia carne descripsit? quis carnem ipsam ex salso et acido, quasi fermento, nervos vero ex osse et carne, ipsum ex terra et medulla, aut medullam ex triangulis confecit? costas compegit? aut cor pyramidatum effecit? quid vero tanta rerum omnium consentiens, conspirans et continuata cognatio? aut quid est tandem in terrestribus rebus, in quo non naturæ umbra intelligentis appareat? Nonne igitur vides ut ipsum infinitum, incomprehensum, ab effectis ostendi possit? Infinita sunt huius generis exempla, unde quasi ex vestigiis et sigillis, Deum ipsum, et ævum, et mundum, et tempus, et ortum, omniaque omnino quæ quidvis effecerint, opportune repetere possis. Nunc id quod subest, ad adiuncta insinuanda traducitur. Sic huius in principatu, communi utilitati consulentis conformatio regnum dabit, non consulentis vero tyrannidem. horum autem paucorum quidem, sed plurium uno, eorumque virtute præditorum informatio, Aristocratiam præstat. Sic populi ad communem utilitatem conspiratio, politeiam, ad patriciorum vero contumeliam, democratiam, ut vos quidem distinguitis, significare parata est. Sic morbi, firmitas, virtutes, opes, pulchritudo, eaque quæ his contraria, e suis illa quidem subiectis exprimuntur. Sic rerum omnium earum quæ natura constant, proprietates et accidentiæ ab ipsis quasi præconibus enunciantur[.] Nunc a rebus adiunctis et accidentiis subiecti commendatio dependet. Sic ab hirundine, a fabæ satione, cæterisque similibus ver habetur: sic toga pro pace, sic arma ac tela pro bello ponuntur. Quo loco et illud etiam observa, communes quidem accidentias, ex alio atque alio subiecto, alia atque alia, ex voluntatis tuæ sententia et arbitratu posse proferre. Nunc etiam a dissentaneo lux affertur. Hic in iis primum quæ sola ratione dissentiunt, ex insigni victoriam, parricidam ex latrone venaberis. Tum iis forte præteritis, quorum unum multis pari ratione videmus opponi, ecce tibi ut ex hæredibus, testatoris, ex eo qui damnum dedit, eius qui tulit, ex coniuge mariti, ex socero generi, eiusque qui locat ex conductore memoria reportatur. Hic si Periclis memoriam repetes, Anaxagoram recognosce. Nam et adulter Hippolitum, et servus libertum, et quod calet frigidum, et qui prodigus parcum, et qui prudens idiotam, et qui secundis rebus utitur calamitosum, cæcus videntem, et sobrium ebrius fortasse designet: ex irrisionis certe elegantia, vel materiam occasione præbente. Atque ut plerique non quidem ex furore, sed iudicio, perpetuas rerum vices reputantes, de altera sorte divinant, et

sperat infestis, metuit secundis

alteram sortem, bene præparatum
pectus,

quidni item, et repetentia quoque succurrat? Sicut etiam natura ipsa, contraria ex contrariis excitat: et adversarum, quam similium rerum familiaritas, appetitio et consequentia maior est. Cæterum in iis rebus quæ comparatione cernuntur, ex multis infinitio, ex Ibice ventus, ex eo quod maius, id quod modicum, et ex modico maius poterit effingi. Nam proportionis officia quis non videt? nihilque certe est in rerum natura, quod similitudinis aliquando luce non possit illustrari. hic igitur ille

os humerosque Deo similis,

Deum, et figulus lutum contrectans, arbitrium eius, principem quoque paterf[amilias] et vetula inter duas adolescentulas constituta, lunæ solisve dabit eclipsim. Sic arbor altissimis defixa radicibus, quæ nulla vi labefactari possit, virtutis speciem præstat: et navis illa cuius

Nudum remigio latus,
et malus celeri saucius africo,
antennæque gemant,

rempublicam male affectam et laborantem animo subiiciet. Sic turbines et procellæ, pericula et calamitatesque designant. Sic si

fulvum fingatur in ignibus aurum,

cognata sententia, de exploranda fide in impetu fortunæ succurrere possit. Atque hic quidem fabularum allegoriæ tanti sunt, ut ea fere sola ratione, in sententiis præsertim, quantum voles efficere queas. Nunc in diversæ qualitatis rebus, Neoptolemus Achillem, et Socrates Anaxagoram excitabit. Et gratis esse placeat, pro exempli utilitate percepta. Postremo, ut distributionis etiam adiumenta recenseam, ecce tibi, tibiæ nuptiales coniugium notant, una turma equitatum, tectum, parietes, mœnia, earumque rerum partes, domum et urbem intelligi volent. Hic ex verbi unius simulacro et imagine, totius sæpe sententiæ conformatio succurrit. quod idem in pictura usuvenire solet. sic Mercurii, Æsculapii, Promethei, Chirones, pro sapientibus: sic Calatini, pro civibus ornatis, iisdemque pauperibus: atque omnino pro suis generibus species assumuntur. Ac ista fere sunt, quæ de rerum absolutarum inflexione dicenda videbantur: nisi forte etiam de institutione expectas. qua quidem in re accurata meorum diligentia viget. Atque ea si naturæ congruentia ponit, placet: sin autem ea mera est, aut raro accedat, aut certe utilitas vincat. Sane omnis necessitati præscriptio cedit: ut mathematicas umbras, et sola inde remedia possis agnoscere.

[Umbræ mathematicæ.]
Res ergo mathematicæ, cum sint abstractæ, et ab omni materiæ concretione separatæ, simplices quidem umbras proiicere nequirent: nec vero etiam superiore ratione inflexas. Nempe hic a nobis numerorum adumbratio intelligenda est: eiusque rei ne suspicio quidem, ex omni observatione naturæ poterat oriri. Ergo hic jure institutio pollet, magni quidem illa momenti, præcepti brevis. Primum itaque elementa eiusmodi esse placet, quæ animi aciem rite ciere possint.

humana ante omnes species est optima: nempe hæc
instrumenta capit quæcunque, et ad omnia nata est.

hos autem ex Zodiaci signorum et errantium umbris, aut literarum etiam ordine apparari placet. ac ne quando similitudo fortasse conturbet, de copia cautum esto. census vero in lævam, ratioque omnis arithmetica certa est: et virgulæ denique supremus calculus esto. Ac de rerum quidem adumbratione satis fere dictum est. Et quoties rem ipsam meminisse placet, si formarum et umbrarum diligenti notatione utere, facile ea quae voles, memoria consequi poteris.

[Verborum inflexio.]
Reliqua est verborum inflexio: quo loco, etsi

Cui lecta potenter erit res,
nec facundia deseret hunc, nec lucidus ordo:

et

Verbaque provisam rem non invita sequantur.

Tamen et huic etiam parti prospicere placeat. etsi res hæc opinionis et fuci potius, quam scientiæ vestigium videtur. Illud igitur primum intelligi par est, plurima quidem ex eorum genere quæ sub sensum cadunt, tum vero etiam eorum quæ non cadunt, eiusmodi esse, ut ex iis ipsis, verba quoque necessario sequantur. hic igitur quæ de rebus dicta sunt, de verbis etiam dicta esse putes. Nunc ubi rerum existet inutilis commendatio, similium verborum conservata et immutata casibus, aut traducta notatio (si exercitatio fiet) omnino fere satis esse possit. Atque cum articuli sua membra sequantur, omnis præterea verborum cura erit inanis, et habitet sane tecum: ea vestra philosophia est. Atqui ne quidquam in hoc genere, et græcus et esuriens sophista desideres, huic etiam parti iuvet indulgere. Primum igitur elementorum facies in certis personis esto: eadem in eorum actionibus propriis, et item in adiunctis. Quibus ante provisis, atque ita quidem provisis, ut prompte et expedite, tot ac talia designet elementa, cum suis effectis et adiunctis, Alledius: eodemque modo in reliquis: quid dubitas ex horum et illorum vice, quascunque compositiones effingere? Rursus, constitue modo consonas, et singulis etiam vocales quinque proprias: finales et liquidas ex gestu quæras: omnia autem personis bene positis notes: quæcumque meminisse opus est, tanquam literis in cera, perscribere certe possis.

[De lege umbrarum.]
Hæc igitur umbrarum quasi consitura fuerit: ad legem et adiuncta veniamus. Cum enim ab unaquaque re, pro luce ingenii, multiplices umbræ produci possint:

Cum præsertim aliis eadem in regione locoque,
Longe dissimiles animus res cogitet omnes:

fitque efformatio simplex secura magis, laboretque sensus umbra reflexa: quod idem etiam utrinque in horizonte contingit: nimirum delectus habendi, et opportunitas expendenda videri possit.

Scilicet arte madent simulacra et docta feruntur.

Et quoniam ea maxime animis affigi certum est, quæ a sensuum instrumentis tradita fuere atque impressa: acerrimus autem est videndi sensus: omnes proinde umbræ simplices, omnes inflexæ, oculorum primum comendatione animis traduntor. luce, colore, figura, et magnitudine descriptæ ac definitæ sunto: quippe alioqui

pars maxima fallit,
propter opinatus animi quos addimus ipsi,
pro visis ut sint, quæ non sint sensibu' visa.

si res ita feret, in suæ dimensionis specie manento: si non feret autem, ex adiunctis modificantor. Cæterum illustres et acres sunto: omninoque eiusmodi, quæ occurrere, celeriterque animum percutere possint. facile enim

uno commovet ictu,
Quælibet una animum nobis subtilis imago.

Ergo insolentibus quidem, aut ridiculis etiam rebus insignitæ sunto, et egregiam pulchritudinis, aut turpitudinis speciem aliquam præ se ferunto:

Creentque
Tenuem animi naturam intus visumque lacessant.

Vagæ ne sunto: interdum enim

Species vanescit iacta in inane.

Si cogitatio creverit, exeunto. Dissimiles forma et dispares ac variæ sunto. Quod si autem ab instrumentis, similes formas sensus acceperit, aut ipse creassit, visionis officiis et opera retractantor. Ac de providentia quidem et apparatu dictum est a nobis.

[Criterium.]
Quid deinde? Nempe criterii vices manent: eaque de re, simili ratione dicendum. Placet igitur primum definire quid ipsum sit. Sed ratio certe diversa est. Nam et vitæ canon et idæa, et veritatis mensura criterium appellatur. Atque hinc quidem omnis vestrarum scolarum est orta dissensio. Aliis enim et esse iudicia visum, et verum in rebus inveniri posse. Parmenidem hic habes, Anaxagoram, Dyonisidorum aliosque permultos. Alii vero nihil sciri aut percipi posse contendere, unde tua manavit versuta dissimulantia. Atque aliis denique assertio esse retinenda visa est unde illud:

Quis novit an hoc vivere sit mori?
an vero mors sit quod vocamus vivere?

Ea nimirum elegantiæ ratio Pyrrhoni, compendio placuit: facillima quidem illa, et quæ ne Sileni, aut Cyllenii quidem asinum excludat. Sed eorum qui iudicia ponunt, minus est alioqui continuata consensio. Illi modo sensus, atque illi ratio placet. unde illud:

Ne te Deus ancipitem iuxta hanc viam cogat,
Iudicare inconsiderato visu, et resonante auditu:
Sed iudices ratione accuratam sententiam.

Nos autem criterium hoc omne, visionis et cogitationis officio et virtute, descriptum esse volumus: ut quæ ex horizonte percepta, vel sensus opera, efficta fuere, iusto impulsu, in memoriam denique insinuari possint. Habet enim animus suam quasi sphæram, et distinctos orbes, sensum, visionem, cogitationem atque memoriam. Atque hæc quidem in centro est in horizonte vero sensuum instrumenta reponimus. Nihil autem ad centrum, nisi per interiectos orbes omnes moverit potest. Non igitur ut instrumenta pulsentur, existit protinus sensus et memoriæ complicatio. Ex quo criterii virtus et accessio denique quæsita videri possit.

[Visionis opus.]
Impulsis igitur instrumentis, ipso etiam sensu in subiectis et umbris impulso, visio pollet: eaque in dispositionis iudicatione tota consumitur. Cum autem subiecta quasi sinus et receptacula posita sint a nobis, certe ordinis ista quæcunque ratio, de ipsis primum demonstranda erit. Ut enim res ipsas ex simulacris, sic ordinem ex subiectis comprehendimus. Primum igitur in subiectis, una si possit idæa statuatur: quæ mox in partes communes sit distribuenda: hæ rursus in alias minus communes, illæ in proprias, propriæ tandem in tribus certo ordine cernantur. Et quamvis fortasse loci natura pugnare videatur, quid est tamen quod impositionis operam possit impedire? Idæam igitur crede idææ, communia communium, propria propriorum, et tribuum tribus observantiæ committe. Insuper novas et decimas etiam, si sit opus, velificationes adhibere licet: idque adiuvantium usibus, et aureæ catenæ ministerio et opportunitate conficitur. Atque hac quidem re nihil est in hac omni consideratione fœcundius. Recto autem animi aspectu, non

certe obliquo, et per diametrum omnia lustranda. Ac denique de spacio et intervallo campi ab oculis animi, ex instrumentorum etiam proportione cavendum. Nunc reliqua est cogitationis in animatione solertia. Sed erro fortasse, nec opus, ut cogitationis operam præterea requiras. Methodum enim qui certe teneat, tantum fortasse quantum volet efficiat: qui vero non teneat, frustra se vexando, nihil prorsus efficere queat. Sane ut in causa hac omni plurimum possit ordo, at certe ut possit, huius artis opus est: et omnia tamen posse, valde negavero: idque ex orbium assumptione repetere licet. Primum igitur ne dormiatur in umbris. subiecta vero in quibus ipsæ reponentur, perfecte et accurate signato. Tum facta acria et circumstantias insignes, superlatio præstet. Non sit autem a natura, neque forte temere, sed ex mera institutione solertia. Tum vero quæ fient, impulsum et affectus vehementes præ se ferant.

[Memoriæ ianitor.]
Mens etiam ipsa, quæ ipsa sensus est, ad ea quæ ipsam moverunt intenderit, et recondere ac retinere velit.

Nam quia tenuia sunt, nisi se contendat acute,
cernere non potis est animus: proinde omnia quæ sunt,
præterea, pereunt.

quod in externis etiam oculis contingit. Denique negatio pollet: ac tui in rem ipsam, rei vero in se ipsam, gemina transformatio. Hæc est illa vivata animi potestas, et accurata solutio. Sic enim informata cogitatio, materiam deserens atque tempus, umbrarum illa quidem ideas et rationes arripit, in ipsam intelligentiam pro facultate propensa. Ac cum omnis solertia admiranda est, tum ea præsertim quæ efficit, ut inanima quæ sunt, quasi vivere et spirare videantur. Habes o Sophronisci fili, de memoria iudicium nostrum reliqua sunt in cura, exercitatione, labore. inde est, ut nihil effugere possit, atque omne quod erit in re, occurrat et incidat: ut Anaxagoræ manum possis agnoscere. Hæc igitur præcipue colenda est tibi, ac semper adhibenda. At tu cum eris in terris, Anaxagoræ huic ipsi, quod etiam ante monui, satisfacere memento. Quamvis hæc tota transitio mihi suspecta est, et hic forte aliquid subesse possit.

FINIS.

Appendix 1
The Mansions of the Moon

In ancient times people were far more aware of the world around them. They knew the sky well and could tell the time of the year and gain orientation with just a glance at the stars.

In the modern-day we all know of the zodiac, which tracks the Sun's motion throughout the year. Few people know of the Lunar Mansions, which track the Moon's motion throughout the month. Think of it as the moon's zodiac.

The Lunar Mansions occur in many cultures including India, China, and the Middle East.

The term 'Mansions' comes from the Arabic word 'manzil' – منازل – meaning 'house', as they are of course the places where the Moon resides. Interestingly enough the Chinese name for the Mansions – 二十八宿 (Èr shí bā xiù) – also has the same meaning.

The Lunar Mansions are divisions of the motions of the Moon circling the Earth. Taking her average daily motion of 12° 51' and 26' and dividing that by the 360 degrees of the zodiac, we arrive at the 28 distinct positions in the sky at which the moon spends time on any given night of a lunar month.

In ancient times the mansions of the moon were not only used as a time keeping device, but also had magical and astrological significance. Every mansion had its own traditional qualities, ruling angel and star to locate the area. Listed below are the auspicious influences, which are the activites or goals best undertaken or avoided during the times when the moon is in this sign. Also included are the mansions' "shadows" meaning what magical effects this image can affect if drawn into the creative memory. The correspondences listed below are the standard for most Renaissance texts, but also include some personal observations.

The First Mansion

Name: Al Nath (The Butting)

Indicator Stars: Sheratan and Mesarthim which mark the horns of Aries, hence the name of the mansion.

Zodiacal Measurement: 0° Aries 00' - 12° Aries 51'

Auspicious Influences: Good for starting a health regime or course of medicine, starting a journey, purchase livestock or pets, create discord between individuals, and imprisonment. Terrible for marriage, partnerships, or the foundation of a meaningful friendship or alliances as one individual usually tries to overpower the other.

Mnemonic Image: A black man with his hair wrapped and encircled, having in his right hand a spear in the manner of a warrior.

Shadows: Good for motivation and completing projects, safety during travel, ending unhealthy relationships, Sex life, murder.

Ruling Angel: Geniel or Geriz

Suffumigation: Liquid storax (styrax)

The Second Mansion

Name: Al Butayn (The Little Belly)

Indicator Star: Botein

Zodiacal Measurement: 12° Aries 51' - 25° Aries 42'

Auspicious Influences: Good for planting and journeys, but bad for marriages and employment ('purchasing slaves').

Mnemonic Image: A crowned king.

Shadows: Removal of anger, supplication, reunification. Finding treasures and underground resources, destroying buildings, and causing strife in relationships.

Ruling Angel: Enediel or Enedil

Suffumigation: Lignum aloes

The Third Mansion

Name: Al Thurayya (The Pleiades)

Indicator Star: Alcyone

Zodiacal Measurement: 25° Aries 42' - 8° Taurus 34'

Auspicious Influences: Good to purchase animals, land travel (not by sea), hunting, alchemical workings, and good works. Bad for marriage, partnerships between unequals, and planting seeds.

Mnemonic Image: A seated woman with her right hand above her head.

Shadows: Acquisition of all good things. Safe travel, imprisoning people, success in hunting and alchemical experiments.

Ruling Angel: Amxiel or Annuncia

Suffumigation: Musk, camphor, mastic, and aromatic oils.

The fourth Mansion

Name: Aldebaran (The Follower)

Indicator Star: Aldebaran

Zodiacal Measurement: 8° Taurus 35' - 21° Taurus 25'

Auspicious Influences: Good for employing others, building, investing, and obtaining offices. Bad for marriage and makes travelling potentially dangerous and difficult.

Mnemonic Image: A knight riding a horse and holding a serpent in his right hand.

Shadows: Destruction, creation of enmity, eradication of pests.

Ruling Angel: Assarez or Azariel.

Suffumigation: Red myrrh and storax.

The Fifth Mansion

Name: Al Haq'ah (A Circle of Hair on a Horse. Supposed to be a reference to a crown)

Indicator Star: Meissa

Zodiacal Measurement: 21° Taurus 26' - 4° Gemini 17'

Auspicious Influences: Good for marriage, education, making medicine, travel, employment, building, getting your haircut or a new hairstyle. Bad for business partnerships.

Mnemonic Image: A head without a body.

Shadows: Assistance in learning, revelations in dream, and favors from superiors.

Ruling Angel: Cabil or Gabiel.

Suffumigation: Sandalwood.

The Sixth Mansion

Name: Al Hanah (The Camel's Brand [as one would brand cattle]), Al Tahayi (The Rainbearers), or Al Maisan (The Shining One).

Indicator Star: Alhena

Zodiacal Measurement: 4° Gemini 18' - 17° Gemini 08'

Auspicious Influences: Good for actions of war and seeking justice ('pursuing enemies and evildoers'), travel, forming partnerships, and hunting. Bad for planting and agricultural work, borrowing money, or depositing something for safekeeping, also bad for therapy, taking medicines and treating injuries.

Mnemonic Image: Two images each of one person. The two images are then tied together.

Shadows: Cultivating love and friendship, destroying cities and fields, improve hunting, bring enemies to justice, and render medicine ineffective.

Ruling Angel: Dirachiel or Nedeyrahe

Suffumigation: Amber and lignum aloes.

The Seventh Mansion

Name: Al Dhira (The Forearm. Arabic astronomy featured a Great Celestial Lion which took up much of the constellations we recognize as Gemini, Cancer, and Leo. This mansion corresponds to one of the Great Lion's front legs)

Indicator Star: Castor and Pollux

Zodiacal Measurement: 17° Gemini 09' - 0° Cancer 00'

Auspicious Influences: Good for asking for help, agricultural pursuits and washing or purifying the body. Bad for buying property or healing the sick.

Mnemonic Image: A man clothed in robes with his hands extended as if in prayer.

Shadows: Increase profit in business (usually through the buying and selling of goods), travel safely, protect crops, create goodwill between individuals, and the gaining of all good things.

Ruling Angel: Siely or Scheliel.

Suffumigation: 'Sweet smelling things'

The Eighth Mansion

Name: Al Nathra (The Tip of the Nose of the Great Celestial Lion)

Indicator Star: Praesepe

Zodiacal Measurement: 0° Cancer 00' - 12° Cancer 51'.

Auspicious Influences: Good for healing, acquiring new goods, and travel. Bad for marriage, partnerships, and employment.

Mnemonic Image: An eagle with the face of a man.

Shadows: Victory, love and friendship, safe travel, hold captives, and pest control. Driving away parasites or infections.

Ruling Angel: Annediex or Amnediel

Suffumigation: Sulfur.

The Ninth Mansion
Name: Al Tarf (The Eye of the Great Celestial Lion)
Indicator Star: Alterf
Zodiacal Measurement: 12° Cancer 51' - 25° Cancer 42'
Auspicious Influences: Basically bad for anything constructive. Bad
for farming, brings deceit in partnerships formed during this time,
and not safe for journeys or inflicting evil on others. Good for
capturing individuals to punish them in captivity and good for
fortifying gates.
Mnemonic Image: A eunuch holding his hands over his eyes.
Shadows: Causing infirmity or protection from being attacked by
others.
Ruling Angel: Raubel or Barbiel
Suffumigation: Pine resin

The Tenth Mansion
Name: Al Jabha (The Forehead of the Great Celestial Lion)
Indicator Star: Regulus
Zodiacal Measurement: 25° Cancer 42' - 8° Leo 34'
Auspicious Influences: Good for marriage and partnerships and good
for building. Not good for travel or lending money.
Mnemonic Image: The head of a lion.
Shadows: To cure illness and ease childbirth, to produce love between
two people, the destruction of enemies, and completing and
strengthening buildings.
Ruling Angel: Aredafir or Ardesiel
Suffumigation: Amber

The Eleventh Mansion
Name: Al Zubra (The Mane of the Great Celestial Lion)
Indicator Star: Zosma
Zodiacal Measurements: 8° Leo 35' - 21° Leo 25'
Auspicious Influences: Good for outside activities, planting, building,
partnerships, and battle, mediocre for journeys and trade.
Mnemonic Image: A man riding a lion with a lance in his right hand
while his left holds the lion's ear.
Shadows: Creating intimidation to receive good things, making

successful demands to authority figures, increasing wealth, fortifying buildings, assisting in battle, freeing captives, and profiting in trade.

Ruling Angel: Necol or Neciel.

Suffumigation: None listed. Maybe saffron.

The Twelfth Mansion

Name: Al Sarfah (The Change or Diversion)

Indicator Star: Denebola

Zodiacal Measurements: 21° Leo 26' - 04° Virgo 17'

Auspicious Influences: Good for construction, renting houses or land, agriculture, marriage, and putting on new garments. Poor for travel and employment.

Mnemonic Image: A man and dragon fighting.

Shadows: Separation of two lovers, increase harvest and cause plants to prosper, destruction of riches, and reinforcing the loyalty of allies.

Ruling Angel: Abdizu or Abdizuel

Suffumigation: Hair of a lion and asafoetida.

The Thirteenth Mansion

Name: Al Awwa (The Barker)

Indicator Star: Zavijava

Zodiacal Measurements: 4° Virgo 18' - 17° Virgo 08'

Auspicious Influences: Good for planting and tilling, journeys, marriage, taking medicine, employment, petitioning authority, and cutting hair.

Mnemonic Image: Separate images of a man and woman tied together

Shadows: Creating love between two people, increase of trade and profit, assisting crops, good and safe journeys, completing buildings, curing sexual dysfunction and freeing captives.

Ruling Angel: Azerut or Jazeriel

Suffumigation: Amber and lignum aloes

The Fourteenth Mansion

Name: Al Simak (The Uplifted)

Indicator Star: Spica

Zodiacal Measurements: 17° Virgo 08' - 00° Libra 00'

Auspicious Influences: Good for marriage, healing, agriculture, employment, partnerships, and travelling by ship.

Mnemonic Image: A dog with its own tail in its mouth.

Shadows: Driving people apart, creating love between spouses, destroying lust, harming crops, assaulting travellers, assisting kings, and developing goodwill between allies.

Ruling Angel: Erdegel or Ergediel.

Suffumigation: Hair of a cat and dog

The Fifteenth Mansion

Name: Al Ghafr (The Covering or Coat of Mail)

Indicator Star: Syrma

Zodiacal Measurements: 00° Libra 00' - 12° Libra 51'

Auspicious Influences: Good to dig wells and canals, heal illnesses caused by windiness, employment, moving house, and buying and selling. Bad for journeys, partnerships, and marriage.

Mnemonic Image: A seated man holding scrolls as if he were reading them.

Shadows: Acquisition of friendship and good will, digging of wells, finding buried treasure, impede travellers, separate spouses, and destroy the reputation of enemies.

Ruling Angel: Achalich or Ataliel

Suffumigation: Frankincense and nutmeg

The Sixteenth Mansion

Name: Al Zubana (The Claws of the Scorpion)

Indicator Star: Zuben Elgenubi and Zuben Eschalami

Zodiacal Measurements: 12° Libra 51' - 25° Libra 42'

Auspicious Influences: Good for employment. Bad for travel, healing, making deals, planting crops, marriage, and partnerships.

Mnemonic Image: A man seated on a throne holding a scale in his hands.

Shadows: Gaining money, destruction of property, merchandise and crops, causing conflict in relationships, impeding travellers, and freeing captives.

Ruling Angel: Azeruch or Azaruel

Suffumigation: 'Fine odours'

The Seventeenth Mansion

Name: Al-Iklil (The Crown)

Indicator Star: Acrab and Deschubba

Zodiacal Measurements: 25° Libra 42' - 08° Scorpio 34'

Auspicious Influences: Good to purchase animals, besiege estates, put on new clothes or armour, love, medicine, building, and tentative travel. Bad for partnerships, grooming, and employment.

Mnemonic Image: A monkey with its arms up over its shoulders.

Shadows: Protecting one's house from thieves, committing crimes and deceptions, besieging cities, reinforcing buildings, protecting friends, creating lasting love and friendship.

Ruling Angel: Adrieb or Adriel

Suffumigation: Hair of a monkey and the hair of a female mouse

The Eighteenth Mansion

Name: Al Qalb (The Heart)

Indicator Star: Antares

Zodiacal Measurements: 08° Scorpio 34' - 21° Scorpio 25'

Auspicious Influences: Good for recovery, renting and purchasing land, building, getting promoted at work. Useful for journeys to the east, good for planting seeds, and taking medicine. Poor for teamwork.

Mnemonic Image: An adder holding its tail above its head.

Shadows: Relieving fevers and diseases of the stomach, conspiring against kings, vengeance against enemies, reinforce buildings, freeing prisoners, and separating friends.

Ruling Angel: Egrebel or Egibiel

Suffumigation: Horn of a stag.

The Nineteenth Mansion

Name: Al Ibrah (The Sting) or Al Shawlah (The Tail)

Indicator Star: Shaula or Lesath

Zodiacal Measurements: 21° Scorpio 25' - 04° Sagittarius 17'

Auspicious influences: Good for sieges, litigation, journeys by land, and planting trees. Bad for partnerships, employment, and travel by sea.

Mnemonic Image: A woman holding her hands in front of her face.

Shadows: Restoring virility, protection during pregnancy and childbirth, besieging cities, destroying wealth, expelling or repelling people, cursing travellers, and increasing harvests or profits.

Ruling Angel: Annucel or Amutiel
Suffumigation: Liquid storax

The Twentieth Mansion
Name: Al Naaim (The Ostriches, a reference to an old asterism
   formed by what we now see as the bow of Sagittarius)
Indicator Star: Ascella
Zodiacal Measurements: 04° Sagittarius 17' - 17° Sagittarius 08'
Auspicious Influences: Good for the purchase or taming of animals,
   mediocre for travel, bad for partnerships.
Mnemonic Image: Figure having the head and arms of a man, body of
   a horse with four feet, and holding a bow and arrow.
Shadows: Hunting, taming wild and disobedient animals (or animal
   like people), protection for travellers, joining people together,
   keep people imprisoned, and destroying resources.
Ruling Angel: Queyhuc or Kyriel
Suffumigation: Hair of a wolf.

The Twenty-First Mansion
Name: Al Balda (The Place, Town, Or City)
Indicator Star: Albaldah
Zodiacal Measurements: 17° Sagittarius 08' - 00° Capricorn 00'
Auspicious Influences: Good for building, planting, and making big
   purchases or investments. Not good for employment.
Mnemonic Image: A man with two faces; one facing forward, the
   other facing behind. [Like Janus]
Shadows: Causing destruction, strengthen buildings, increase
   harvests, make a profit, and separate lovers.
Ruling Angel: Bectue or Bethnael
Suffumigation: Sulfur and carabe

The Twenty-Second Mansion
Name: Sa'd al-Dhabih (Luck of the Slayer)
Indicator Star: Prima Giedi
Zodiacal Measurements: 00° Capricorn 00' - 12° Capricorn 51'
Auspicious Influences: Good for escaping things, healing others,
   journeys, good for partnerships. Bad for marriage and
   employment.
Mnemonic Image: A man with winged feet wearing a helmet.

Shadows: To disperse rumors and restore reputations, free captives, cure illness, create hostilities or goodwill between individuals.
Ruling Angel: Geliel
Suffumigation: Mercury

The Twenty-Third Mansion
Name: Sa'd Bula (Luck of the Swallower)
Indicator Star: Al Bali
Zodiacal Measurement: 12° Capricorn 51' – 25° Capricorn 42'
Auspicious Influences: Good for donning clothes, taking medicine or having therapy, making partnerships. Bring abuse in relationships. Bad in journeys, and depositing something with someone for safekeeping.
Mnemonic Image: A cat with the head of a dog.
Shadows: Destruction and devastation, healing illness, ruining marriages or friendships, and freeing captives.
Ruling Angel: Zequebin or Requiel
Suffumigation: The hair of a cat and dog

The Twenty-Fourth Mansion
Name: Sa'd al Su'ud (Luck of the Lucks)
Indicator Star: Sadalsuud
Zodiacal Measurement: 25° Capricorn 42' – 8° Aquarius 34'
Auspicious Influences: Good for healing, dispatching troops and organising battles, employment, and freeing those captured. Mediocre for travel. Bad for marriage and partnerships.
Mnemonic Image: A woman holding a child in her arms as if she were nursing.
Shadows: Increase herds and growing groups, increase merchandise, profit, increase goodwill between spouses, bringin morale, destroying the resources of others, and prevent officials from fulfilling their office correctly.
Ruling Angel: Abrine or Abrinael
Suffumigation: Bull or ram horn.

The Twenty-Fifth Mansion
Name: Sa'd al-Akhbiyah (Luck of the Tents)
Indicator Star: Sadalbachia
Zodiacal Measurement: 8° Aquarius 34' – 21° Aquarius 25'

Auspicious Influences: Good for fighting, revenge on enemies, good for safety in travel but causes delays, also good for fortifying buildings. Bad for marriage, planting, partnerships, purchasing animals and employment.

Mnemonic Image: A man planting trees.

Shadows: Protection of crops, attacking enemies, cursing the body, destroying harvests, protecting staff and messengers on their travel, and for separating spouses.

Ruling Angel: Aziel

Suffumigation: The flowers of trees.

The Twenty-Sixth Mansion

Name: Al-Fargh al-Muqaddam (The Preceding Spout), Al-Fargh al-Awwal (The First Spout)

Indicator Star: Markab

Zodiacal Measurements: 21° Aquarius 25' – 04° Pisces 17'

Auspicious Influences: Good for employment, building, and journeys. Difficult for marriage and bad for partnerships.

Mnemonic Image: A woman washing or combing her hair in a vessel.

Shadows: Creating of love, protecting travellers, strengthening buildings, and holding people at bay or in prison.

Ruling Angel: Tagriel

Suffumigation: Sweet-smelling odours.

The Twenty-Seventh Mansion

Name: Al-Fargh al-Muakhkhar (The Following Spout)

Indicator Star: Algenib and Alpheratz

Zodiacal Measurements: 04° Pisces 17' – 17° Pisces 08'

Auspicious Influences: Good for gardening, business, and marriage. Bad for travel, employment, and giving or taking loans.

Mnemonic Image: A winged man holding a perforated dish, raising it towards his mouth.

Shadows: Destroying or drying up springs and wells, increasing sales or making deals, acquiring profit, increasing harvest, heal illness, impeding buildings, harming resources, cursing people.

Ruling Angel: Abliemel or Alheniel

Suffumigation: Asafoetida and liquid storax.

The Twenty-Eighth Mansion

Name: Batn al-Hut (Belly of the Fish)

Indicator Star: Mirach

Zodiacal Measurements: 17° Pisces 08' – 00° Aries 00'

Auspicious Influences: Good for trade, planting, healing and marriage. Bad for giving loans or taking loans. Mediocre for travel. Partnerships formed under this influence start well but end poorly.

Mnemonic Image: A fish with a colored spine.

Shadows: Summoning fish, inflicting damage on sailors at sea, increasing trade, besieging cities, bringing good harvests, cause things to become lost, destroy areas, bring safety to travellers, increase love between spouses, and keep captives imprisoned.

Ruling Angel: Anuxi or Amnixiel

Suffumigation: Fish skin

Appendix 2
The 32 Decans of the Zodiac

From *Three Books of Occult Philosophy* by Henry Cornelius Agrippa and *Astrolabium Planum* by Johannes Engel (see overleaf).

Aries, the Ram

Third Decan 21-30°
In the third face ariseth the figure of a white man, pale, with reddish hair, and clothed with a red garment, who is

First Decan 1-10°
Therefore it is said, that in the first face of Aries, ascendeth the image of a black man, standing and cloathed in a white garment, girdled about, of a great body, with reddish eyes, and great strength, and like one that is angry; and this image signifieth and causeth boldness, fortitude, loftiness and shamelessness.

Associated Constellation: The Girdle of Andromeda
Planet: Mars
Suffumigation: Myrtle
Angel: Zazer (Extending Border)
Spirit: Rarum

Second Decan 11-20°
In the second face ascendeth a form of a woman, outwardly cloathed with a red garment, and under it a white, spreading abroad over her feet, and this image causeth nobleness, height of a Kingdom, and greatness of dominion.

Associated Constellation: Cassiopeia
Planet: Sun
Suffumigation: Stammonia
Angel: Bahhemei (Silent Sound)
Spirit: Gibsir

carrying on the one hand a golden Bracelet, and holding forth a wooden staff, is restless, and like one in wrath, because he cannot perform that good he would. This image bestoweth wit, meekness, joy and beauty. (Variant image pictured a woman playing a lute under an oak tree).

Associated Constellation: The Throne of Cassiopeia
Planet: Mercury
Suffumigation: Black Pepper
Angel: Satander (Radiance in Adversity)
Spirit: Rahol

Taurus, the Bull

First Decan 1-10°
In the first face of Taurus ascendeth a naked man, an Archer, Harvester or Husbandman, and goeth forth to sow, plough, build, people, and divide the earth, according to the rules of Geometry.

*Associated
   Constellation:*
   Perseus
Planet: Venus
Suffumigation:
   Costum
Angel: Kadmedie
   (Half-filled
   Container)
Spirit: Adica

Second Decan 11-20°
In the second face ascendeth a naked man, holding in his hand a key; it giveth power, nobility, and dominion over people.

*Associated
   Constellation:*
   Eridanus (the River)
Planet: Moon
Suffumigation:
   Codamorns
Angel: Manachraie
   (Bestowal of Vision)
Spirit: Agricol

Third Decan 21-30°
In the third face, ascendeth a man in whose hand is a Serpent, and a dart, and is the image of necessity and profit, and also of misery & slavery. Alternative imagine pictured is a slave with a peg leg and lame arm.

*Associated
   Constellation:*
   Auriga (the
   Shepherd, also
   called the
   Charioteer)
Planet: Saturn
Suffumigation: Cassia
Angel: Yaksagnotz
   (Rapid
   Suppression by
   Authority)
Spirit: Fifal

Gemini, the Twins

First Decan 1-10°
In the first face of Gemini ascendeth a man in whose hand is a rod, and he is, as it were, serving another; it granteth wisdom, and the knowledge of numbers and arts in which there is no profit.

Associated Constellation: Orion
Planet: Jupiter
Suffumigation: Mastick
Angel: Siegrash (Baseness and Poverty)
Spirit: Imini

Second Decan 11-20°
In the second face ascendeth a man in whose hand is a Pipe, and another being bowed down, digging the earth: and they signify infamous and dishonest agility, as that of Jesters and Juglers [jugglers]; it also signifies labours and painful searchings.

Associated Constellation: Canis Major (the Greater Dog)
Planet: Mars
Suffumigation: Cinnamon
Angel: Shahadnie (Confirmed Suffering)
Spirit: Kolluir

Third Decan 21-30°
In the third, ascendeth a man seeking for Arms, and a fool holding in the right hand a Bird, and in his left a pipe, and they are the significations of forgetfulness, wrath, boldness, jeasts [jests], scurrilities, and unprofitable words.

Associated Constellation: Canis Minor (the Lesser Dog)
Planet: Sun
Suffumigation: Cypress
Angel: Betor (In a State of Seeking)
Spirit: Ibnahim

Cancer, the Crab

First Decan 1-10°
In the first face of Cancer ascendeth the form of a young Virgin, adorned with fine cloathes [clothes], and having a Crown on her head; it giveth acuteness of senses, subtilty of wit, and the love of men.

Associated Constellation: Argo Navis (the Ship Argo – Puppis, the Stern)
Planet: Mercury
Suffumigation: Camphor
*Angel:*Mitraos (The Dead See the Sun & Are Strong)
Spirit: Ititz

Second Decan 11-20°
In the second face ascendeth a man clothed in comely apparel, or a man and woman sitting at the table and playing; it bestoweth riches, mirth, gladness, and the love of women.

Associated Constellation: Ursa Minor (the Lesser Bear – the Neck of the Bear)
Plant: Venus
Suffumigation: Succum / Anise
Angel: Rahadea (Tremble with Knowledge)
Spirit: Urodu

Third Decan 21-30°
In the third face ascendeth a man a Hunter with his lance and horne, bringing out dogs for to hunt; the significance of this is the contention of men, the pursuing of those who fly, the hunting and possessing of things by arms and brawlings.

Associated Constellation: Ursa Major (the Greater Bear – the Flank of the Bear)
Planet: Moon
Suffumigation: Anise
Angel: Elinakier (God is Known)
Spirit: Irkamon

Leo, the Lion

First Decan 1-10°
In the first face of Leo ascendeth a man riding on a Lion; it signifieth boldness, violence, cruelty, wickedness, lust and labours to be sustained.

Associated Constellation: Leo Minor (the Lesser Lion)
Planet: Saturn
Suffumigation: Olibanum
Angel: Laosanhar Desire (Thorn of the Mountain)
Spirit: Oksos

Second Decan 11-20°
In the second ascendeth an image with hands lifted up, and a man on whose head is a Crown; he hath the appearance of an angry man, and one that threatneth, having in his right hand a Sword drawn out of the scabbard, & in his left a buckler; it hath signification upon hidden contentions, and unknown victories, & upon base men, and upon the occasions of quarrels and battels [battles].

Associated Constellation: Ursa Major (the Tail of the Great Bear)
Planet: Jupiter
Suffumigation: Lyn Balsami
Angel: Zachaay (Remove the Ruinous)
Spirit: Otobir

Third Decan 21-30°
In the third face ascendeth a young man in whose hand is a Whip, and a man very sad, and of an ill aspect; they signifie love and society, and the loss of one's right for avoiding strife. Alternative image pictured is a man making mocking humour.

Associated Constellation: Canes Venatici (the Hunting Dogs)
Planet: Mars
Suffumigation: Muces Muscator
Angel: Sachieber (Vile is Purified)
Spirit: Kutruc

Virgo, the Virgin

First Decan 1-10°
In the first face of Virgo ascendeth the figure of a good maide, and a man casting seeds; it signifieth getting of wealth, ordering of diet, plowing, sowing, and peopling.

Associated Constellation: Crater (the Cup)
Planet: Sun
Suffumigation: Santal Flav
Angel: Annaorah (Breath Trembles with Desire)
Spirit: Idia

Second Decan 11-20°
In the second face ascendeth a black man cloathed with a skin, and a man having a bush of hair, holding a bag; they signifie gain, scraping together of wealth and covetousness.

Associated Constellation: Corvus (the Raven)
Planet: Mercury
Angel: Reayahyah (God Beholds God)
Suffumigation: Srorus
Spirit: Abodir

Third Decan 21-30°
In the third face ascendeth a white woman and deaf, or an old man leaning on a staff; the signification of this is to shew weakness, infirmity, loss of members, destruction of trees, and depopulation of lands.

Associated Constellation: Hydra (the Serpent – Tail of the Serpent)
Planet: Venus
Suffumigation: Mastick
Angel: Mispar (Number)
Spirit: Idida

Libra, the Scales

First Decan 1-10°
In the first face of Libra ascendeth the form of an angry man, in whose hand is a Pipe, and the form of a man reading in a book; the operation of this is in justifying and helping the miserable and weak against the powerful and wicked.

Associated Constellation: Boötes (the Ploughman
Planet: Moon
Suffumigation: Galbanum
Angel: Tarsani (Fresh Thorn)
Spirit: Cibor

Second Decan 11-20°
In the second face ascend two men furious and wrathful and a man in a comely garment, sitting in a chair; and the signification of these is to shew indignation against the evil, and quietness and security of life with plenty of good things.

Associated Constellation: Corona (Northern Crown) and Crux (Southern Cross)
Planet: Saturn
Suffumigation: Bofor
Angel: Saharnaz (Tower of the Hawk)
Spirit: Asor

Third Decan 21-30°
In the third face ascendeth a violent man holding a bow, and before him a naked man, and also another man holding bread in one hand, and a cup of wine in the other; the signification of these is to shew wicked lusts, singings, sports and gluttony.

Associated Constellation: Centaurus (the Centaur)
Planet: Jupiter
Suffumigation: Mortum
Angel: Shehdar (Goat of the Age)
Spirit: Abodil

Scorpio, the Scorpion

First Decan 1-10°
In the first face of
Scorpio ascendeth a
woman of good face
and habit, and two
men striking her; the
operations of these are
for comliness, beauty,
and for strifes,
treacheries, deceits,
detractations, and
perditions.

*Associated
Constellation:*
Lupus (the Wolf –
the Sacrifice)
Planet: Mars
Suffumigation:
Opoponax
Angel: Kamotz (Much
Oppression)
Spirit: Skorpia

Second Decan 11-20°
In the second face
ascendeth a man
naked, and a woman
naked, and a man
sitting on the earth,
and before him two
dogs biting one
another; and their
operation is for
impudence, deceit,
and false dealing, and
for to lend mischief
and strife amongst
men.

*Associated
Constellation:*
Hercules
Planet: Sun
Suffumigation:
Opoponax
Angel: Hiendohar
(Weak Child of the
Mountain)
Spirit: Vilusia

Third Decan 21-30°
In the third face
ascendeth a man
bowed downward
upon his knees, and a
woman striking him
with a staff, and it is
the signification of
drunkenness,
fornication, wrath,
violence, and strife.

*Associated
Constellation:*
Ophiucus (the
Serpent Bearer)
Planet: Mercury
Suffumigation:
Opoponax
Angel: Natarvadaiel
(Tremble, be Filled
with God)
Spirit: Koroum

Sagittarius, the Archer

First Decan 1-10°
In the first face of Sagittariys ascendeth the form of a man armed with a coat of male [mail], and holding a naked sword in his hand; the operation of this is for boldness, malice, and liberty.

Associated Constellation: Ara (the Altar)
Planet: Venus
Suffumigation: Lign-aloes
Angel: Masharat (Divided Sign)
Spirit: Sagitor

Second Decan 11-20°
In the second face ascendeth a woman weeping, and covered with cloathes; the operation of this is for sadness and fear of his own body.

Associated Constellation: Corona Australis (the Southern Crown)
Planet: Moon
Suffumigation: Foi Lori
Angel: Vahrin (God Overcomes)
Spirit: Agilah

Third Decan 21-30°
In the third face ascendeth a man like in colour to gold, or an idle man playing with a staff; and the signification of this is in following our own wills, and obstinacy in them, and in activeness for evil things, contentions, and horrible matters.

Associated Constellation: Lyra (the Lyre)
Planet: Saturn
Suffumigation: Gaxisphilium
Angel: Abuha (Father of Interjection)
Spirit: Boram

Capricorn, the Goat

First Decan 1-10°
In the first face of
Capricorn ascendeth
the form of a woman,
and a man carrying
full bags; and the
signification of these
is for to go forth and
to rejoyce [rejoice], to
gain and to lose with
weakness and
baseness.

*Associated
   Constellation:*
   Aquila (the Eagle)
Planet: Jupiter
Suffumigation:
   Assafœtida
Angel: Masnin
   (Tribute of
   Posterity)
Spirit: Absalom

Second Decan 11-20°
In the second face
ascendeth two women,
and a man looking
towards a Bird flying
in the Air; and the
signification of these
is for the requiring
those things which
cannot be done, and
for the searching after
those things which
cannot be known.

*Associated
   Constellation:*
   Sagitta (the Arrow)
Planet: Mars
Suffumigation:
   Colophonum
Angel: Yasisyah
   (God's Swallow)
Spirit: Istriah

Third Decan 21-30°
In the third face
ascendeth a woman
chast [chaste] in body,
and wise in her work,
and a banker gathering
his mony [money]
together on the table;
the signification of
this is to govern in
prudence, in
covetousness of
money, and in avarice.

*Associated
   Constellation:*
   Delphinus (the
   Dolphin)
Planet: Sun
Suffumigation: Cubel
   Pepper
Angel: Ysgadibarodiel
   (Adore the Chosen
   & Sufficient of
   God)
Spirit: Abdomon

Aquarius, the Waterman

First Decan 1-10°
In the first face of Aquarius ascendeth the form of a prudent man, and of a woman spinning; and the signification of these is in the thought and labour for gain, in poverty and baseness.

Associated Constellation: Piscis Australis (the Southern Fish)
Planet: Mercury
Suffumigation: Euphorbium
Angel: Sasfem (Mouth of a Moth)
Spirit: Anator

Second Decan 11-20°
In the second face ascendeth the form of a man with a long beard; and the signification of this belongeth to the understanding, meeknes, modesty, liberty and good maners. Alternative image pictured is a holy man teaching.

Associated Constellation: Cygnus (the Swan)
Planet: Venus
Suffumigation: Euphorbium
Angel: Abadron (Forsake Victory)
Spirit: Ilutria

Third Decan 21-30°
In the third face ascendeth a black and angry man; and the signification of this is in expressing insolence; and impudence.

Associated Constellation: Pegasus (the Winged Horse)
Planet: Moon
Suffumigation: Rhubarb
Angel: Geradiael (Strangeness and of God)
Spirit: Obola

Pisces, the Fishes

First Decan 1-10°
In the first face of Pisces ascendeth a man carrying burthens [burdens] on his shoulder, and well cloathed; it hath his significion in journeys, change of place, and in carefulness of getting wealth and cloaths.

Associated Constellation: the Square of Pegasus (the Body of the Winged Horse)
Planet: Saturn
Suffumigation: Thyme
Angel: Biehalmi (Flow Rapidly)
Spirit: Pisiar

Second Decan 11-20°
In the second face ascendeth a woman of a good countenance, and well adorned; and the signification is to desire and put oneself on about high and great matters. Alternative image pictured is a astrologer pointing to the sky.

Associated Constellation: Cepheus (the Crowned King)
Planet: Jupiter
Suffumigation: Coxium
Angel: Auron (Light Overcomes)
Spirit: Filista

Third Decan 21-30°
In the third face ascendeth a man naked, or a youth, and nigh him a beautiful maide, whose head is adorned with flowers, and it hath his significance for rest, idleness, delight, fornication, and for imbracings of women.

Associated Constellation: Andromeda
Planet: Mars
Suffumigation: Santal Alb
Angel: Satrip (Giants Roam)
Spirit: Odorom

A Note on Terminology

Though Frances Yates seems to have had a low opinion of the expository part of Dicsone's *De Umbra*, calling it an 'impressionistic reflection' of Giordano Bruno's famous work[1], and had an even lower opinion of the *Thamus*, which she sees as nothing more than a re-tread of the *De Umbra* (when it is, in fact, a distinct work), Dicsone's original and sometimes challenging terminology makes it clear that he was striking out on his own and seeking to develop his own system independently of his master. As a result, although he sometimes uses Brunonian terminology (most obviously, *umbra*), he does not always use it in a strictly Brunonian sense (e.g. *horizon*).

Below we have provided a list of the principal terms used in the expository sections of the two texts, along with our choice of English equivalents and, in some cases, brief explanations. Many of the terms are further explained in the extensive footnotes to the two texts, and in some cases we have added cross-references to these (U = *De Umbra*, T = *Thamus* and the number refers to the relevant footnote).

Sir Hugh Platt, an unimpressed student of Dicsone's, refers in *The Jewell House of Art and Nature*, published in London in 1594, to 'the Art of memorie which master Dicsone the Scot did teach of late yeres in England, and whereof he hath written a figurative and obscure treatise'[2]. 'Figurative and obscure' – that certainly hits the nail on the head.

A
absolutum subiectum absolute subject
accidentia accident
accipere to accept
acies animi gaze of the mind *T207*
actus action (opposed to *requies*), e.g. *in actum educere* to lead forth into action
adiuvans adjuvant
adjuncta an adjunct

adumbratio adumbration *T23*
æterna permanent (a characteristic of an adjuvant)
affectus condition
allocare to assemble
anima soul (as the vivifying substance of every human being)
animare to animate
animatio animation
animus mind (as the fount of feeling, desire and thinking)

antecedens antecedent
appendix adjunct
aspectus view
aspectus iudicium judgement of vision *U134 T165*
assumere to select (a shadow or subject)
assumptio selection

C

campus field
cathena aurea Golden Chain *U123 T154*
centrum centre (opposed to *horizon,* boundary)
character character *U111 T140*
cogitatio thinking, faculty of thought
cogitandum reflection
cogitationis apparatus the thinking apparatus
cognitio understanding
cognoscere to recognise
cohærentia coherence
cohærere to cohere
commendare to approve
commendatio approval (see *oculorum*)
commercium exchange
communis accidentia common accidental
communis animus world-mind *U99 T121*
communis utilitas general welfare *U156 T188*
comparatio comparison
complexio connection
complicatio folding-together (of the senses and the memory)

U199 T237
compositio matching
conformatio construction *U136 T167*
congruentia naturæ harmony of Nature
coniugatio etymological connection
coniunctus conjoined
coniuratio alliance
consequi to retrieve
conserere to compose
consistens a stop (linguistics)
contentio contention
corporum expers disencumbered
credere to assign (a shadow to a subject), (with *fides,* to entrust)
criterium discrimination
custos guard

D

decemviratus decemvirate *U122 T151*
declinatio variation
decuria tenth
delectus selection
diametrum diameter
dimensio dimension
dispositio arrangement
dissentaneum something that differs
distinctus distinct (of a subject)
doctrina learning
Draconis Luna Lunar Dragon *U175*

E

effectum effect

efficacia efficacy
efficiens efficient cause
efficiens causa efficient cause
efficientia effect
efficta simulachra representative
    simulacrum
efficta species representation
effictum represented
effingere to represent
efformatio formation
elementum 1) a letter of the
    alphabet
    2) an element
emanare to emanate
enunciatum proposition
eventus occurrence
exercitatio practice
exhibitio example
expeditus unencumbered (of the
    memory, unencumbered by
    the body or the senses)
explicatus expanded (of a
    retention)
externi oculi external eyes (as
    opposed to the 'inner' eyes of
    the mind or intellect)

F

factorum communio association
    of events *U161*
factum act
facultas ability
familia rationis family of reason
fides faith
figura figure *U111 T140*
finalis a final
fingere to create
firma perceptio firm perception
firma retentio firm retention

forma form
forma externa external form
fortuna Fortune
fucus dissimulation

G

gemina transformatio dual
    transformation *U204 T249*
generatio generative process
genus genus
gestus gesture
gigni to be brought forth (of a
    shadow)

H

horizon boundary
hospes guest *T145*

I

idea idea *U111 T140*
imago image *U111 T140*
imbecillitas impotence
imitatum simulachrum imitative
    simulacrum
impellere to project
impositio naming
impulsus stimulus
incomprehensum
    incomprehensible
indicium token *U111 T140*
inflexio inflection
inflexus inflected
informata cogitatio informed
    thinking
informatio conception (in
    Thamus)
insinuare to insinuate
insitus innate
inspectio inspection (of an object)

institutio arrangement
institutio ruda basic arrangement
intelligentia intelligence
internuncio intermediary
intervallum space (between)
intuendum inspection
inventio invention
involutum abstruse
iudicatio (the act of) judgement
iudicium (the faculty of)
    judgement ('the capacity to
    retain what you have learned
    or what you yourself have
    conceived, even if you do not
    find it congenial material for
    reflection' (*De Umbra*)
iustus impulsus regular stimulus

L
lex umbrarum principle of the
    shadows
liquidum a liquid (linguistics)
locus memory-locus
lunæ mansionum imagines
    images of the lunar mansions
lux light (as opposed to *tenebræ*)

M
materia material
materiæ concretio concretion of
    the material
mediæ areæ central areas
memor rememberance (a 'thing
    remembered')
memoria memory
mens intellect ('*Mens* implies
    merely the intellect, or
    rational faculty, under the
    government of which are the

affections, passions, appetites,
and sentiments of *Animus*.
When opposed to each other,
Animus refers to the
sentiments and passions; *Mens*
to the reason' – Rev.
Alexander Crombie,
*Gymnasium sive Symbola
Critica. Intended to assist the
classical student in his
endeavours to attain a correct
Latin prose style*, 2nd edition,
p. 246).
mens prima First Mind, Primal
    Mind *U125 T156*
mentis oculi eyes of the intellect
    U137 T168
modificata modified
modificata absoluta absolute
    modified shadow
modificata Mathematica
    mathematical modified
    shadow
modificata umbra modified
    shadow
modificatio modification
momentum influence
motus movement
multiplicatio multiplication
munus function
mutuatio borrowing

N
negatio negation
negotium memory-activity
nota mark *U111 T140*
notatio notation

O

oblivio forgetfulness
oculi animi eyes of the mind *T243*
oculorum com[m]endatio approval of the eyes *U133 T164*
opportunitas arrangement
optica corpora visible bodies, bodies that can be seen with the naked eye
orbis orb
ordo organisation
ortus origination

P

partes communes common parts *U200 T238*
partes propriæ particular parts *U200 T238*
perceptio perception
peripheria periphery
persona mask
perspexisse insight
perspicere insight
positio position (term from logic = positing, assertion) *U131 T162*
potentia power, capacity of the boundary
potentia horizontis in aspectu visual strength of the boundary
præceptio preceding notion
præfectus (of a decan) commander
præsentatio representation
princeps (of a decan) prince
progressio progression
proiicere to project

pronunciare to recite
proportio analogy *U111 T140*
proprius characteristic
proprietates properties
prospectere foresight
prospexisse foresight
providentia foreknowledge
prudentia prudence
pulsare to stimulate
pulsus stimulus
pulsus cogitationis (see *animatio*) stimulus of thought

R

ratio reason
ratiocinans memoria rational memory *U101 T123*
rationis instrumentum rational instrument
rationis insula Island of Reason
receptaculum receptacle
recolere to go over in one's mind
recondere to put away
recordatio recollection
repetentia reminiscence
reputare to calculate
requies rest (opposed to *actus*)
res object
res absolutæ absolute objects
res facta created object
respexisse hindsight
respicere hindsight
respicientia hindsight
retentio retention
retinere to retain
revocans process of revocation

S

sensibilia objects knowable by

the senses
sensibilis perceptible
sensilis endowed with sensation
sensum thought
sensus sense (and, occasionally, 'sensation')
sensus apparatus sensory apparatus
sensus instrumenta sensory apparatus
sensuum instrumenta sensory apparatus
sententia disposition
sigillum seal
signum sign *U111 T140*
similitudo resemblance
simplex umbra simple shadow
simulac[h]rum simulacrum
simulac[h]rum effictum represented simulacrum
simulac[h]rum imitatum imitated simulacrum
singulum a single (as opposed to an *adjunct*)
sinus pocket
socius companion
species representation
sphæra sphere
spirans aspirate
subiectum subject ('a sort of pocket or receptacle into which the shadows are placed' – *De Umbra*)
subiectum absolutum absolute subject (contains the shadows)
subiectum adiuvans adjuvant subject
subiectum continens containing subject

superior ratio higher reason
superum radii rays from the heavens
superlatio exaggeration
tenebræ darkness

T

tradere to hand over
traducere to convey
transformatio transformation
transitio transition
translatio metaphor
tribus a third-part (of an astrological sign, i.e. a decan)
tropus a metaphor

U

umbra shadow ('the representation of an object allocated to a subject and selected so as to ensure a firm perception of it' – *De Umbra*) *U111 T140*
umbra boni shadow of the Good
umbra inflexa inflected shadow
umbra iudicii shadow of judgement
umbra modificata modified shadow
umbra reflexa reflected shadow
universa natura universal nature
usus purpose

V

velificatio veiling *U201 T239*
verborum inflexio verbal inflection
vestigium trace *U111 T140*
vicis interchange (used in *Thamus*

instead of *mutuatio*)
virtus virtue (in the old sense of a power or strength)
visio vision

visum mental image
vocale vowel
vox expression

1   Yates, *The Art of Memory,* Routledge 1999, p. 272.

2   Yates, op. cit., pp. 284-285.

A note on Dicsone's sources and some suggestions for further reading

Classical Latin

Apart from the Latin plays (by Plautus, Terence and the Neo-Latin humanist George Buchanan), epigrams (Martial) and poetry (Virgil, Horace and Ovid) with which any educated man of that time and place would have been familiar Dicsone draws most heavily in his two texts on the Art of Memory on the works of the orator and supreme Latin stylist Cicero. He seems to have ransacked Cicero's works for anything connected with the subject, and at least a dozen texts by or attributed to him seem to have been on his bookshelf, including the earliest known treatise on rhetoric, the *Rhetorica ad Herennium* (dating from the late 80s BCE), formerly attributed to Cicero, which contains a famous section on the Art of Memory in Book III, 16-24.

But the main point of difference between the *De Umbra* and the *Thamus* in terms of source material is Dicsone's recourse to the *De Rerum Natura* of the Epicurean philosopher Lucretius, especially its Third Book which deals mostly with the *animus* (mind) and the *anima* (soul) and the Fourth Book (concerned with the senses, sleep and dreams). In the *De Umbra* there are no direct references to Lucretius at all; in the *Thamus* there are more than twenty. Although the great French scholar Denis Lambin's annotated edition of Lucretius had appeared in 1563, Dicsone seems not to have made its acquaintance until the 1590s. The fact that one of Dicsone's Lucretian paraphrases is uncannily similar to an annotation in Michel de Montaigne's personal copy of Lambin's Lucretius (see footnotes 7 and 148 of the *Thamus*) suggests that Dicsone may even have come into possession of Montaigne's copy[1] after his death in 1592. Dicsone was certainly influenced in this choice of reading material by his master Bruno who, as Alexandre Koyré notes, was 'the first man to take Lucretian cosmology seriously'[2]. Dicsone's enthusiasm for Lucretius may also have been prompted by his growing interest in the natural sciences in the years following the publication of the *De Umbra* (see the section below on natural philosophy). Perhaps he felt the need for a more intellectually rigorous underpinning of his ideas, which may explain why the *Thamus* is, in general, a tauter and more readily comprehensible text than the *De Umbra*.

Almost all these Classical Latin works are available in various English translations, many of them obtainable on-line without cost from the Internet Archive or Google Books.

Giordano Bruno

Unsurprisingly, both of Dicsone's texts draw heavily on the works of his master, Giordano Bruno. Dicsone quotes from *De umbris idearum* (*The Shadows of Ideas*, Paris, 1582), including the *Triginta Intentiones Umbrarum* (*The Thirty Intentions*) and the *Ars Memoriæ* (*The Art of Memory*); *Cantus Circaeus* (*The Incantation of Circe*, 1582); *Lo Spaccio de la Bestia Trionfante* (*Expulsion of the Triumphant Beast*, 1584); *De la causa, principio, et uno* (*Concerning Cause, Principle, and Unity*, 1584); *De imaginum, signorum et idearum compositione* (*On the Composition of Images, Signs and Ideas*, 1591); *De monade numero et figura* (*On the Monad, Number, and Figure*, Frankfurt, 1591); *De innumerabilibus, immenso et infigurabili* (*Of Innumerable Things, Vastness and the Unrepresentable*, 1591); and the *Summa terminorum metaphysicorum* (*Handbook of Metaphysical Terms*, 1595). Unfortunately only some of Bruno's works have been translated into English.

Neo-Latin: Petrus Ramus

The French 'scholastic anti-scholastic' Petrus Ramus was, of course, one of Dicsone's *bêtes noires*, but he shows a close familiarity with several of his works, including the *Scholæ in liberales artes*, the *Dialecticæ libri duo*, the *Præfatio Tertia de Cæsaris Militia* and the *Aristotelicæ animadversiones*.

Latin translations of and commentaries on Greek texts

Dicsone seems to have preferred reading Latin translations or paraphrases of Greek authors to tackling the Greek originals. Some of his distinctive terminology seems to have been drawn from Latin paraphrases of (or commentaries on) works by Aristotle, especially the *Metaphysics* and Book III of *On the Soul (De Anima)*, e.g. the analysis of the *Metaphysics* by Jacobus Cheyne (*Analysis in XIV libros Aristotelis de prima seu divina philosophia*); Marco Antonio (or Marcantonio) Flaminio's *Paraphrasis in duodecimum Aristotelis librum* of 1536; Latin translations by Giovanni Faseolo and Evangelista Longo Asulano of the commentary on *De Anima* formerly attributed to the 6th century Neoplatonist Simplicius; and the *Super Aristotelis libro V, de physica auscultatione lucidissima commentaria, cum nova interpretatione* by the English scholastic philosopher Walter Burley (c.1275-1344/5) in the Venice edition of 1589. He also seems to have studied Denis Lambin's translations of Aristotle's *Politics* and works by the Middle Platonist Alcinous. He makes extensive use of a Latin translation (by Ambrogio Traversari?) of the Βίοι καὶ γνῶμαι τῶν ἐν φιλοσοφίᾳ εὐδοκιμησάντων (*Lives of the Eminent Philosophers*) of Diogenes Laertius as well as a translation (possibly by Henri Estienne) of the Πυρρώνειοι ὑποτυπώσεις (*Outlines of Pyrrhonism*) of Sextus Empiricus. He also quotes from an anonymous Latin translation of *De natura* by Parmenides and may have been influenced by the 1571 Latin paraphrase of the fourteen books mistakenly attributed to Aristotle on the secret wisdom of Ancient Egypt, *Libri quatuordecim qui Aristotelis esse dicuntur, De secretiore parte divinae sapientiae secundum Aegyptios*, by Jacques Charpentier.

The long-winded dialogues which serve as a prelude to both texts obviously draw heavily on Plato, and one assumes that the Latin translations of them by Marsilio Ficino published in 1484 were Dicsone's source of inspiration. He also made use of Cicero's uncompleted translation of Plato's *Timaeus* (usually known as *De Universitate*).

Outside of philosophy Dicsone also seems to have relied on Henri Estienne's famous 1566 edition of Homer's *Iliad*.

Neo-Latin: natural philosophy

In the interval between the publication of *De Umbra* and the *Thamus* Dicsone seems to have made a serious study of natural philosophy, drawing on works by the founder of physiology Jean Fernel (*Physiologia*, 1567[3]) and the Flemish Franciscan Frans Titelmans (*Libri duodecim de consyderatione rerum naturalium*, 1530). Dicsone was, of course, writing against the background of the Copernican Revolution in cosmology to which Bruno also contributed, and Dicsone's 'map of the mind' may well have been influenced by heliocentric ideas.

Catholic writings

As befits a double-agent (he acted as a go-between between the Catholic rebel Francis Hay Earl of Erroll and the Scottish Kirk), Dicsone oscillated between Catholicism and Presbyterianism, but by 1592 (nine years after publication of the *De Umbra* and five years before the *Thamus*) he had made up his mind that he was a Catholic. Both St. Augustine (*De Trinitate XI and XII)* and St. Thomas Aquinas feature in Dicsone's texts. He may also have read Nicholas of Cusa's epistemological treatise *De Beryllo* which compares human and divine creativity. Cusa was familiar with the *Corpus Hermeticum*, from which he sometimes quotes.

Esoteric literature

Besides Giordano Bruno, Dicsone drew heavily on the *Corpus Hermeticum*, presumably in the Latin translation by Marsilio Ficino of 1471, as well as Marsilio's assessment of the rapture of St. Paul, *De raptu Pauli*, and, perhaps, an esoterically-inspired work by the Huguenot Philippe de Mornay (*Traité de la vérité de la religion chrétienne contre les athées, épicuriens, payens, juifs, mahométans et autres infidèles*, Antwerp, 1581) which quotes extensively from the *Divine Pimander*. He may even have been familiar with the bizarre works on 'occult jurisprudence' of the lawyer, satirist and Neo-Latin poet Étienne Forcadel.

As for suggestions for further reading, readers are referred to the extensive footnotes in the two translations, but we must also mention the remarkable work by the late Romanian scholar Ioan Petru Culianu (or Couliano), *Eros and Magic in the Renaissance* (translated by Margaret Cook for the University of Chicago Press, 1987; original title *Eros et magie à la Renaissance*, Flammarion 1984). For Culianu, 'At its greatest degree of development, reached in the work of Giordano Bruno, magic is a means of control over the individual and the masses based on deep knowledge of personal and collective erotic impulses. We can observe in it not only the distant ancestor of psychoanalysis but also, first and foremost, that of applied psychosociology and mass psychology.'

Michael Storch's thesis entitled *Applied Imagination: Giordano Bruno and the Creation of Magical Images*[4] which, in the words of the author, 'is a departure from much of the current scholarship on Bruno which has focused on his contribution to scientific thought, and downplayed or ignored the Hermetic and magical elements which pervade his work' is also worthy of careful study by everyone who wishes to explore the esoteric as well as the mnemotechnical dimension of these fascinating works.

More general works worthy of warm recommendation include Marsha Keith Schuchard, *Restoring the Temple of Vision: Cabalistic Freemasonry and Stuart Culture*, Brill's Studies in Intellectual History vol. 110, 2002; and Mary Carruthers, *The Book of Memory: A Study of Memory in Medieval Culture*, Cambridge 1990.

For the transcription and translation of the *De Umbra* and the *Thamus* we used the Google Books digitisations.

Further Reading

We have not supplied a bibliography as we feel that the works mentioned in the introductory material and the footnotes, many of which are freely available on-line, provide the reader with sufficient pointers for further exploration. We do however consider the works by Ioan Petru Culianu (*Eros and Magic in the Renaissance*) and Michael Storch (*Applied Imagination*) to be indispensable starting-points for readers wishing to seriously explore the esoteric rather than the purely mnemonistic aspects of this subject.

It is also hoped that future titles in this series will include transcriptions and footnoted translations of Dr. Robert Fludd's *De animæ memorativæ scientia*; the polemic by "G.P." of Cambridge attacking Dicsone's ideas, together with Dicsone's riposte; Peter of Ravenna's *Phoenix seu artificiosa memoria*, and other classics in this field.

1   A digitisation of Montaigne's copy of Lucretius will be found at https://cudl.lib.cam.ac.uk/view/PR-MONTAIGNE-00001-00004-00004/1

2   Alexandre Koyré, *From the Closed World to the Infinite Universe*, John Hopkins Press, 1957, p. 6.

3   Translated into English by John M. Forrester as *The Physiologia of Jean Fernel* and available *gratis* at the Internet Archive.

4   Available online at http://digitool.library.mcgill.ca/R/?func=dbin-jump-full&object_id=102846&local_base=GEN01-MCG02

BV - #0006 - 210520 - C0 - 210/148/15 - PB - 9780853185734